CASEBOOK SE

PUBLISHED

Jane Austen: *Emma* DAVID LODGE

Jane Austen: *'Northanger Abbey' & 'Persuasio*

Jane Austen: *'Sense and Sensibility', 'Pride and Prejudice' & Mansfield Park*
B.C. SOUTHAM

Beckett: *Waiting for Godot* RUBY COHN

William Blake: *Songs of Innocence and Experience* MARGARET BOTTRALL

Charlotte Brontë: *'Jane Eyre' & 'Villette'* MIRIAM ALLOTT

Emily Brontë: *Wuthering Heights* MIRIAM ALLOTT

Browning: *'Men and Women' & Other Poems* J.R. WATSON

Bunyan: *The Pilgrim's Progress* ROGER SHARROCK

Chaucer: *Canterbury Tales* J.J. ANDERSON

Coleridge: *'The Ancient Mariner' & Other Poems* ALUN R. JONES & WILLIAM TYDEMAN

Congreve: *Comedies* PATRICK LYONS

Conrad: *'Heart of Darkness', 'Nostromo' & 'Under Western Eyes'* C.B. COX

Conrad: *The Secret Agent* IAN WATT

Dickens: *Bleak House* A.E. DYSON

Dickens: *'Hard Times', 'Great Expectations' & 'Our Mutual Friend'* NORMAN PAGE

Dickens: *'Dombey and Son' & 'Little Dorrit'* ALAN SHELSTON

Donne: *Songs and Sonets* JULIAN LOVELOCK

George Eliot: *Middlemarch* PATRICK SWINDEN

George Eliot: *'The Mill on the Floss' & 'Silas Marner'* R.P. DRAPER

T.S. Eliot: *Four Quartets* BERNARD BERGONZI

T.S. Eliot: *'Prufrock', 'Gerontion', 'Ash Wednesday' & Other Shorter Poems*
B.C. SOUTHAM

T.S. Eliot: *The Waste Land* C.B. COX & ARNOLD P. HINCHLIFFE

T.S. Eliot: *Plays* ARNOLD P. HINCHLIFFE

Henry Fielding: *Tom Jones* NEIL COMPTON

E.M. Forster: *A Passage to India* MALCOLM BRADBURY

William Golding: *Novels 1954-64* NORMAN PAGE

Hardy: *The Tragic Novels* R.P. DRAPER

Hardy: *Poems* JAMES GIBSON & TREVOR JOHNSON

Hardy: *Three Pastoral Novels* R.P. DRAPER

Gerard Manley Hopkins: *Poems* MARGARET BOTTRALL

Henry James: *'Washington Square' & 'The Portrait of a Lady'* ALAN SHELSTON

Jonson: *Volpone* JONAS A. BARISH

Jonson: *'Every Man in his Humour' & 'The Alchemist'* R.V. HOLDSWORTH

James Joyce: *'Dubliners' & 'A Portrait of the Artist as a Young Man'* MORRIS BEJA

Keats: *Odes* G.S. FRASER

Keats: *Narrative Poems* JOHN SPENCER HILL

D.H. Lawrence: *Sons and Lovers* GAMINI SALGADO

D.H. Lawrence: *'The Rainbow' & 'Women in Love'* COLIN CLARKE

Lowry: *Under the Volcano* GORDON BOWKER

Marlowe: *Doctor Faustus* JOHN JUMP

Marlowe: *'Tamburlaine the Great', 'Edward the Second' & 'The Jew of Malta'*
JOHN RUSSELL BROWN

Marvell: *Poems* ARTHUR POLLARD

Milton: *Paradise Lost* A.E. DYSON & JULIAN LOVELOCK

O'Casey: *'Juno and the Paycock', 'The Plough and the Stars' & 'The Shadow of a Gunman'* RONALD AYLING

Eugene O'Neill: *Three Plays* NORMAND BERLIN

John Osborne: *Look Back in Anger* JOHN RUSSELL TAYLOR

The English Novel

Developments in Criticism
since Henry James

A CASEBOOK

EDITED BY

STEPHEN HAZELL

MACMILLAN

Selection, editorial matter and Introduction
© Stephen Hazell 1978

First published 1978
Reprinted 1986, 1990

Published by
MACMILLAN EDUCATION LTD
Houndmills, Basingstoke, Hampshire RG21 2XS
and London
Companies and representatives
throughout the world

Printed in Hong Kong

British Library Cataloguing in Publication Data

The English novel. – (Casebook series).
1. English fiction – History and criticism –
Addresses, essays, lectures
I. Hazell, Stephen II. Series
823'.009   PR823
ISBN 0–333–21473–0 Pbk

CONTENTS

ACKNOWLEDGEMENTS

The editor and publishers wish to thank the following, who have kindly given permission for the use of copyright material: Wayne Booth, extract from *The Rhetoric of Fiction* (1961), reprinted by permission of The University of Chicago Press. Malcolm Bradbury, extract from *Possibilities: Essays on the State of the Novel* (1973) pp. 256–71, reprinted by permission of Oxford University Press. David Craig, extract from *The Real Foundations* (1973), reprinted by permission of Chatto & Windus Ltd. John Fowles, extracts from *The French Lieutenant's Woman* (Jonathan Cape Ltd, 1969), reprinted by permission of Anthony Sheil Associates Ltd. Barbara Hardy, extract from *The Novels of George Eliot* (1959), reprinted by permission of the The Athlone Press of The University of London. Norman Holland, extract from *The Dynamics of Literary Response* (1969), copyright © 1968 by Norman Holland, reprinted by permission of Oxford University Press Inc. Frank Kermode, extract from *Puzzles and Epiphanies* (1962), reprinted by permission of Routledge & Kegan Paul Ltd. D. H. Lawrence, extracts 'Morality and the Novel' and 'John Galsworthy' from *Phoenix* published by William Heinemann Ltd, reprinted by permission of Laurence Pollinger Ltd and the Estate of the late Mrs Frieda Lawrence. F. R. Leavis, extract from *The Living Principle* (1975), reprinted by permission of the author and Chatto and Windus Ltd. F. R. Leavis, extract from 'The Novel as Dramatic Poem IV', from *Scrutiny*, XVII, reprinted by permission of the author and Cambridge University Press. David Lodge, essay 'Samuel Beckett: Some Ping Understood' from *Encounter* (1968), reprinted by permission of the author and the publisher. Iris Murdoch, essay 'Against Dryness' from *Encounter* (1961), reprinted by permission of the author and publisher. Robert Scholes, extract from *The Fabulators*, copyright © 1967 by Robert Scholes, reprinted by permission of the author. Lionel Trilling, essay on 'Manners, Morals, and the Novel', from *Kenyon Review* (1948), reprinted by permission of Mrs Diana Trilling. Raymond Williams, extract from *The Country and The City* (1973), reprinted by permission of Chatto & Windus Ltd.

Angus Wilson, extract from *The Wild Garden* (1963), reprinted by permission of Martin Secker & Warburg Ltd.

GENERAL EDITOR'S PREFACE

The Casebook series, launched in 1968, has become a well-regarded library of critical studies. The central concern of the series remains the 'single-author' volume, but suggestions from the academic community have led to an extension of the original plan, to include occasional volumes on such general themes as literary 'schools' and genres.

Each volume in the central category deals either with one well-known and influential work by an individual author, or with closely related works by one writer. The main section consists of critical readings, mostly modern, collected from books and journals. A selection of reviews and comments by the author's contemporaries is also included, and sometimes comment from the author himself. The Editor's introduction charts the reputation of the work or works from the first appearance to the present time.

Volumes in the 'general themes' category are variable in structure but follow the basic purpose of the series in presenting an integrated selection of readings, with an Introduction which explores the theme and discusses the literary and critical issues involved.

A single volume can represent no more than a small selection of critical opinions. Some critics are excluded for reasons of space, and it is hoped that readers will pursue the suggestions for further reading in the Select Bibliography. Other contributions are severed from their original context, to which some readers may wish to turn. Indeed, if they take a hint from the critics represented here, they certainly will.

A. E. DYSON

INTRODUCTION

A critic, if he's good, can offer to show the reader things about novels he might not see for himself. If he's too good, the unwary reader may be in danger of having his own reading of a novel drowned out (as against willingly modified) by the other's compelling vision. Criticism can be powerful; that is one of the underlying assumptions in the making of this anthology. Another is that good criticism is a creative act, though of a different status from, and necessarily secondary to, the creative act of fiction itself. One power of a good novel is, indeed, to 'take over' our minds as we read, and we allow it that privileged entry because we recognize that our first (and altogether inviting) duty to a novel is to experience it. This is not a passive experience, for we are recreating the world of the novel from the signs on the page, and the level of our active co-operation with the novel is the level of its power. If we then wish to increase the value of our experience, our further duty is to evaluate it: to reflect, discuss, reread – and read critics. A powerful critic can remap and re-evaluate a novel for us: individually our reading habits can be enriched, and generally good novels can be given greater currency. However, it is our duty not to allow him the same privilege over us as we at first allow the novelist, but to test the critic against the novel. This anthology, then, wants both to put the reader in touch with some powerful critical voices, and to encourage an independence from them.

The essays collected here are from the last one hundred years, and one of the principles of selection is the illustration of developments in novel criticism. Such developments are creative but not necessarily progressive (in contrast to scientific thought, which is creative *by* progressing to higher levels of verification). So to tell the history of these developments is itself a matter of interpretation rather than certainty, and the telling seems to me to have all the problems associated with narrative: questions of pace, focus, emphasis; choice of detail, principal characters and their relationships.[1] To organise under theoretical headings seems wrong: there is a muddling variety of kinds of heading[2] because there is no agreed theoretical framework, and anyway most good critics transcend any single label. On the other hand a comprehensive chronological account flattens out the living issues. So, while trying to do a measure of justice to theory and history, I shall spend most time on major figures, and use as a recurring focus the kind of reading attention the critics variously call for. Integral to this focus, it proves, is a consideration of the way critics themselves use language.

As a preliminary indication of what I have in mind, let me point to ·divergent positions on the question of reading attention. The extremes would be the encouragement of total absorption in a novel and the encouragement of unceasing analytical consciousness. Scholes, in the essay reprinted here, contends that fiction works in a similar way to dream and that the exercising of the faculty of imagination is 'quite enough justification' for fiction. Holland, the psychological critic represented in this collection, writes elsewhere, in a particularly Freudian sentence, 'It is by fusing with the literary work as we once fused with another source of nourishment that we take its process of transformation into ourselves.'[3] Though both have often to be analytical in means, the end in view is, in Scholes's words, 'to suggest what we as readers need in the way of equipment and expectations' in order to possess imaginative literature. Lawrence thought the novel was 'supremely important' because it can 'make the whole man alive tremble' as nothing else can.[4] At its best it can help us live.

On these views, the fullest relationship between reader and fiction is like the intensest moments of human contact. Trilling reveals a more diurnal view, but maintains the human analogy: we should 'read the work of literature with a lively sense of its latent and ambiguous meanings, as if it were, as indeed it is, a being no less alive and contradictory than the man who created it'.[5] The complex middle view – James and Leavis come to mind, and can serve to show that by 'middle' I mean a difficult search for the right response, not easy-going eclecticism – holds a conscious, intelligent attentiveness to the novel as verbal and formal art as an essential prerequisite for perceiving its bearing on life. As we move to the other end of my scale, there is increasing analytical awareness of the novel as text – as a complex communication, indeed, whose conventions or rhetoric require our attention (as in Booth, represented here), but still material for the rational enquiring mind like other verbal messages. For the far extreme we probably have to go to France, where some writers and critics, recognising that realism in the novel has only a qualified objectivity, because human language itself is irremediably soaked in human value and prejudice, seek and praise techniques for liberating the novel as far as may be from its past, from its tyrannical richness of form and language. Better still they go off the end into cinema, Robbe-Grillet being the most obvious example. Such a scale will not serve as a comprehensive account, but can be a helpful frame in which to place some historically recurrent debates – for example, the old humanism versus new ideologies, or the demand for 'organic form' and the 'illusion of life' verşus an equal valuation of overt strategy and explicit statement by the novelist, matters that will be touched on later. And finally, before turning to my introduction of the specific material in this collection, let me exemplify how a critic's language constantly and implicitly places him.

If one believes that the novel offers unique possibilities for the enlargement of consciousness and the intensification of being, then one will resist treating it as a particular kind of literary pigeon-hole, no matter how capacious, and will see the form in a non-generic and ahistorical way . . . [the] neo-classical epic framework [of *Tom Jones*] scarcely contains the novel's sense of freedom and irrepressible vitality. The picaresque novel, originally a distinctive genre, soon burst its bounds . . . one can see the development of the European novel in the eighteenth and nineteenth centuries as the successive opening up of tracts of unexplored territory.[6]

This passage from Bergonzi's *The Situation of the Novel* is fairly explicit to start with: the tone welcomes the role the novel played in the deepening of post-Renaissance individualism. The metaphors are also of a piece with the analysis: the bursting of bounds and the opening up of unexplored territory are a welcome for new personal freedoms and self-discovery. If we had to label Bergonzi we should say he was a liberal humanist like Trilling. It becomes clear in his book that one of its drives is anxiety about how to accommodate a situation where liberal humanist values look to be in retreat, as though all the territory of freedom has been explored, and, as with empires, contraction follows. So the situation of the novel that strikes Bergonzi is this: 'In the last few decades, the novel has, I think, abandoned freedom for genre, in various important but unremarked ways.'[7]

The action of a comedy moves towards an identity which is usually a social identity. In Dickens the family, or a group analogous to a family, is the key to

social identity. Hence his recognition scenes are usually genealogical, concerned with discovering unknown fathers and mothers or articulating the
correct family relationships.[8]

This is from Northrop Frye, and it is immediately evident that the
underlying drive is quite different. The manner is of explication, not
judgement. The explication is conducted in language that aspires to the
technical: for Frye 'the action of a comedy', 'identity', and 'recognition
scenes' are the kind of accurate and objective terms in which novel
description should be carried on. The relation between his sentences is
dictated by the logic of his developing description: for example, the
'hence' at the beginning of the third sentence is totally confident in
ascribing the characteristic endings of Dickens's novels to the particular
comic genre in which they are written. Indeed, Frye sees criticism to
literature as grammar is to language, musicology to music, physics to
the natural world.

   These are rather obvious and explicit examples of radically different
modes of discourse, but I take it to be generally true that we can
profitably attend to a critic's own characteristic use of language. These
two passages can illustrate one further point of relevance to this
anthology: the provisional sorting of recent critics into a set which
concentrates on the 'art' of fiction (e.g. Frye), and a set which
concentrates on fiction's bearing on our experience of reality (e.g.
Bergonzi). Thorough systematising of criticism misrepresents its character as a communal debate, but the above division is one of the more
obvious and pressing ones available.

   First, however, I must turn to an account of the most striking line of
development in the last century.

A MAJOR TRADITION

Modern criticism of the English novel took its major impetus from
Henry James. There was intelligent commentary and review in
existence – recent studies have shown just how much[9] – but, as the first
essay reprinted below shows, James felt the need to bring discussion
through to higher levels of consistency and articulacy. James is a
turning-point in the consciously-developed reading of novels, and his
consistency of devotion to the task was, in effect, new. One of his aims
was to win for novels, not least his own, the seriousness of attention

which had previously been largely reserved for the long-standing literary forms, poetry and drama. The shadow of these older forms still falls across novel criticism, as witnessed by the continuing call for a 'poetics' or 'rhetoric' of fiction, but from James onwards there was at least to be no lack of voices claiming a high status for the novel.

James, in making new initiatives in criticism, was also calling for a change in the relationship between novelist and reader. He characterises the earlier relationship as 'the comfortable, good-humoured feeling abroad that a novel is a novel, as a pudding is a pudding, and that our only business with it could be to swallow it'.[10] The earlier reader would certainly have looked for a 'good read' (and that's fair enough), and, if the novel proved instructive also, so much the better: the reader could judge the moral that the novelist drew from the reality he presented by comparison with his own moral beliefs and his experience of the same reality. Radical doubts about how much we do, in fact, perceive 'the same reality' are part of a change in the novel. The problem of consciousness is crucial to the modern movement. And this doubt fosters the further one as to whether moral beliefs can be separable from perception, and so in turn whether questions about the moral value of a novel can be separated from questions about its artistic (i.e. perceptual) mode. From say 1880 to 1930 the novel has a major and difficult period of innovation, formulating new ways of looking at the world to supersede the earlier implicit assumption that the novel could be a transparent window on life. It is not accidental that the first big growth in novel criticism corresponds with this period. Indeed, much recent criticism of the novel is still a response to that crucial era of transition: it tries to articulate what is central to the innovations and achievements of such writers as James, Conrad, Lawrence, Joyce and Woolf, so that they remain shaping forces of modern consciousness.

James, then, is decisive, both for the modern novel and its criticism. His 1884 essay 'The Art of Fiction' is the first essay in the present collection. It was strategically conceived. It aimed to cajole and to tug leading men of letters along with him into a new arena of discussion,[11] for he saw that the opportunity might then exist to get beyond the dominant Victorian moralism and sentiment, stifling as he felt they were of both life and art. He worked to stretch attitudes into greater openness, especially to the complexities and paradoxes of what the novelist has to do by way of art in the very effort to capture life, and concern for getting this interconnection right stands at the centre of a major tradition of novel criticism.

'The only reason for the existence of a novel is that it does attempt to represent life'; 'the only distinction [is] between bad novels and good novels' (as against distinctions like 'novels of incident' and 'novels of character'); 'the only classification of the novel that I can understand is into that which has life and that which has it not'; 'the only condition that I can think of attaching to the composition of a novel is . . . that it be sincere'. The repeated phrase here, in some of James's most forceful assertions, is a measure of how strongly he was struggling for freedom from dead categories and restrictive judgements. Artistically, the novelist must be granted freedom in his subject and general mode of treatment. This granted, a major criterion of success is how 'organic' the work of art is – here the insight of Romantic poetry criticism is brought to bear – so that the novel should present a convincing and coherent created world, not a narrative manipulated by the author for local effect or to illustrate preconceived precepts. (Trollope, in once going so far as to call his art 'only make-believe', an art of controlled effects, is found guilty by James of 'betrayal of a sacred office'.) Coleridge's notion of the intuitive growth of the work of art from a 'seed' is nonetheless characteristically transmuted by James, who associates a high level of conscious intelligence with the development of his corresponding 'germ'. His Prefaces to the New York edition of his novels[12] abound with a wealth of technical discussion of his means of giving shape, coherence, pattern and emphasis to his work. And in his Preface to *The Portrait of a Lady* he elaborates a fine image – the section is reprinted below – for the novelist's position: chosen form and authorial viewpoint are part of the substance of fiction, no reality existing except as part of a means of perception. Yet the fictive reality must in the end be tested against the reader's own sense of life; his consciousness of art once raised, the tests are interest, 'solidity of specification', inclusiveness, representativeness.

James then looks to the reader for an attention which will not relax into sentiment and moral precept. Morality lies in the whole means of apprehension. 'The essence of moral energy is to survey the whole field.' 'Art lives upon discussion, upon experiment, upon curiosity, upon variety of attempt, upon the exchange of views and the comparison of stand-points.' The novelist must have this intelligence *in* his art, and the reader *about* it.

Discussion did advance. Novelists – Conrad, say, and Ford Madox Ford – became more explicit about the nature and problems of their art. An essential document in a comprehensive history of this development would be Virginia Woolf's essay 'Modern Fiction' (1919), in which she sees the highly-detailed realism of writers like Bennett and Galsworthy as examples of the continued existence of a way of writing from which real life has, in fact, leaked away: the novel's grasp on life can be maintained only by continuing formal experiment. Major critical efforts by men not themselves novelists begin to appear; for example, Percy Lubbock's *The Craft of Fiction* (1921) expanded James's ideas on the construction of novels, though, like American followers of this line in America twenty and more years later, he becomes more prescriptive of the formal qualities good novels must have than can safely be deduced from James (the 'autonomy' of the novel, the demand that it only *show* its meaning and never *tell* it, becomes all). E. M. Forster's *Aspects of the Novel* (1927) enlarges on the modern impetus towards asserting the superior fruitfulness of having an essentially symbolic or motif-based structure over the traditional narrative primacy – this even while maintaining an aggressively amateur tone. Aggressive in a different way, and opposed to professionalised criticism, is D. H. Lawrence, in whom I find a surprising community of concern with Henry James – surprising given the very wide difference in their novels and modes of critical address – and his work is next represented in this anthology.

He, even more than James, avoids any strict conceptual framework for his writings about the novel. At centre he calls upon those standards of judgement which also inform his creative writing: for example, 'quickness', the response of 'man alive'. Like James, he relegates the classification of novels to unimportance compared with sincere and intelligent judgement. In the essay on Galsworthy reprinted below he opens with an attack on any notion that criticism can be scientific ('classifying . . . in an imitation-botanical fashion is mere impertinence and mostly dull jargon') and asserts that the critic 'must be emotionally alive in every fibre, intellectually capable and skilful in essential logic, and then morally very honest'. He finds good critics to be rare.

He creates a rich range of vocabulary for trying to enforce the sense of life which is to be the standard for judging a novel: 'vital', 'honourable', in harmony with the 'passional inspiration', in 'good faith', showing 'relatedness' all revealing that the novel can be 'the one bright book of life'. Like James, he draws on the idea of the novel's being good when organic ('inter-related in all its parts, vitally, organically'). By that standard the author 'can't fool the novel': the imposition of didactic purpose will show through, the living relatedness of all the parts will fail. The essay on Galsworthy exemplifies the principle. Lawrence shows how a satiric intelligence builds up towards vital novel-writing, but then collapses in its collusion with sentiment and precept. Lawrence's best-known dictum is on this topic of the imposed moral and the true novel pulling in opposite directions: 'Never trust the artist. Trust the tale. The proper function of the critic is to save the tale from the artist who created it.'[13]

In this matter of the autonomy of the work of literature, later critics have gone farther than James and Lawrence, most famously Wimsatt and Beardsley in their 1946 essay 'The Intentional Fallacy'. Their arguments seem to work best for poetry, and a later 'neo-Aristotelian' counter-attack works best with the novel. Wayne Booth has probably worked hardest at restoring the author's importance, of which more below. The earlier critics held more to the complexity of the novel's having both personal and impersonal characteristics. The circle that has to be squared in Lawrence is that while he's against the novelist putting his 'thumb in the pan' for some absolute belief, against, for example, his manipulating his novel to show the supremacy of romantic love in human values, he finds other kinds of purpose acceptable. We are left with the problem of construing the sentence 'If only the "purpose" be large enough, and not at outs with the passional inspiration.'[14] Lawrence's novels hope to enact a purpose rather than preach directly (his success varies), and his criticism may best be read as an enactment of the aliveness he calls for: it has the qualities of a vivacious mind in free address to the reader; he invents suggestive but unpolished phrases, has frequent changes of tone, repeats key ideas and images cumulatively. All this demands a relationship with the reader, and depends as much on personal response as on impersonal ideas. To read Lawrence's criticism is to have the intelligence and the feelings moved, surprised and irritated into awareness.

James and Lawrence, then, are two great writers who saw the value to the novel's development of sincere and intelligent critics, and it seems natural to turn next to F. R. Leavis, for whose novel-criticism those two writers are major informing spirits.[15] In developing their kind of concern he has become one of the most important and challenging of modern critics, and the pugilistic energy he has given to his task has made him both revered and reviled. He has been deeply committed to intelligence in and about the novel. and to linking this with judgements about the essential qualities of our civilisation; he sees evaluation of life as uniquely possible in the novel's density. His critical standards draw heavily on both James and Lawrence − he looks for high art written by man alive, so to speak − and goes on to lay a stress peculiarly his own on the importance of evaluation, of 'placing' writers in degrees of relative weight and life-helpfulness.

Leavis rejects exact theoretical statements; his language and his style are of his essence; but indications of the area of his concern can be given. We have seen that James and Lawrence felt that the novel should address itself to, and be judged in terms of, 'morality', but that this word is very widely defined in each case. Leavis likewise will not allow morality to be pinned down to precepts, but does see it as the governing significance of good novel structures: the 'formal perfection' of *Emma*, he writes in *The Great Tradition*, is only to be appreciated 'in terms of moral preoccupations'. Novels which simply generate a lot of lifelikeness (whether naturalistic as in Bennett or caricatured as often in Dickens) are likely to be 'placed' less highly than those where the creative talent serves, and is served by, moral significance. Such significance is seen only in the achievement and integrity of the art, not as explicit assertion. The essay on *St. Mawr* reprinted below is an example of Leavis making out this case specifically. In that short novel of Lawrence's the critique of civilisation often rises to explicitness; but the explicitness is seen as earned by the substance, and the true core of the work is seen in the 'affirmation of life' which comes through only in the art. Another way that Leavis puts this is in making 'presentment' superior to description (see the penultimate paragraph of the piece on Conrad's prose).

We thus run into the same paradox encountered by James and Lawrence: the conviction that novels must be created as independent organic worlds in which the reader's judgement can operate without authorial interference, together with a conviction that the fineness of the author's mind, the largeness of his sincere purpose, the richness of his moral preoccupations, all have a bearing on the novel's value. Thus we must use non-literary criteria in the same breath as literary ones.

In Leavis this makes for vivid criticism partly because the sheer effort of urging together literary sensitivity and moral-social apprehension is always evident: the effort keeps the intelligence of both Leavis and his reader alive. Indeed, the feeling of combat with the text, with the reader, and with other critics is central to his critical achievement. He is dedicated to the notion of critical collaboration, the 'common pursuit of true judgment' (a seminal phrase of Eliot's). Critical judgements are offered to other competent readers who then respond with a 'Yes, but . . .' – this process has occurred widely, however much Leavis himself may incline to impatience with the but-clauses of others.

Leavis has addressed himself to cultural problems directly in such works as *Nor Shall my Sword*, as well as through literature. The notion that he is a Practical Critic, pinning his faith above all on detailed textual analysis, is a misapprehension. He would agree that a novel is deeper than any paraphrase of it, and often uses long quotation and concrete analysis, but the conjunction of this method with strong social – moral convictions makes him quite other.

Leavis's combative strategy is to pin up the current critical judgements that he finds unacceptable – for example, Eliot's judgement in *After Strange Gods* that Lawrence has 'an incapacity for what we ordinarily call thinking' – and to crystallise his analysis and argument around that – in this case by demonstrating the need to rethink the meaning of 'intelligence' so that it covers the mode of perception which is so fruitful in Lawrence. His over-all aim in *D. H. Lawrence: Novelist* is to 'win clear recognition' for Lawrence's greatness, to 'insist' on the strengths of his art. In doing so Lawrence's work will, variously: commend, enforce, refute, develop, demonstrate, challenge, manifest, affirm, realise, bear irrefutable witness, testify, and so on. The reader is drawn into the debate, encouraged to 'take what is offered', to place the major and the achieved, the vital and the healthy. This is the language to engender in the reader that evaluative attention which yet remains responsive to the details of the art (Leavis is fond of James's phrase, the 'solidity of specification'). Leavis has been a central influence on novel-criticism, producing followers, dissentient sympathisers, and opponents. Trilling here represents the second category: those who feel that fiction does have the cultural importance Leavis ascribes to it, but who also feel that he is too parochially English, too 'personal' in his combative style, too much inclined to neglect the importance of other sources of ideas besides literature.

In Trilling's work, indeed, ideas play an altogether larger part than in the critics we have looked at so far – for example ideas drawn from

philosophy, politics, and psychology, as well as those implicit in
literature. In the Preface to *The Liberal Imagination* (1950) he writes
persuasively of the intimate connection between literature and politics.
His own politics are roughly 'liberal humanist', though part of his task
was to provide a critique of liberalism from within, since there was then,
unfortunately as he saw it, no intelligent conservatism to oppose it. His
basic tenet remains in the tradition of Matthew Arnold: literature 'must
always, for us now, be the criticism of life' he writes, his own
characteristic interpretation of the phrase being 'the illumination and
refinement of . . . Reason by which man might shape the conditions of
his own existence.' This confident (one feels like adding 'American' and
perhaps even 'old-fashioned') version of the tradition sees the real
possibility of the individual shaping his culture by creating or critically
maintaining its stock of motivating ideas. Later liberals – like Bradbury, discussed below – hold such positions more uneasily. More left-
wing writers tend to see ideas as the result of more powerful cultural
factors, economic and social, and to rate their causative power lower if
they are not integral to some economic or social necessity.

Trilling's style and approach derive, therefore, from standing on high
ground, and his essay is one of the most generally discursive included in
this volume. He is prepared to tackle the largest ideas, such as how the
idea of 'reality' has changed, and so sees literature in a wide context, not
as isolated texts for analysis. He is particularly concerned to posit the
lines of development of a distinctively modern consciousness: one
characteristic essay reveals him struggling with modern literature's
'canonization of the primal non-ethical energies' and its 'hostility to
civilization'.[16] Of past literature, he wishes to show us how to look for
the context of manners and morals in which it was written, the
'unrecorded hum of implication' that once surrounded it. And, further
to bring out the imaginative fullness of fiction, he wishes us to respond to
the latent ambiguous meanings. He has tried to respond creatively to
the major modern intellectual developments, and has absorbed into his
critical manner what he found relevant and liberating in psychoanalytic theory. For example, in *Sincerity and Authenticity* (1972) he advances
the idea of sincerity in terms of truth to self where self must be newly
understood. At the same time, he shows the development of these
modern notions from Diderot via Goethe, Hegel, Marx and Freud.

What Trilling gains in breadth he loses in intensity. He is more the
urbane and eloquent intellectual and less the awkward and compelling

visionary than Lawrence and Leavis, but still it seems to me that the
figures I have discussed so far are the main representatives of a central
tradition of novel criticism which tries to retain the strengths of an
English and American line of moral thought while rejecting its potential
narrowness by looking for the authentic realisation in art of modern life.
Few other critics or groups have quite the inclusiveness of this central
tradition. The narrowing of focus which has in varying degrees
occurred has, however, produced some very interesting insights, even if
it also stands in danger of addressing too specialised an audience.

THE ART OF FICTION

It's a salient point that of my representatives of the 'major tradition' the
first two are primarily novelists and the latter two are primarily
academics. The steady growth, from the inter-war period onwards, of
English Literature as a discipline in its own right has naturally had a
major effect on criticism. The greater part of post-war writing has been
both in and for universities. Leavis and Trilling themselves, it must be
said, are particularly conscious of the university's potential contribution to the state of a nation and so wish to press home arguments
about the national culture which will be felt by a wider educated
public. Many academic critics, however, suit their style either to a
student audience – in which case the personal tone or the drive of
general argument is often muffled by the needs for exposition and
coverage of the field – or to an audience of fellow academics – in
which case the purely scholarly or methodological often comes to the
fore. They may see themselves, on an implicit analogy with the sciences,
as field-workers. They may take a particular approach a step further
(many efforts are made under titles like 'Towards a Poetics of Fiction',
'Towards a Science of the Text'), or approach novels from an ever-
wider range of non-literary disciplines (say anthropology, or structuralism). The best of such criticism can be creative. The over-all danger
in the modern critical scene is the combination of spurious objectivity
with hectic pluralism, where the objectivity flattens out debate and the
pluralism loses sight of any central area on which debate might focus.
Academic precision of observation and restraint from easy general-
isation are real gains for the reader, but he needs at the same time to
keep a close eye on how important the issues are to which those qualities
are addressed.

    In my two main sections of post-war criticism, all the writers are academics, though some are also novelists (e.g. Malcolm Bradbury), and some are closely associated with 'higher' journalism (e.g. Frank Kermode). But, although the manner of writing is less immediately personal than, say, Lawrence's, an eye and an ear can be developed for quite sharp distinctions between them.

My grouping of some critics under 'The Art of Fiction' derives whatever justification it can claim from the large number of them who have wished to increase awareness of verbal and formal artifice in the novel, often with the intention of confirming its status as an art as complex as poetry. One side of Henry James's thinking has had continuing influence, the side represented by the Prefaces. His full discussion of dramatic and pictorial effects for creating a shapely and impersonal whole has been a constant source of authority. Lubbock, as already mentioned, made a near dogma of impersonal 'showing' as against personal 'telling', and there is a similar line of American New Criticism. There has also been a counter-movement. Barbara Hardy in England quietly demonstrated in 1959 the disfavour the Lubbock approach can do to an author such as George Eliot, who composed on different principles from James, and Wayne Booth soon after made a major theoretical contribution to the debate. A thumbnail sketch of his position is needed here to supplement the brief extract of his work reprinted below, though neither can do justice to the comprehensiveness of his argument.

Booth seeks to demonstrate that the ideal of showing as against telling is unattainable. If the novelist rejects direct commentary on the action in his own voice, we may be offered instead the inner thoughts of various characters – a device which is artificial and selective, and, in fact, another way of telling the reader how to interpret. If inner commentary is rejected, we may be guided through the narrative indirectly by being given, in description, the relative reliability of the characters and their comments. And so Booth goes on to analyse progressively more indirect expressions, to show that any selection of events, metaphors, or formal patterns serves an authorial purpose. (This conclusion yields quite a different model for novel-making from that which sees it as the product of the organic imagination.) 'We must never forget', he concludes, 'that though the author can to some extent choose his disguises, he can never choose to disappear.'[17] But attitudes implied in a novel may themselves be a choice and not those of the actual author: in sum, a novel is the statement of an 'implied author'. The statement is achieved by a wealth of specific narrative techniques that we should attend to, and these constitute the rhetoric of fiction.

Booth is probably too confident that a novel can be seen as embodied statement, and neglects its potential ambiguity, its openness, its quality as something recreated by the reader – all its more poetic functions, one might say – but he effectively undermines exclusive positions about what novels should be like, and broadens our descriptive vocabulary.

Barbara Hardy is also concerned to rescue authors from inappropriate criteria. She demonstrates George Eliot's relatively disregarded power of form as the product of 'a particular kind of generalising and qualifying vision of the human lot' which leads to the novelist 'always being very much in evidence in her novels'.[18] On the other hand she places less stress on the conscious use of rhetoric than does Booth. She writes elsewhere, 'narrative . . . is not to be regarded as an aesthetic invention used by artists to control, manipulate, and order experience, but as a primary act of mind transferred to art from life'.[19] None the less, she and Booth, and David Lodge as well, all require a technically educated attentiveness in novel-reading. 'This formal attentiveness to words may well go beyond the kind of attentiveness we expect to give to the novel, and it is certainly true that it comes out of reading novels many times and at varying speeds. Yet the unusually attentive reader is doing no more than approach the detailed attentiveness which even the uncreative writer usually gives to his writing.'[20]

David Lodge's attention is to the novelist's verbal art, language being taken to be pre-eminent in importance over other aspects of the novel, structure included. He also typifies a growing trend amongst recent critics in providing himself with full theoretical justification, exemplified in various essays reprinted in *The Language of Fiction* (1968) and *The Novelist at the Crossroads* (1971). He gives an interesting account of theoretical developments in England and America and on the Continent. In calling for an increased recognition of the primacy of the verbal, he still finds himself close to Leavis as to why the novel is important. It is the balance between analysis and evaluation that has changed. He, Booth and Hardy look for an adequately articulated descriptive method as a precondition of judgement rather than as something inseparable from judgement.

Scholes also calls for a heightened attentiveness to the art of fiction, but stands out amongst my chosen critics in assuming a persuader's role on behalf of certain new developments in fiction: what he calls fabulation. We attend to his criticism in order to attune our minds to the new genre; that done we subsume our consciousness into the world of the novel, we 'swallow' it, to use James's word. Fabulation is justified simply in the exercising and enriching of the imagination. The fiction of the future will increasingly abandon the techniques of realism, but this does not mean that it has abandoned reality. Fabulation 'tends away from the representation of reality, but returns toward actual human life by way of ethically controlled fantasy'.[21] Scholes is a vigorous apologist for romance, picaresque, allegory, science fiction and kindred forms. His style is naturally more boisterous than that of the others in this section because it is more specifically special pleading. His arguments have grown in favour, especially in America. His more recent writing calls structuralism into the witness box, and his critical demeanour has at the same time grown more visionary.[22] In the English critical tradition fantasy has received a disproportionately small amount of attention to its strong contribution to fiction. Scholes's voice is thus an important one; his strong taste for one kind of literature may be a general limitation, but it is also a source of specific strength.

There has, then, been a variety of increased attention to the art of fiction: a delight in the novel-making skills, a concern for the 'poetics' of fiction, an academic desire for precise methods of description. These developments have gone along with increasing doubts that the novel is a simple realistic or objective form, doubts that go deeper than James envisaged, and doubts shared also by many of those who continue to write more directly of the novel and reality than do the critics I have just been discussing.

FICTION AND REALITY

'Reality' is one of those words – like 'Nature' in the sixteenth and seventeenth centuries – which are altogether indispensable, and altogether without an agreed meaning or reference. Hopes, fears, judgements, insights, prejudices, all go into shaping each writer's use of the word, just because it is such a central and powerful word. So my remarks here are necessarily of a preliminary kind. It is widely agreed, though, that the novel has a specially intimate connection, amongst literary forms, with reality, generally through its 'solidity of specification'. Realism is seen as the single most dominant aspect of the development of the novel, but since Henry James the understanding of it has become more interestingly complex. It is not now often held to be the objective representation of an objectively existing reality, for reality itself is felt to be less securely objective; for any one of us, it depends on what our language and experience allow us to see. An author may be realistic in faithfully reporting what he sees, but his novel is an instrument of perception more like a lens than a mirror.

So we soon get realisms rather than Realism; the most common category in fiction can provisionally be labelled bourgeois realism. The novel is assumed to be intimately related with the rise of the bourgeoisie, with its generally individualistic view of life, and other associated values: the typical centre of interest is thus character in relation to social placing. This general view is shared by critics of widely differing ideological attitude, and one of the arguments deriving from this view is that the decline of power of the realistic novel over the last few decades relates to the declining relevance of the bourgeois world-view. It does, at least, seem clear that most writing about realism has ideological content, either explicit or implicit, and that the defence or exploration of a set of social values is the underlying drive which gives such criticism its force. The clearest division of attitude apparent at this moment is between the liberal humanist and Marxist positions; the latter is usually explicit, the former often implicit, partly because it flows from a longer tradition, so that its assumptions seem axiomatic until challenged. A few approaches to reality may appear to be non-ideological – the psychological approach is one that springs to mind as having significantly influenced novel-criticism, though even here one might note that Freudian approaches dominate, and there must be a certain egalitarian drive to a doctrine that judges universal inner motives to be more significant than outward social position. The debate about the interplay of novels and reality is a specific branch of the general discussion of society's nature and purposes.

Much recent fiction, however, is not realistic in any traditional sense, and this is another fact that critics whose driving interest is in the relation of fiction to reality have been anxious to attend to; some have found a way to welcome the new as wholeheartedly as does Scholes (say) from his more purely aesthetic point of view. The critics in this anthology represent a range of interested response to the development of, and crisis in, realism.

Frank Kermode has consistently attempted to elaborate the specifically modern sense of reality shown in fiction. His very wide reading range and his correlating habit of mind give him to see the novel in relation to an internationally evolving sensibility. He has brought some order to this large topic partly by historical means, where he has distinguished phases by pioneering vocabulary such as 'palaeo-modernism' and 'neo-modernism', and partly by non-historical means, showing how powerfully the novel draws on permanent myths of the human imagination. Kermode brings many subjects – psychology, anthropology, theology and so on – to the elucidation of man as a fiction-making animal. His most notable work in this field is *The Sense of an Ending* (1966), on fiction and apocalypse. The very sense of a crisis in realism is therefore grist to his mill, to his epochal view. The sheer breadth of Kermode's context for explaining literature seems to make literature's power of explaining the world – especially in articulating for us our modern sense of crisis – its central value, the critic's duty being to 'provide the means by which the reader may be put in possession of the valuable book'. His interests are so plural that he comes closer than most to transcending any implicit ideological commitment. His style is thus very open, free in making surprising and interesting connections; and also difficult to engage with for readers trying to test out against the critics a more specific set of values or judgements. His central achievement has been to call for the reader to be as widely aware as possible of modern realities when reading the novel, and in turn to bring to the reader's attention books he might otherwise neglect; his review essays have been important in this.

Another means of largely avoiding an implicitly committed position is to take the structure of reality as provided by some objective discipline and apply it to the novel. It unsurprisingly turns out that this works best with disciplines that in truth approximate to the humane more closely than the scientific. It would be widely conceded that Freudian psychology, in much of its terminology, is a brilliant metaphorical construct, with roots in the same cultural situation that produced modernism in literature. It turns out to be a sympathetic way of considering many modern developments – the ambiguity of both experience and motive, the indirectness of language, the importance of symbol, for example – even though it also carries the risk of always unearthing these things in material that is barely susceptible to its approach. Norman Holland, who has an essay on Conrad in this collection, is a discriminating user of Freudian explanation. He is able to incorporate a full sense of style and symbol into his account of a novel, even while accounting for these features in terminology like 'drive' and 'defense'.

Other potentially sympathetic disciplines (like structuralism) – sympathetic to a certain area of the novel – are beginning to make their presence felt, but the central criticism of realism is still based in a sense of the novel's relation to social values and an observable social reality, even if modernistic doubts are now more abounding than once.

The first chapter of Malcolm Bradbury's *Possibilities* (1973), from which the essay on John Fowles reprinted here is taken, is called 'The Open Form: The Novel and Reality'. The openness of the novel, its capacities as a vehicle for an enormous range of individual voices, is central to a liberal view. Bradbury's general air, though, is not so much James's of championing new freedoms against old restrictions as of defending established freedoms against new restrictions. The essay on Fowles shows Bradbury trying to accommodate where he can and resist where he must the new French criticism, which, very roughly, sees the author's style and narrative structures as imposition, a kind of individualistic tyranny. He also recognises strengths in, and feels compelled to resist, the Marxist historicist view. In talking of the 'primary centre of literature' he asserts that 'it surely lies in the creative play of individuals, responding not to "history" but to life, a response capable of generating forms, orders, or fictions of extraordinary range and variety'.[23] Bradbury's awareness of other critics is so keen that a certain awkward allusiveness results: if he uses the word 'writerly' he is nodding in the direction of Roland Barthes's *écriture*; the quotation marks around 'history' in the above sentence signal the reference to the Marxist approach. An awkwardness is also to be noticed in the work of Raymond Williams, though here it results from the intensity of the effort required to bring together differing kinds of criticism. In particular he has sought his own way of uniting Marxism and the approach of Leavis's *Scrutiny*, social inclusiveness with the criteria from individual experience, to simplify the matter. To show how novels are both culturally shaped and at the same time create·our cultural understanding so that the shaper may also be shaped has been a central achievement. He makes repeated phrases like 'knowable community' (for a social grouping that the novel has uniquely made readers inward with) do a lot of work, and gives to words like 'improvement' and 'cultivation' the full aura of their often chilling social history. He values literature where it extends the range of social sympathy and perception by presentation of convincing experience. His theoretical bent does extend to showing, for example, that country and city in the novel should be seen not as opposing symbols but as different expressions of the same limiting social relationships, but his most personal stress is on finding a place for the history of ordinary people in the critical apparatus we set up for reading novels.

At present, the most theoretical of English Marxist critics is Terry Eagleton, though even he quite recently showed how influential the main English tradition remains. He can write, for example, 'It is integral to the imaginative achievements of Blake, Wordsworth, Dickens and Eliot that they can "totalise" and "transcend" those pressures without damage to the quickness and specificity of their feel for concrete life.'[24] Totalisation and transcendence are the Marxist goals of having an overall interpretation of society not limited by class perceptions; quickness (a Lawrence word), specificity (James) and concrete life (Leavis) derive from the appeal to experience of a quite different tradition. Even if Eagleton himself may now consciously reject such bringing together, and find Williams to be in internal contradiction, there are yet Marxist critics whose concern for concrete life is to the fore, given shape indeed by underlying theory, but not led by it into the attempt to make criticism scientific. David Craig is one such, and an essay of his on Victorian fiction is included here. I suspect that one force which keeps Leavis, Williams and Craig within sight of each other despite deep differences is a background in religious nonconformism, combining social radicalism and respect for the individual.

Critics of fiction and reality, then, differ in style and implicit values in quite specific ways, and the general reader may pick his own way amongst the critics by attending to these qualities in their writing.

CRITICISM AND THE READER

In concluding this introduction, I should first like to note that I have included extracts from three recent novelists. They help to show that novels continue to be written in a critical context (as they clearly were in the earlier cases of, say, James, Ford, Conrad, Lawrence, Woolf, Forster), and that the interests of novelists do intersect with those of critics. The extracts are brief – the writers are not quite major critics in themselves – but interesting in showing the author's version of critical topics. Angus Wilson shows from personal experience how the meaning of a story may prove independent of its author's intention; Iris Murdoch indicates sympathy with the liberal humanist defence of form; John Fowles shows the heightened self-consciousness characteristic of recent developments, and indeed the extracts are from a novel of his: he has incorporated the critical theory for judging the action of his own narrative.

Finally, a note about the status of this anthology. It aims, as I said at the beginning, to put the student or general reader in touch with some powerful critical voices while encouraging an independence from them. It is to fulfil the latter part of this aim that the essays are generally of a reasonable length, so that the reader may judge strategy, texture of thinking, and characteristic vocabulary – short extracts would mean picking out the main 'ideas' and would distort the whole sense of personal engagement. It follows that this anthology does not attempt any comprehensive account of novel theory (some such anthologies do exist – see the Select Bibliography). It does offer an account of some main events in the history of novel criticism since Henry James in England and America, but the decision to offer decent-length essays from the critics who are included has entailed painful decisions to omit some historically significant critics like E. M. Forster in England or Mark Schorer in the U. S. A. My essential hopes are that a reading of the selected critics in sequence will progressively involve the reader in an understanding of the living debate about the nature and value of the English novel; will help enrich his reading habits; and will help him form personal standards of judgement through grappling with the standards of others.

NOTES

1. See, for example, David Lodge's 'Crosscurrents in Modern English Criticism' in his *The Novelist at the Crossroads* (London, 1971) pp. 247–86. Conceding that there are 'many ways of categorising and distinguishing literary critics, according to their methods and principles', he constructs a narrative account based on general types rather than methods: the academic critics, the creator-critics, and the freelance critics.

2. For example, the general heading 'perspectives on fiction' would suggest subdivision into psychological, sociological, etc.; while division by ideological approach – liberal humanist, Marxist, etc. – would produce a quite different ordering of critics; so would distinguishing 'schools of criticism' – the New Critics, the neo-Aristotelians, and so forth.

3. Norman Holland, 'The "Unconscious" of Literature', in *Stratford-upon-Avon Studies 12: Contemporary Criticism* (London, 1970) p. 153.

4. D. H. Lawrence, 'Why the Novel Matters', first published in *Phoenix* (London, 1936) p. 535.

5. Lionel Trilling, 'Freud and Literature', in his *The Liberal Imagination* (New York, 1950; London, 1951) p. 39 (of 1951 edition).

6. Bernard Bergonzi, *The Situation of the Novel* (London, 1970) pp. 15, 16.

7. Ibid., p. 20.

8. Northrop Frye, *The Stubborn Structure* (London, 1970) p. 231.

9. Richard Stang in *The Theory of the Novel in England, 1850–1870* (New York, 1959) shows that there was a widespread interest during that period in the nature of the novel. See also Kenneth Graham, *English Criticism of the Novel 1865–1900* (London, 1965).

10. See 'The Art of Fiction', reprinted below.

11. See the historical setting provided by Mark Spilka, 'Henry James and Walter Besant: "The Art of Fiction" Controversy', *Novel*, VI 2 (Winter 1973), 101–19.

12. The Prefaces are collected and introduced by R. P. Blackmur as *The Art of the Novel* (New York, 1934).

13. D. H. Lawrence, 'The Spirit of Place, *Studies in Classic American Literature* (London, 1924) p. 9.

14. D. H. Lawrence, 'The Novel', *Reflections on the Death of a Porcupine* (Philadelphia, 1925) p. 104.

15. At the time of writing, a new book by Leavis on Lawrence has just appeared *Thought, Words, and Creativity* (London, 1976).

16. The essay is 'On the Teaching of Modern Literature', *Beyond Culture* (London, 1966) pp. 3–30.

17. This is the closing sentence of chapter 1 of Booth's *The Rhetoric of Fiction* (Chicago, 1961).

18. Barbara Hardy, *The Novels of George Eliot* (London, 1959; reprinted with corrections 1963) pp. 10, 12 (of 1963 edition).

19. Hardy, 'Towards a Poetics of Fiction: 3) An Approach through Narrative', *Novel*, II 1 (Fall 1968) 5.

20. Hardy, *The Novels of George Eliot*, p. 11.

21. Robert Scholes, *The Fabulators* (New York, 1967) p. 11.

22. See, for example, Scholes, 'The Fictional Criticism of the Future', *Triquarterly*, XXXIV (Fall 1975) 233–47.

23. Malcolm Bradbury, *Possibilities* (London, 1973) p. 27.

24. Terry Eagleton, *Exiles and Emigrés* (London, 1970) p. 10.

PART ONE

A Major Tradition

Henry James

1. THE ART OF FICTION (1884)

I should not have affixed so comprehensive a title to these few remarks, necessarily wanting in any completeness upon a subject the full consideration of which would carry us far, did I not seem to discover a pretext for my temerity in the interesting pamphlet lately published under this name by Mr Walter Besant. Mr Besant's lecture at the Royal Institution – the original form of his pamphlet – appears to indicate that many persons are interested in the art of fiction, and are not indifferent to such remarks, as those who practise it may attempt to make about it. I am therefore anxious not to lose the benefit of this favourable association, and to edge in a few words under cover of the attention which Mr Besant is sure to have excited. There is something very encouraging in his having put into form certain of his ideas on the mystery of story-telling.

It is a proof of life and curiosity – curiosity on the part of the brotherhood of novelists as well as on the part of their readers. Only a short time ago it might have been supposed that the English novel was not what the French call *discutable*. It had no air of having a theory, a conviction, a consciousness of itself behind it – of being the expression of an artistic faith, the result of choice and comparison. I do not say it was necessarily the worse for that: it would take much more courage than I possess to intimate that the form of the novel as Dickens and Thackeray (for instance) saw it had any taint of incompleteness. It was, however, *naïf* (if I may help myself out with another French word); and evidently if it be destined to suffer in any way for having lost its *naïveté* it has now an idea of making sure of the corresponding advantages. During the period I have alluded to there was a comfortable, good-humoured feeling abroad that a novel is a novel, as a pudding is a pudding, and that our only business with it could be to swallow it. But within a year or two, for some reason or other, there have been signs of returning animation – the era of discussion would appear to have been to a certain extent opened. Art lives upon discussion, upon experiment, upon curiosity, upon variety of attempt, upon the exchange of views and the comparison of stand-points; and there is a presumption that those times when no one has anything particular to say about it, and has no reason to give for practice or preference, though they may be times of honour, are not times of development – are times, possibly even, a little of dullness. The successful application of any art is a delightful spectacle, but the theory too is interesting; and though there is a great deal of the latter without the former I suspect there has never been a genuine success that has not had a latent core of conviction. Discussion, suggestion, formulation, these things are fertilizing when they are frank and sincere. Mr Besant has set an excellent example in saying what he thinks, for his part, about the way in which fiction should be written, as well as about the way in which it should be published; for his view of the 'art', carried on into an appendix, covers that too. Other labourers in the same field will doubtless take up the argument, they will give it the light of their experience, and the effect will surely be to make our interest in the novel a little more what it had for some time threatened to fail to be – a serious, active, inquiring interest, under protection of which this delightful study may, in moments of confidence, venture to say a little more what it thinks of itself.

It must take itself seriously for the public to take it so. The old superstition about fiction being 'wicked' has doubtless died out in England; but the spirit of it lingers in a certain oblique regard directed toward any story which does not more or less admit that it is only a joke. Even the most jocular novel feels in some degree the weight of the prescription that was formerly directed against literary levity: the jocularity does not always succeed in passing for orthodoxy. It is still expected, though perhaps people are ashamed to say it, that a production which is after all only a 'make-believe' (for what else is a 'story'?) shall be in some degree apologetic – shall renounce the pretension of attempting really to represent life. This, of course, any sensible, wide-awake story declines to do, for it quickly perceives that the tolerance granted to it on such a condition is only an attempt to stifle it disguised in the form of generosity. The old evangelical hostility to the novel, which was as explicit as it was narrow and which regarded it as little less favourable to our immortal part than a stage-play, was in reality far less insulting. The only reason for the existence of a novel is that it does attempt to represent life. When it relinquishes this attempt, the same attempt that we see on the canvas of the painter, it will have arrived at a very strange pass. It is not expected of the picture that it will make itself humble in order to be forgiven; and the analogy between the art of the painter and the art of the novelist is, so far as I am able to see, complete. Their inspiration is the same, their process (allowing for the different quality of the vehicle) is the same, their success is the same. They may learn from each other, they may explain and sustain each other. Their cause is the same, and the honour of one is the honour of another. The Mahometans think a picture an unholy thing, but it is a long time since any Christian did, and it is therefore the more odd that in the Christian mind the traces (dissimulated though they may be) of a suspicion of the sister art should linger to this day. The only effectual way to lay it to rest is to emphasize the analogy to which I just alluded – to insist on the fact that as the picture is reality, so the novel is history. That is the only general description (which does it justice) that we may give of the novel. But history also is allowed to represent life; it is not, any more than painting, expected to apologize. The subject-matter of fiction is stored up likewise in documents and records, and if it will not give itself away, as they say in California, it must speak with assurance, with the tone of the historian. Certain accomplished novelists have a habit of giving themselves away which must often bring tears to the eyes of people who take their fiction seriously. I was lately struck, in reading over many pages of Anthony Trollope, with his want of discretion in this particular. In a digression, a parenthesis or an aside, he concedes to the reader that he and this trusting friend are only 'making believe'. He admits that the events he narrates have not really happened, and that he can give his narrative any turn the reader may like best. Such a betrayal of a sacred office seems to me, I confess, a terrible crime; it is what I mean by the attitude of apology, and it shocks me every whit as much in Trollope as it would have shocked me in Gibbon or Macaulay. It implies that the novelist is less occupied in looking for the truth (the truth, of course I mean, that he assumes, the premises that we must grant him, whatever they may be) than the historian, and in doing so it deprives him at a stroke of all his standing-room. To represent and illustrate the past, the actions of men, is the task of either writer, and the only difference that I can see is, in proportion as he succeeds, to the honour of the novelist, consisting as it does in his having more difficulty in collecting his evidence, which is so far from being purely literary. It seems to me to give him a great character, the fact that he has at once so much in common with the philosopher and the painter; this double analogy is a magnificent heritage.

It is of all this evidently that Mr Besant is full when he insists upon the fact that fiction is one of the *fine* arts, deserving in its turn of all the honours and emoluments that have hitherto been reserved for the successful profession of music, poetry, painting, architecture. It is impossible to insist too much on so important a truth, and the place that Mr Besant demands for the work of the novelist may be represented, a trifle abstractly, by saying that he demands not only that it shall be reputed artistic, but that it shall be reputed very artistic indeed. It is excellent that he should have struck this note, for his doing so indicates that there was need of it, that his proposition may be to many people a novelty. One rubs one's eyes at the thought; but the rest of Mr Besant's essay confirms the revelation. I suspect in truth that it would be possible to confirm it still further, and that one would not be far wrong in saying that in addition to the people to whom it has never occurred that a novel ought to be artistic, there are a great many others who, if this principle were urged upon them, would be filled with indefinable mistrust. They would find it difficult to explain their repugnance, but it would operate strongly to put them on their guard. 'Art', in our Protestant communities, where so many things have got so strangely twisted about, is supposed in certain circles to have some vaguely injurious effect upon those who make it an important consideration, who let it weigh in the balance. It is assumed to be opposed in some mysterious manner to morality, to amusement, to instruction. When it is embodied in the work of the painter (the sculptor is another affair!) you know what it is: it stands there before you, in the honesty of pink and green and a gilt frame; you can see the worst of it at a glance, and you can be on your guard. But when it is introduced into literature it becomes more insidious – there is danger of its hurting you before you know it. Literature should be either instructive or amusing, and there is in many minds an impression that these artistic preoccupations, the search for form contribute to neither end, interfere indeed with both. They are too frivolous to be edifying, and too serious to be diverting; and they are moreover priggish and paradoxical and superfluous. That, I think, represents the manner in which the latent thought of many people who read novels as an exercise in skipping would explain itself if it were to become articulate. They would argue, of course, that a novel ought to be 'good', but they would interpret this term in a fashion of their own, which indeed would vary considerably from one critic to another. One would say that being good means representing virtuous and aspiring characters, placed in prominent positions; another would say that it depends on a 'happy ending', on a distribution at the last of prizes, pensions, husbands, wives, babies, millions, appended paragraphs, and cheerful remarks. Another still would say that it means being full of incident and movement, so that we shall wish to jump ahead, to see who was the mysterious stranger, and if the stolen will was ever found, and shall not be distracted from this pleasure by any tiresome analysis or 'description'. But they would hold it accountable for all the description, another would see it revealed in the absence of sympathy. Its hostility to a happy ending would be evident, and it might even in some cases render any ending at all impossible. The 'ending' of a novel is, for many persons, like that of a good dinner, a course of dessert and ices, and the artist in fiction is regarded as a sort of meddlesome doctor who forbids agreeable aftertastes. It is therefore true that this conception of Mr Besant's of the novel as a superior form encounters not only a negative but a positive indifference. It matters little that as a work of art it should really be as little or as much of its essence to supply happy endings, sympathetic characters, and an objective tone, as if it were a work of mechanics: the association of ideas, however incongruous, might easily be too much for it if an eloquent voice were not sometimes raised to call attention to the fact that it is at once as free and as serious a branch of literature as any other.

Certainly this might sometimes be doubted in presence of the enormous number of works of fiction that appeal to the credulity of our generation, for it might easily seem that there could be no great character in a commodity so quickly and easily produced. It must be admitted that good novels are much compromised by bad ones, and that the field at large suffers discredit from overcrowding. I think, however, that this injury is only superficial, and that the super-abundance of written fiction proves nothing against the principle itself. It has been vulgarized, like all other kinds of literature, like everything else to-day, and it has proved more than some kinds accessible to vulgarization. But there is as much difference as there ever was between a good novel and a bad one: the bad is swept with all the daubed canvases and spoiled marble into some unvisited limbo, or infinite rubbish-yard beneath the back-windows of the world, and the good subsists and emits its light and stimulates our desire for perfection. As I shall take the liberty of making but a single criticism of Mr Besant, whose tone is so full of the love of his art, I may as well have done with it at once. He seems to me to mistake in attempting to say so definitely beforehand what sort of an affair the good novel will be. To indicate the danger of such an error as that has been the purpose of these few pages; to suggest that certain traditions on the subject, applied *a priori*, have already had much to answer for, and that the good health of an art which undertakes so immediately to reproduce life must demand that it be perfectly free. It lives upon exercise, and the very meaning of exercise is freedom. The only obligation to which in advance we may hold a novel, without incurring the accusation of being arbitrary, is that it be interesting. That general responsibility rests upon it, but it is the only one I can think of. The ways in which it is at liberty to accomplish this result (of interesting us) strike me as innumerable, and such as can only suffer from being marked out or fenced in by prescription. They are as various as the temperament of man, and they are successful in proportion as they reveal a particular mind, different from others. A novel is in its broadest definition a personal, a direct impression of life: that, to begin with, constitutes its value, which is greater or less according to the intensity of the impression. But there will be no intensity at all, and therefore no value, unless there is freedom to feel and say. The tracing of a line to be followed, of a tone to be taken, of a form to be filled out is a limitation of that freedom and a suppression of the very thing that we are most curious about. The form, it seems to me, is to be appreciated after the fact: then the author's choice has been made, his standard has been indicated; then we can follow lines and directions and compare tones and resemblances. Then in a word we can enjoy one of the most charming of pleasures, we can estimate quality, we can apply the test of execution. The execution belongs to the author alone; it is what is most personal to him, and we measure him by that. The advantage, the luxury, as well as the torment and responsibility of the novelist, is that there is no limit to what he may attempt as an executant – no limit to his possible experiments, efforts, discoveries, successes. Here it is especially that he works, step by step, like his brother of the brush, of whom we may always say that he has painted his picture in a manner best known to himself. His manner is his secret, not necessarily a jealous one. He cannot disclose it as a general thing if he would; he would be at a loss to teach it to others. I say this with a due recollection of having insisted on the community of method of the artist who paints a picture and the artist who writes a novel. The painter *is* able to teach the rudiments of his practice, and it is possible, from the study of good work (granted the aptitude), both to learn how to paint and to learn how to write. Yet it remains true, without injury to the *rapprochement*, that the literary artist would be obliged to say to his pupil much more than the other, 'Ah, well, you must do it as you can!' It is a question of degree, a matter of delicacy. If there are exact sciences, there are also exact arts, and the grammar of painting is so much more definite that it makes the difference.

I ought to add, however, that if Mr Besant says at the beginning of his essay that the 'laws of fiction may be laid down and taught with as much precision and exactness as the laws of harmony, perspective, and proportion', he mitigates what might appear to be an extravagance by applying his remark to 'general' laws, and by expressing most of these rules in a manner with which it would certainly be unaccommodating to disagree. That the novelist must write from his experience, that his 'characters must be real and such as might be met with in actual life': that 'a young lady brought up in a quiet country village should avoid descriptions of garrison life', and 'a writer whose friends and personal experiences belong to the lower middle-class should carefully avoid introducing his characters into society'; that one should enter one's notes in a common-place book; that one's figures should be clear in outline; that making them clear by some trick of speech or of carriage is a bad method, and 'describing them at length' is a worse one; that English Fiction should have a 'conscious moral purpose'; that 'it is almost impossible to estimate too highly the value of careful workmanship – that is, of style'; that 'the most important point of all is the story', that 'the story is everything': these are principles with most of which it is surely impossible not to sympathize. That remark about the lower middle-class writer and his knowing his place is perhaps rather chilling; but for the rest I should find it difficult to dissent from any one of these recommendations. At the same time, I should find it difficult positively to assent to them, with the exception, perhaps, of the injunction as to entering one's notes in a common-place book. They scarcely seem to me to have the quality that Mr Besant attributes to the rules of the novelist – the 'precision and exactness' of 'the laws of harmony, perspective, and proportion'. They are suggestive, they are even inspiring, but they are not exact, though they are doubtless as much so as the case admits of: which is a proof of that liberty of interpretation for which I just contended. For the value of these different injunctions - so beautiful and so vague – is wholly in the meaning one attaches to them. The characters, the situation, which strike one as real will be those that touch and interest one most, but the measure of reality is very difficult to fix. The reality of Don Quixote or of Mr Micawber is a very delicate shade; it is a reality so coloured by the author's vision that, vivid as it may be, one would hesitate to propose it as a model: one would expose one's self to some very embarrassing questions on the part of a pupil. It goes without saying that you will not write a good novel unless you possess the sense of reality; but it will be difficult to give you a recipe for calling that sense into being. Humanity is immense, and reality has a myriad forms; the most one can affirm is that some of the flowers of fiction have the odour of it, and others have not; as for telling you in advance how your nosegay should be composed, that is another affair. It is equally excellent and inconclusive to say that one must write from experience; to our suppositious aspirant such a declaration might savour of mockery. What kind of experience is intended, and where does it begin and end? Experience is never limited, and it is never complete; it is an immense sensibility, a kind of huge spider-web of the finest silken threads suspended in the chamber of consciousness, and catching every air-borne particle in its tissue. It is the very atmosphere of the mind; and when the mind is imaginative – much more when it happens to be that of a man of genius – it takes to itself the faintest hints of life, it converts the very pulses of the air into revelations. The young lady living in a village has only to be a damsel upon whom nothing is lost to make it quite unfair (as it seems to me) to declare to her that she shall have nothing to say about the military. Greater miracles have been seen than that, imagination assisting, she should speak the truth about some of these gentlemen. I remember an English novelist, a woman of genius, telling me that she was much commended for the impression she had managed to give in one of her tales of the nature and way of life of the French Protestant youth. She had been asked where she learned so much about this recondite being, she had been congratulated on her peculiar opportunities. These opportunities consisted in her having once, in Paris, as she ascended a staircase, passed an open door where, in the household of a *pasteur*, some of the young Protestants were seated at table round a finished meal. The glimpse made a picture: it lasted only a moment, but that moment was experience. She had got her direct personal impression, and she turned out her type. She knew what youth was, and what Protestantism; she also had the advantage of having seen what it was to be French, so that she converted these ideas into a concrete image and produced a reality. Above all, however, she was blessed with the faculty which when you give it an inch takes an ell, and which for the artist is a much greater source of strength than any accident of residence or of place in the social scale. The power to guess the unseen from the seen, to trace the implication of things, to judge the whole piece by the pattern, the condition of feeling life in general so completely that you are well on your way to knowing any particular corner of it – this cluster of gifts may almost be said to constitute experience, and they occur in country and in town and in the most differing stages of education. If experience consists of impressions, it may be said that impressions *are* experience, just as (have we not seen it?) they are the very air we breathe. Therefore, if I should certainly say to a novice, 'Write from experience and experience only', I should feel that this was rather a tantalizing monition if I were not careful immediately to add, 'Try to be one of the people on whom nothing is lost!'

I am far from intending by this to minimize the importance of exactness – of truth of detail. One can speak best from one's own taste, and I may therefore venture to say that the air of reality (solidity of specification) seems to me to be the supreme virtue of a novel – the merit on which all its other merits (including that conscious moral purpose of which Mr Besant speaks) helplessly and submissively depend. If it be not there they are all as nothing, and if these be there, they owe their effect to the success with which the author has produced the illusion of life. The cultivation of this success, the study of this exquisite process form, to my taste, the beginning and the end of the art of the novelist. They are his inspiration, his despair, his reward, his torment, his delight. It is here in very truth that he competes with life; it is here that he competes with his brother the painter in *his* attempt to render the look of things, the look that conveys their meaning, to catch the colour, the relief, the expression, the surface, the substance of the human spectacle. It is in regard to this that Mr Besant is well inspired when he bids him take notes. He cannot possibly take too many, he cannot possibly take enough. All life solicits him, and to 'render' the simplest surface, to produce the most momentary illusion, is a very complicated business. His case would be easier, and the rule would be more exact, if Mr Besant had been able to tell him what notes to take. But this, I fear, he can never learn in any manual; it is the business of his life. He has to take a great many in order to select a few, he has to work them up as he can, and even the guides and philosophers who might have most to say to him must leave him alone when it comes to the application of precepts, as we leave the painter in communion with his palette. That his characters 'must be clear in outline', as Mr Besant says – he feels that down to his boots; but how he shall make them so is a secret between his good angel and himself. It would be absurdly simple if he could be taught that a great deal of 'description' would make them so, or that on the contrary the absence of description and the cultivation of dialogue, or the absence of dialogue and the multiplication of 'incident', would rescue him from his difficulties. Nothing, for instance, is more possible than that he be of a turn of mind for which this odd, literal opposition of description and dialogue, incident and description, has little meaning and light. People often talk of these things as if they had a kind of internecine distinctness, instead of melting into each other at every breath, and being intimately associated parts of one general effort of expression. I cannot imagine composition existing in a series of blocks, nor conceive, in any novel worth discussing at all, of a passage of description that is not in its intention narrative, a passage of dialogue that is not in its intention descriptive, a touch of truth of any sort that does not partake of the nature of incident, or an incident that derives its interest from any other source than the general and only source of the success of a work of art – that of being illustrative. A novel is a living thing, all one and continuous, like any other organism, and in proportion as it lives will it be found, that in each of the parts there is something of each of the other parts. The critic who over the close texture of a finished work shall pretend to trace a geography of items will mark some frontiers as artificial, I fear, as any that have been known to history. There is an old-fashioned distinction between the novel of character and the novel of incident which must have cost many a smile to the intending fabulist who was keen about his work. It appears to me as little to the point as the equally celebrated distinction between the novel and the romance – to answer as little to any reality. There are bad novels and good novels, as there are bad pictures and good pictures; but that is the only distinction in which I see any meaning, and I can as little imagine speaking of a novel of character as I can imagine speaking of a picture of character. When one says picture one says of character, when one says novel one says of incident, and the terms may be transposed at will. What is character but the determination of incident? What is incident but the illustration of character? What is either a picture or a novel that is *not* of character? What else do we seek in it and find in it? It is an incident for a woman to stand up with her hand resting on a table and look out at you in a certain way; or if it be not an incident I think it will be hard to say what it is. At the same time it is an expression of character. If you say you don't see it (character in *that – allons donc!*), this is exactly what the artist who has reason of his own for thinking he *does* see it undertakes to show you. When a young man makes up his mind that he has not faith enough after all to enter the church as he intended, that is an incident, though you may not hurry to the end of the chapter to see whether perhaps he doesn't change once more. I do not say that these are extraordinary or startling incidents. I do not pretend to estimate the degree of interest proceeding from them, for this will depend upon the skill of the painter. It sounds almost puerile to say that some incidents are intrinsically much more important than others, and I need not take this precaution after having professed my sympathy for the major ones in remarking that the only classification of the novel that I can understand is into that which has life and that which has it not.

The novel and the romance, the novel of incident and that of character – these clumsy separations appear to me to have been made by critics and readers for their own convenience, and to help them out of some of their occasional queer predicaments, but to have little reality or interest for the producer, from whose point of view it is of course that we are attempting to consider the art of fiction. The case is the same with another shadowy category which Mr Besant apparently is disposed to set up – that of the 'modern English novel'; unless indeed it be that in this matter he has fallen into an accidental confusion of stand-points. It is not quite clear whether he intends the remarks in which he alludes to it to be didactic or historical. It is as difficult to suppose a person intending to write a modern English as to suppose him writing an ancient English novel: that is a label which begs the question. One writes the novel, one paints the picture, of one's language and of one's time, and calling it modern English will not, alas! make the difficult task any easier. No more, unfortunately, will calling this or that work of one's fellow-artist a romance – unless it be, of course, simply for the pleasantness of the thing, as for instance when Hawthorne gave this heading to his story of *Blithedale*. The French, who have brought the

theory of fiction to remarkable completeness, have but one name for the
novel, and have not attempted smaller things in it, that I can see, for
that. I can think of no obligation to which the 'romancer' would not be
held equally with the novelist; the standard of execution is equally high
for each. Of course it is of execution that we are talking – that being the
only point of a novel that is open to contention. This is perhaps too often
lost sight of, only to produce interminable confusions and cross-
purposes. We must grant the artist his subject, his idea, his *donnée*: our
criticism is applied only to what he makes of it. Naturally I do not mean
that we are bound to like it or find it interesting: in case we do not our
course is perfectly simple – to let it alone. We may believe that of a
certain idea even the most sincere novelist can make nothing at all, and
the event may perfectly justify our belief; but the failure will have been a
failure to execute, and it is in the execution that the fatal weakness is
recorded. If we pretend to respect the artist at all, we must allow him his
freedom of choice, in the face, in particular cases, of innumerable
presumptions that the choice will not fructify. Art derives a considerable part of its beneficial exercise from flying in the face of presumptions, and some of the most interesting experiments of which it is
capable are hidden in the bosom of common things. Gustave Flaubert
has written a story about the devotion of a servant-girl to a parrot, and
the production, highly finished as it is, cannot on the whole be called a
success. We are perfectly free to find it flat, but I think it might have
been interesting; and I, for my part, am extremely glad he should have
written it; it is a contribution to our knowledge of what can be done – or
what cannot. Ivan Turgénieff has written a tale about a deaf and dumb
serf and a lap-dog, and the thing is touching, loving, a little masterpiece.
He struck the note of life where Gustave Flaubert missed it – he flew in
the face of a presumption and achieved a victory.

Nothing, of course, will ever take the place of the good old fashion of
'liking' a work of art or not liking it: the most improved criticism will not
abolish that primitive, that ultimate test. I mention this to guard myself
from the accusation of intimating that the idea, the subject, of a novel or
a picture, does not matter. It matters, to my sense, in the highest degree,
and if I might put up a prayer it would be that artists should select none
but the richest. Some, as I have already hastened to admit, are much
more remunerative than others, and it would be a world happily
arranged in which persons intending to treat them should be exempt
from confusions and mistakes. This fortunate condition will arrive only,

I fear, on the same day that critics become purged from error. Meanwhile, I repeat, we do not judge the artist with fairness unless we say to him,

Oh, I grant you your starting-point, because if I did not I should seem to prescribe to you, and heaven forbid I should take that responsibility. If I pretend to tell you what you must not take, you will call upon me to tell you then what you must take; in which case I shall be prettily caught. Moreover, it isn't till I have accepted your data that I can begin to measure you. I have the standard, the pitch; I have no right to tamper with your flute and then criticize your music. Of course I may not care for your idea at all; I may think it silly, or stale, or unclean; in which case I wash my hands of you altogether. I may content myself with believing that you will not have succeeded in being interesting, but I shall, of course, not attempt to demonstrate it, and you will be as indifferent to me as I am to you. I needn't remind you that there are all sorts of tastes: who can know it better? Some people, for excellent reasons, don't like to read about courtesans. Many object to Americans. Others (I believe they are mainly editors and publishers) won't look at Italians. Some readers don't like quiet subjects; others don't like bustling ones. Some enjoy a complete illusion, others the consciousness of large concessions. They choose their novels accordingly, and if they don't care about your idea they won't, *a fortiori*, care about your treatment.

So that it comes back very quickly, as I have said, to the liking: in spite of M. Zola, who reasons less powerfully than he represents, and who will not reconcile himself to this absoluteness of taste, thinking that there are certain things that people ought to like, and that they can be made to like. I am quite at a loss to imagine anything (at any rate in this matter of fiction) that people *ought* to like or to dislike. Selection will be sure to take care of itself, for it has a constant motive behind it. That motive is simply experience. As people feel life, so they will feel the art that is most closely related to it. This closeness of relation is what we should never forget in talking of the effort of the novel. Many people speak of it as a factitious, artificial form, a product of ingenuity, the business of which is to alter and arrange the things that surround us, to translate them into conventional, traditional moulds. This, however, is a view of the matter which carries us but a very short way, condemns the art to an eternal repetition of a few familiar *clichés*, cuts short its development and leads us straight up to a dead wall. Catching the very note and trick, the strange irregular rhythm of life, that is the attempt whose strenuous force keeps Fiction upon her feet. In proportion as in what she offers us we see life *without* rearrangement do we feel that we are touching the truth; in proportion as we see it *with* arrangement do we feel that we are being put off with a substitute, a compromise and convention. It is not uncommon to hear an extraordinary assurance of remark in regard to this matter of rearranging, which is often spoken of as if it were the last word of art. Mr Besant seems to me in danger of falling into the great error with his rather unguarded talk about 'selection'. Art is essentially selection, but it is a selection whose main care is to be typical, to be inclusive. For many people art means rose-coloured window-panes, and selection means picking a bouquet for Mrs Grundy. They will tell you glibly that artistic considerations have nothing to do with the disagreeable, with the ugly; they will rattle off shallow common-places about the province of art and the limits of art till you are moved to some wonder in return as to the province and the limits of ignorance. It appears to me that no one can ever have made a seriously artistic attempt without becoming conscious of an immense increase – a kind of revelation – of freedom. One perceives in that case – by the light of a heavenly ray – that the province of art is all life, all feeling, all observation, all vision. As Mr Besant so justly intimates, it is all experience. That is a sufficient answer to those who maintain that it must not touch the sad things of life, who stick into its divine unconscious bosom little prohibitory inscriptions on the end of sticks, such as we see in public gardens – 'It is forbidden to walk on the grass; it is forbidden to touch the flowers; it is not allowed to introduce dogs or to remain after dark; it is requested to keep to the right.' The young aspirant in the line of fiction whom we continue to imagine will do nothing without taste, for in that case his freedom would be of little use to him; but the first advantage of his taste will be to reveal to him the absurdity of the little sticks and tickets. If he have taste, I must add, of course he will have ingenuity, and my disrespectful reference to that quality just now was not meant to imply that it is useless in fiction. But it is ony a secondary aid; the first is a capacity for receiving straight impressions.

Mr Besant has some remarks on the question of 'the story' which I shall not attempt to criticize, though they seem to me to contain a singular ambiguity, because I do not think I understand them. I cannot see what is meant by talking as if there were a part of a novel which is the story and part of it which for mystical reasons is not – unless indeed the distinction be made in a sense in which it is difficult to suppose that any one should attempt to convey anything. 'The story', if it represents anything, represents the subject, the idea, the *donnée* of the novel; and there is surely no 'school' – Mr Besant speaks of a school – which urges that a novel should be all treatment and no subject. There must assuredly be something to treat; every school is intimately conscious of that. This sense of the story being the idea, the starting-point, of the novel, is the only one that I see in which it can be spoken of as something different from its organic whole; and since in proportion as the work is successful the idea permeates and penetrates it, informs and animates it, so that every word and every punctuation-point contribute directly to the expression, in that proportion do we lose our sense of the story being a blade which may be drawn more or less out of its sheath. The story and the novel, the idea and the form, are the needle and thread, and I never heard of a guild of tailors who recommended the use of the thread without the needle, or the needle without the thread. Mr Besant is not the only critic who may be observed to have spoken as if there were certain things in life which constitute stories, and certain others which do not. I find the same odd implication in an entertaining article in the *Pall Mall Gazette*, devoted, as it happens, to Mr Besant's lecture. 'The story is the thing!' says this graceful writer, as if with a tone of opposition to some other idea. I should think it was, as every painter who, as the time for 'sending in' his picture looms in the distance, finds himself still in quest of a subject – as every belated artist not fixed about his theme will heartily agree. There are some subjects which speak to us and others which do not, but he would be a clever man who should undertake to give a rule – an *index expurgatorius* – by which the story and the no-story should be known apart. It is impossible (to me at least) to imagine any such rule which shall not be altogether arbitrary. The writer in the *Pall Mall* opposes the delightful (as I suppose) novel of *Margot la Balafrée* to certain tales in which 'Bostonian "nymphs" appear to have "rejected English dukes for psychological reasons" '. I am not acquainted with the romance just designated, and can scarcely forgive the *Pall Mall* critic for not mentioning the name of the author, but the title appears to refer to a lady who may have received a scar in some heroic adventure. I am inconsolable at not being acquainted with this episode, but am utterly at a loss to see why it is a story when the rejection (or acceptance) of a duke is not, and why a reason, psychological or other, is not a subject when a cicatrix is. They are all particles of the multitudinous life with which the novel deals, and surely no dogma which pretends to make it lawful to touch the one and unlawful to touch the other will stand for a moment on its feet. It is the special picture that must stand or fall, according as it seem to possess truth or to lack it. Mr Besant does not, to my sense, light up the subject by intimating that a story must, under penalty of not being a story, consist of 'adventures'. Why of adventures more than of green spectacles? He mentions a category of impossible things, and among them he places 'fiction without adventure'. Why without adventure, more than without matrimony, or celibacy, or parturition, or cholera, or hydropathy, or Jansenism? This seems to me to bring the novel back to the hapless little *rôle* of being an artificial, ingenious thing – bring it down from its large, free character of an immense and exquisite correspondence with life. And what *is* adventure, when it comes to that, and by what sign is the listening pupil to recognize it? It is an adventure – an immense one – for me to write this little article; and for a Bostonian nymph to reject an English duke is an adventure only less stirring, I should say, than for an English duke to be rejected by a Bostonian nymph. I see dramas within dramas in that, and innumerable points of view. A psychological reason is, to my imagination, an object adorably pictorial; to catch the tint of its complexion – I feel as if that idea might inspire one to Titianesque efforts. There are few things more exciting to me, in short, than a psychological reason, and yet, I protest, the novel seems to me the most magnificent form of art. I have just been reading at the same time, the delightful story of *Treasure Island*, by Mr Robert Louis Stevenson and, in a manner less consecutive, the last tale from M. Edmond de Goncourt, which is entitled *Chérie*. One of these works treats of murders, mysteries, islands of dreadful renown, hair-breadth escapes, miraculous coincidences and buried doubloons. The other treats of a little French girl who lived in a fine house in Paris, and died of wounded sensibility because no one would marry her. I call *Treasure Island* delightful, because it appears to me to have succeeded wonderfully in what it attempts; and I venture to bestow no epithet upon *Chérie*, which strikes me as having failed deplorably in what it attempts – that is in tracing the development of the moral consciousness of a child. But one of these productions strikes me as exactly as much of a novel as the other, and as having a 'story' quite as much. The moral consciousness of a child is as much a part of life as the islands of the Spanish Main, and the one sort of geography seems to me to have those 'surprises' of which Mr Besant speaks quite as much as the other. For myself (since it comes back in the last resort, as I say, to the preference of the individual), the picture of the child's

experience has the advantage that I can at successive steps (an immense
luxury, near to the 'sensual pleasure' of which Mr Besant's critic in the
Pall Mall speaks) say Yes or No, as it may be, to what the artist puts
before me. I have been a child in fact, but I have been on a quest for a
buried treasure only in supposition, and it is a simple accident that with
M. de Goncourt I should have for the most part to say No. With George
Eliot, when she painted that country with a far other intelligence, I
always said Yes.

The most interesting part of Mr Besant's lecture is unfortunately the
briefest passage – his very cursory allusion to the 'conscious moral
purpose' of the novel. Here again it is not very clear whether he be
recording a fact or laying down a principle; it is a great pity that in the
latter case he should not have developed his idea. This branch of the
subject is of immense importance, and Mr Besant's few words point to
considerations of the widest reach, not to be lightly disposed of. He will
have treated the art of fiction but superficially who is not prepared to go
every inch of the way that these considerations will carry him. It is for
this reason that at the beginning of these remarks I was careful to notify
the reader that my reflections on so large a theme have no pretension to
be exhaustive. Like Mr Besant, I have left the question of the morality of
the novel till the last, and at the last I find I have used up my space. It is
a question surrounded with difficulties, as witness the very first that
meets us, in the form of a definite question, on the threshold. Vagueness,
in such a discussion, is fatal, and what is the meaning of your morality
and your conscious moral purpose? Will you not define your terms and
explain how (a novel being a picture) a picture can be either moral or
immoral? You wish to paint a moral picture or carve a moral statue: will
you not tell us how you would set about it? We are discussing the Art of
Fiction; questions of art are questions (in the widest sense) of execution;
questions of morality are quite another affair, and will you not let us see
how it is that you find it so easy to mix them up? These things are so clear
to Mr Besant that he has deduced from them a law which he sees
embodied in English Fiction, and which is 'a truly admirable thing and
a great cause for congratulation'. It is a great cause for congratulation
indeed when such thorny problems become as smooth as silk. I may add
that in so far as Mr Besant preceives that in point of fact English Fiction
has addressed itself preponderantly to these delicate questions he will
appear to many people to have made a vain discovery. They will have
been positively struck, on the contrary, with the moral timidity of the

usual English novelist; with his (or with her) aversion to face the difficulties with which on every side the treatment of reality bristles. He is apt to be extremely shy (whereas the picture that Mr Besant draws is a picture of boldness), and the sign of his work, for the most part, is a cautious silence on certain subjects. In the English novel (by which of course I mean the American as well), more than in any other, there is a traditional difference between that which people know and that which they agree to admit that they know, that which they see and that which they speak of, that which they feel to be a part of life and that which they allow to enter into literature. There is the great difference, in short, between what they talk of in conversation and what they talk of in print. The essence of moral energy is to survey the whole field, and I should directly reverse Mr Besant's remark and say not that the English novel has a purpose, but that it has a diffidence. To what degree a purpose in a work of art is a source of corruption I shall not attempt to inquire; the one that seems to me least dangerous is the purpose of making a perfect work. As for our novel, I may say lastly on this score that as we find it in England to-day it strikes me as addressed in a large degree to 'young people', and that this in itself constitutes a presumption that it will be rather shy. There are certain things which it is generally agreed not to discuss, not even to mention, before young people. That is very well, but the absence of discussion is not a symptom of the moral passion. The purpose of the English novel – 'a truly admirable thing, and a great cause for congratulation' – strikes me therefore as rather negative.

There is one point at which the moral sense and the artistic sense lie very near together; that is in the light of the very obvious truth that the deepest quality of a work of art will always be the quality of the mind of the producer. In proportion as that intelligence is fine will the novel, the picture, the statue partake of the substance of beauty and truth. To be constituted of such elements is, to my vision, to have purpose enough. No good novel will ever proceed from a superficial mind; that seems to me an axiom which, for the artist in fiction, will cover all needful moral ground: if the youthful aspirant take it to heart it will illuminate for him many of the mysteries of 'purpose'. There are many other useful things that might be said to him, but I have come to the end of my article, and can only touch them as I pass. The critic in the *Pall Mall Gazette*, whom I have already quoted, draws attention to the danger, in speaking of the art of fiction, of generalizing. The danger that he has in mind is rather, I imagine, that of particularizing, for there are some comprehensive remarks which, in addition to those embodied in Mr Besant's suggestive lecture, might without fear of misleading him be addressed to the ingenuous student. I should remind him first of the magnificence of the form that is open to him, which offers to sight so few restrictions and such innumerable opportunities. The other arts, in comparison, appear confined and hampered; the various conditions under which they are exercised are so rigid and definite. But the only condition that I can think of attaching to the composition of the novel is, as I have already said, that it be sincere. This freedom is a splendid privilege, and the first lesson of the young novelist is to learn to be worthy of it.

Enjoy it as it deserves [I should say to him]; take possession of it, explore it to its utmost extent, publish it, rejoice in it. All life belongs to you, and do not listen either to those who would shut you up into corners of it and tell you that it is only here and there that art inhabits, or to those who would persuade you that this heavenly messenger wings her way outside of life altogether, breathing a superfine air, and turning away her head from the truth of things. There is no impression of life, no manner of seeing it and feeling it, to which the plan of the novelist may not offer a place; you have only to remember that talents so dissimilar as those of Alexandre Dumas and Jane Austen, Charles Dickens and Gustave Flaubert have worked in this field with equal glory. Do not think too much about optimism and pessimism; try and catch the colour of life itself. In France to-day we see a prodigious effort (that of Emile Zola, to whose solid and serious work no explorer of the capacity of the novel can allude without respect), we see an extraordinary effort vitiated by a spirit of pessimism on a narrow basis. M. Zola is magnificent, but he strikes an English reader as ignorant; he has an air of working in the dark; if he had as much light as energy, his results would be of the highest value. As for the aberrations of a shallow optimism, the ground (of English fiction especially) is strewn with their brittle particles as with broken glass. If you must indulge in conclusions, let them have the taste of a wild knowledge. Remember that your first duty is to be as complete as possible – to make as perfect a work. Be generous and delicate and pursue the prize.

SOURCE: *Longman's Magazine,* IV (September 1884); reprinted with minor corrections in *Partial Portraits* (London, 1888) pp. 78–97.

2. 'THE HOUSE OF FICTION' (1908)

. . . There is, I think, no more nutritive or suggestive truth in this connection [viz. whether 'subjects' for a novel can be of themselves moral or immoral – Ed.] than that of the perfect dependence of the 'moral' sense of a work of art on the amount of felt life concerned in producing it. The question comes back thus, obviously, to the kind and the degree of the artist's prime sensibility, which is the soil out of which his subject springs. The quality and capacity of that soil, its ability to 'grow' with due freshness and straightness any vision of life, represents, strongly or weakly, the projected morality. That element is but another name for the more or less close connexion of the subject with some mark made on the intelligence, with some sincere experience. By which, at the same time, of course, one is far from contending that this enveloping air of the artist's humanity – which gives the last touch to the worth of the work – is not a widely and wondrously varying element; being on one occasion a rich and magnificent medium and on another a comparatively poor and ungenerous one. Here we get exactly the high price of the novel as a literary form – its power not only, while preserving that form with closeness, to range through all the differences of the individual relation to its general subject-matter, all the varieties of outlook on life, of disposition to reflect and project, created by conditions that are never the same from man to man (or, so far as that goes, from man to woman), but positively to appear more true to its character in proportion as it strains, or tends to burst, with a latent extravagance, its mould.

The house of fiction has in short not one window, but a million – a number of possible windows not to be reckoned, rather; every one of which has been pierced, or is still pierceable, in its vast front, by the need of the individual vision and by the pressure of the individual will. These apertures, of dissimilar shape and size, hang so, all together, over the human scene that we might have expected of them a greater sameness of report than we find. They are but windows at the best, mere holes in a dead wall, disconnected, perched aloft; they are not hinged doors opening straight upon life. But they have this mark of their own that at each of them stands a figure with a pair of eyes, or at least with a field-glass, which forms, again and again, for observation, a unique instrument, insuring to the person making use of it an impression distinct from every other. He and his neighbours are watching the same show, but one seeing more where the other sees less, one seeing black where the other sees white, one seeing big where the other sees small, one seeing coarse where the other sees fine. And so on, and so on; there is fortunately no saying on what, for the particular pair of eyes, the window may *not* open; 'fortunately' by reason, precisely, of this incalculability of range. The spreading field, the human scene, is the 'choice of subject'; the pierced aperture, either broad or balconied or slit-like and low-browed, is the 'literary form'; but they are, singly or together, as nothing without the posted presence of the watcher – without, in other words, the consciousness of the artist. Tell me what the artist is, and I will tell you of what he has *been* conscious. Thereby I shall express to you at once his boundless freedom and his 'moral' reference. . . .

SOURCE: extract from Preface to *The Portrait of a Lady*, vol. III of the New York edition of James's novels (1908) pp. 45–7.

D. H. Lawrence

1. MORALITY AND THE NOVEL (1925)

The business of art is to reveal the relations between man and his circumambient universe, at the living moment. As mankind is always struggling in the toils of old relationships, art is always ahead of the 'times', which themselves are always far in the rear of the living moment.

When van Gogh paints sunflowers, he reveals, or achieves, the vivid relation between himself, as man, and the sunflower, as sunflower, at that quick moment of time. His painting does not represent the sunflower itself. We shall never know what the sunflower itself is. And the camera will *visualize* the sunflower far more perfectly than van Gogh can.

The vision on the canvas is a third thing, utterly intangible and inexplicable, the offspring of the sunflower itself and van Gogh himself. The vision on the canvas is for ever incommensurable with the canvas, or the paint, or van Gogh as a human organism, or the sunflower as a botanical organism. You cannot weigh nor measure nor even describe the vision on the canvas. It exists, to tell the truth, only in the much-debated fourth dimension. In dimensional space it has no existence.

It is a revelation of the perfected relation, at a certain moment, between a man and a sunflower. It is neither man-in-the-mirror nor flower-in-the-mirror, neither is it above or below or across anything. It is in between everything, in the fourth dimension.

And this perfected relation between man and his circumambient universe is life itself, for mankind. It has the fourth-dimensional quality of eternity and perfection. Yet it is momentaneous.

Man and the sunflower both pass away from the moment, in the process of forming a new relationship. The relation between all things changes from day to day, in a subtle stealth of change. Hence art, which reveals or attains to another perfect relationship, will be for ever new.

At the same time, that which exists in the non-dimensional space of pure relationship is deathless, lifeless, and eternal. That is, it gives us the *feeling* of being beyond life or death. We say an Assyrian lion or an Egyptian hawk's head 'lives'. What we really mean is that it is beyond life, and therefore beyond death. It gives us that feeling. And there is something inside us which must also be beyond life and beyond death, since that 'feeling' which we get from an Assyrian lion or an Egyptian hawk's head is so infinitely precious to us. As the evening star, that spark of pure relation between night and day, has been precious to man since time began.

If we think about it, we find that our life *consists in* this achieving of a pure relationship between ourselves and the living universe about us. This is how I 'save my soul' by accomplishing a pure relationship between me and another person, me and other people, me and a nation, me and a race of men, me and the animals, me and the trees or flowers, me and the earth, me and the skies and sun and stars, me and the moon: an infinity of pure relations, big and little, like the stars of the sky: that makes our eternity, for each one of us, me and the timber I am sawing, the lines of force I follow; me and the dough I knead for bread, me and the very motion with which I write, me and the bit of gold I have got. This, if we knew it, is our life and our eternity. the subtle, perfected relation between me and my whole circumambient universe.

And morality is that delicate, for ever trembling and changing *balance* between me and my circumambient universe, which precedes and accompanies a true relatedness.

Now here we see the beauty and the great value of the novel. Philosophy, religion, science, they are all of them busy nailing things down, to get a stable equilibrium. Religion, with its nailed down One God, who says *Thou shalt, Thou shan't,* and hammers home every time; philosophy, with its fixed ideas; science with its 'laws': they, all of them, all the time, want to nail us on to some tree or other.

But the novel, no. The novel is the highest example of subtle inter-relatedness that man has discovered. Everything is true in its own time, place, circumstance, and untrue outside of its own place, time, circumstance. If you try to nail anything down, in the novel, either it kills the novel, or the novel gets up and walks away with the nail.

Morality in the novel is the trembling instability of the balance. When the novelist puts his thumb in the scale, to pull down the balance to his own predilection, that is immorality.

The modern novel tends to become more and more immoral, as the novelist tends to press his thumb heavier and heavier in the pan: either on the side of love, pure love: or on the side of licentious 'freedom'.

The novel is not, as a rule, immoral because the novelist has any dominant *idea*, or *purpose*. The immorality lies in the novelist's helpless, unconscious predilection. Love is a great emotion. But if you set out to write a novel, and you yourself are in the throes of the great predilection for love, love as the supreme, the only emotion worth living for, then you will write an immoral novel.

Because *no* emotion is supreme, or exclusively worth living for. *All* emotions go to the achieving of a living relationship between a human being and the other human being or creature or thing he becomes purely related to. All emotions, including love and hate, and rage and tenderness, go to the adjusting of the oscillating, unestablished balance between two people who amount to anything. If the novelist puts his thumb in the pan, for love, tenderness, sweetness, peace, then he commits an immoral act: he *prevents* the possibility of a pure relationship, a pure relatedness, the only thing that matters: and he makes inevitable the horrible reaction, when he lets his thumb go, towards hate and brutality, cruelty and destruction.

Life is so made that opposites sway about a trembling centre of balance. The sins of the fathers are visited on the children. If the fathers drag down the balance on the side of love, peace, and production, then in the third or fourth generation the balance will swing back violently to hate, rage, and destruction. We must balance as we go.

And of all the art forms, the novel most of all demands the trembling and oscillating of the balance. The 'sweet' novel is more falsified, and therefore more immoral, than the blood-and-thunder novel.

The same with the smart and smudgily cynical novel, which says it doesn't matter what you do, because one thing is as good as another, anyhow, and prostitution is just as much 'life' as anything else.

This misses the point entirely. A thing isn't life just because somebody does it. This the artist ought to know perfectly well. The ordinary bank clerk buying himself a new straw hat isn't 'life' at all: it is just existence, quite all right, like everyday dinners: but not 'life'.

By life we mean something that gleams, that has the fourth-dimensional quality. If the bank clerk feels really piquant about his hat, if he establishes a lively relation with it, and goes out of the shop with the new straw on his head, a changed man, be-aureoled, then that is life.

The same with the prostitute. If a man establishes a living relation to her, if only for one moment, then it is life. But if it *doesn't*: if it is just money and function, then it is not life, but sordidness, and a betrayal of living.

If a novel reveals true and vivid relationships, it is a moral work, no matter what the relationships may consist in. If the novelist *honours* the relationship in itself, it will be a great novel.

But there are so many relationships which are not real. When the man in *Crime and Punishment* murders the old woman for sixpence, although it is *actual* enough, it is never quite real. The balance between the murderer and the old woman is gone entirely; it is only a mess. It is actuality, but it is not 'life', in the living sense.

The popular novel, on the other hand, dishes up a réchauffé of old relationships: *If Winter Comes*. And old relationships dished up are likewise immoral. Even a magnificent painter like Raphael does nothing more than dress up in gorgeous new dresses relationships which have already been experienced. And this gives a gluttonous kind of pleasure to the mass: a voluptuousness, a wallowing. For centuries, men say of their voluptuously ideal woman: 'She is a Raphael Madonna.' And women are only just learning to take it as an insult.

A new relation, a new relatedness hurts somewhat in the attaining; and will always hurt. So life will always hurt. Because real voluptuousness lies in re-acting old relationships, and at the best, getting an alcoholic sort of pleasure out of it, slightly depraving.

Each time we strive to a new relation, with anyone or anything, it is bound to hurt somewhat. Because it means the struggle with and the displacing of old connexions, and this is never pleasant. And moreover, between living things at least, an adjustment means also a fight, for each party, inevitably, must 'seek its own' in the other, and be denied. When in the two parties, each of them seeks his own, her own, absolutely, then it is a fight to the death. And this is true of the things called 'passion'. On the other hand, when, of the two parties, one yields utterly to the other, this is called sacrifice, and it also means death. So the Constant Nymph died of her eighteen months of constancy.

It isn't the nature of nymphs to be constant. She should have been constant in her nymph-hood. And it is unmanly to accept sacrifices. He should have abided by his own manhood.

There is, however, the third thing, which is neither sacrifice nor fight to the death: when each seeks only the true relatedness to the other.

Each must be true to himself, herself, his own manhood, her own womanhood, and let the relationship work out of itself. This means courage above all things: and then discipline. Courage to accept the life-thrust from within oneself, and from the other person. Discipline, not to exceed oneself any more than one can help. Courage, when one has exceeded oneself, to accept the fact and not whine about it.

Obviously, to read a really new novel will *always* hurt, to some extent. There will always be resistance. The same with new pictures, new music. You may judge of their reality by the fact that they do arouse a certain resistance, and compel, at length, a certain acquiescence.

The great relationship, for humanity, will always be the relation between man and woman. The relation between man and man, woman and woman, parent and child, will always be subsidiary.

And the relation between man and woman will change for ever, and will for ever be the new central clue to human life. It is the *relation itself* which is the quick and the central clue to life, not the man, nor the woman, nor the children that result from the relationship, as a contingency.

It is no use thinking you can put a stamp on the relation between man and woman, to keep it in the *status quo*. You can't. You might as well try to put a stamp on the rainbow or the rain.

As for the bond of love, better put it off when it galls. It is an absurdity, to say that men and women *must love*. Men and women will be for ever subtly and changingly related to one another; no need to yoke them with any 'bond' at all. The only morality is to have man true to his manhood, woman to her womanhood, and let the relationship form of itself, in all honour. For it is, to each, *life itself*.

If we are going to be moral, let us refrain from driving pegs through anything, either through each other or through the third thing, the relationship, which is for ever the ghost of both of us. Every sacrificial crucifixion needs five pegs, four short ones and a long one, each one an abomination. But when you try to nail down the relationship itself, and write over it *Love* instead of *This is the King of the Jews*, then you can go on putting in nails for ever. Even Jesus called it the Holy Ghost, to show you that you can't lay salt on its tail.

The novel is a perfect medium for revealing to us the changing rainbow of our living relationships. The novel can help us to live, as nothing else can: no didactic Scripture, anyhow. If the novelist keeps his thumb out of the pan.

But when the novelist *has* his thumb in the pan, the novel becomes an unparalleled perverter of men and women. To be compared only, perhaps, to that great mischief of sentimental hymns, like 'Lead, Kindly Light', which have helped to rot the marrow in the bones of the present generation.

SOURCE: *The Calendar of Modern Letters* (December 1925); reprinted in *Phoenix* (London, 1936) pp. 527–32.

2. ON JOHN GALSWORTHY (1928)

Literary criticism can be no more than a reasoned account of the feeling produced upon the critic by the book he is criticizing. Criticism can never be a science: it is, in the first place, much too personal, and in the second, it is concerned with values that science ignores. The touchstone is emotion, not reason. We judge a work of art by its effect on our sincere and vital emotion, and nothing else. All the critical twiddle-twaddle about style and form, all this pseudo-scientific classifying and analysing of books in an imitation-botanical fashion, is mere impertinence and mostly dull jargon.

A critic must be able to *feel* the impact of a work of art in all its complexity and its force. To do so, he must be a man of force and complexity himself, which few critics are. A man with a paltry, impudent nature will never write anything but paltry, impudent criticism. And a man who is *emotionally* educated is rare as a phoenix. The more scholastically educated a man is generally, the more he is an emotional boor.

More than this, even an artistically and emotionally educated man must be a man of good faith. He must have the courage to admit what he feels, as well as the flexibility to *know* what he feels. So Sainte-Beuve remains, to me, a great critic. And a man like Macaulay, brilliant as he is, is unsatisfactory, because he is not honest. He is emotionally very alive, but he juggles his feelings. He prefers a fine effect to the sincere statement of the æsthetic and emotional reaction. He is quite intellectually capable of giving us a true account of what he feels. But not morally. A critic must be emotionally alive in every fibre, intellectually capable and skilful in essential logic, and then morally very honest.

Then it seems to me a good critic should give his reader a few standards to go by. He can change the standards for every new critical attempt, so long as he keeps good faith. But it is just as well to say: This and this is the standard we judge by.

Sainte-Beuve, on the whole, set up the standard of the 'good man'. He sincerely believed that the great man was essentially the good man in the widest range of human sympathy. This remained his universal standard. Pater's standard was the lonely philosopher of pure thought and pure æsthetic truth. Macaulay's standard was tainted by a political or democratic bias, he must be on the side of the weak. Gibbon tried a purely moral standard, individual morality.

Reading Galsworthy again – or most of him, for all is too much – one feels oneself in need of a standard, some conception of a real man and a real woman, by which to judge all these Forsytes and their contemporaries. One cannot judge them by the standard of the good man, nor of the man of pure thought, nor of the treasured humble nor the moral individual. One would like to judge them by the standard of the human being, but what, after all, is that? This is the trouble with the Forsytes. They are human enough, since anything in humanity is human, just as anything in nature is natural. Yet not one of them seems to be a really vivid human being. They are social beings. And what do we mean by that?

It remains to define, just for the purpose of this criticism, what we mean by a social being as distinct from a human being. The necessity arises from the sense of dissatisfaction which these Forsytes give us. Why can't we admit them as human beings? Why can't we have them in the same category as Sairey Gamp for example, who is satirically conceived, or of Jane Austen's people, who are social enough? We can accept Mrs Gamp or Jane Austen's characters or even George Meredith's Egoist as human beings in the same category as ourselves. Whence arises this repulsion from the Forsytes, this refusal, this emotional refusal, to have them identified with our common humanity?

Why do we feel so instinctively that they are inferiors?

It is because they seem to us to have lost caste as human beings, and to have sunk to the level of the social being, that peculiar creature that takes the place in our civilization of the slave in the old civilizations. The human individual is a queer animal, always changing. But the fatal change today is the collapse from the psychology of the free human individual into the psychology of the social being, just as the fatal change in the past was a collapse from the freeman's psyche to the psyche of the slave. The free moral and the slave moral, the human moral and the social moral: these are the abiding antitheses.

While a man remains a man, a true human individual, there is at the core of him a certain innocence or naïveté which defies all analysis, and which you cannot bargain with, you can only deal with it in good faith from your own corresponding innocence or naïveté. This does not mean that the human being is nothing but naïve or innocent. He is Mr Worldly Wiseman also to his own degree. But in his essential core he is naïve, and money does not touch him. Money, of course, with every man living goes a long way. With the alive human being it may go as far as his penultimate feeling. But in the last naked him it does not enter.

With the social being it goes right through the centre and is the controlling principle no matter how much he may pretend, nor how much bluff he may put up. He may give away all he has to the poor and still reveal himself as a social being swayed finally and helplessly by the money-sway, and by the social moral, which is inhuman.

It seems to me that when the human being becomes too much divided between his subjective and objective consciousness, at last something splits in him and he becomes a social being. When he becomes too much aware of objective reality, and of his own isolation in the face of a universe of objective reality, the core of his identity splits, his nucleus collapses, his innocence or his naïveté perishes, and he becomes only a subjective – objective reality, a divided thing hinged together but not strictly individual.

While a man remains a man, before he falls and becomes a social individual, he innocently feels himself altogether within the great continuum of the universe. He is not divided nor cut off. Men may be against him, the tide of affairs may be rising to sweep him away. But he is one with the living continuum of the universe. From this he cannot be swept away. Hamlet and Lear feel it, as does Œdipus or Phædra. It is the last and deepest feeling that is in a man while he remains a man. It is there the same in a deist like Voltaire or a scientist like Darwin: it is there, imperishable, in every great man: in Napoleon the same, till material things piled too much on him and he lost it and was doomed. It is the essential innocence and naïveté of the human being, the sense of being at one with the great universe-continuum of space – time – life, which is vivid in a great man, and a pure nuclear spark in every man who is still free.

But if man loses his mysterious naïve assurance, which is his innocence; if he gives *too* much importance to the external objective reality and so collapses in his natural innocent pride, then he becomes obsessed with the idea of objectives or material assurance; he wants to *insure* himself, and perhaps everybody else: universal insurance. The impulse rests on fear. Once the individual loses his naive at-oneness with the living universe he falls into a state of fear and tries to insure himself with wealth. If he is an altruist he wants to insure everybody, and feels it is the tragedy of tragedies if this can't be done. But the whole necessity for thus materially insuring oneself with wealth, money, arises from the state of fear into which a man falls who has lost his at-oneness with the living universe, lost his peculiar nuclear innocence and fallen into fragmentariness. Money, material salvation is the only salvation. What is salvation is God. Hence money is God. The social being may rebel even against this god, as do many of Galsworthy's characters. But that does not give them back their innocence. They are only anti-materials instead of positive materialists. And the anti-materialist is a social being just the same as the materialist, neither more nor less. He is castrated just the same, made a neuter by having lost his innocence, the bright little individual spark of his at-oneness.

When one reads Mr Galsworthy's books it seems as if there were not on earth one single human individual. They are all these social beings, positive and negative. There is not a free soul among them, not even Pendyce, or June Forsyte. If money does not actively determine their being, it does negatively. Money, or property, which is the same thing. Mrs Pendyce, lovable as she is, is utterly circumscribed by property. Ultimately, she is not lovable at all, she is part of the fraud, she is prostituted to property. And there is nobody else. Old Jolyon is merely a sentimental materialist. Only for one moment do we see a man, and that is the road-sweeper in *Fraternity* after he comes out of prison and covers his face. But even *his* manhood has to be explained away by a wound in the head: an abnormality.

Now it looks as if Mr Galsworthy set out to make that very point: to show that the Forsytes were not full human individuals but social beings fallen to a lower level of life. They have lost that bit of free manhood and free womanhood which makes men and women. *The Man of Property* has the elements of a very great novel, a very great satire. It sets out to reveal the social being in all his strength and inferiority. But the author has not the courage to carry it through. The greatness of the book rests in its new and sincere and amazingly profound satire. It is the ultimate satire on modern humanity, and done from inside, with really consummate skill and sincere creative passion, something quite new. It seems to be a real effort to show up the social being in all his weirdness. And then it fizzles out.

Then, in the love affair of Irene and Bosinney, and in the sentimentalizing of old Jolyon Forsyte, the thing is fatally blemished. Galsworthy had not quite enough of the superb courage of his satire. He faltered, and gave in to the Forsytes. It is a thousand pities. He might have been the surgeon the modern soul needs so badly, to cut away the proud flesh of our Forsytes from the living body of men who are fully alive. Instead, he put down the knife and laid on a soft, sentimental poultice, and helped to make the corruption worse.

Satire exists for the very purpose of killing the social being, showing him what an inferior he is and, with all his parade of social honesty, how subtly and corruptly debased. Dishonest to life, dishonest to the living universe on which he is parasitic as a louse. By ridiculing the social being, the satirist helps the true individual, the real human being, to rise to his feet again and go on with the battle. For it is always a battle, and always will be.

Not that the majority are necessarily social beings. But the majority is only *conscious* socially: humanly, mankind is helpless and unconscious, unaware even of the thing most precious to any human being, that core of manhood or womanhood, naïve, innocent at-oneness with the living universe-continuum, which alone makes a man individual and, as an individual *essentially* happy, even if he be driven mad like Lear. Lear was essentially happy, even in his greatest misery. A happiness from which Goneril and Regan were excluded as lice and bugs are excluded from happiness, being social beings, and, as such, parasites, fallen from true freedom and independence.

But the tragedy today is that men are only materially and socially conscious. They are unconscious of their own manhood, and so they let it be destroyed. Out of free men we produce social beings by the thousand every week.

The Forsytes are all parasites, and Mr Galsworthy set out, in a really magnificent attempt, to let us see it. They are parasites upon the thought, the feelings, the whole body of life of really living individuals who have gone before them and who exist alongside with them. All they can do, having no individual life of their own, is out of fear to rake together property, and to feed upon the life that has been given by living men to mankind. They have no life, and so they live for ever, in perpetual fear of death, accumulating property to ward off death. They can keep up convention, but they cannot carry on a tradition. There is a tremendous difference between the two things. To carry on a tradition you must add something to the tradition. But to keep up a convention needs only the monotonous persistency of a parasite, the endless endurance of the craven, those who fear life because they are not alive, and who cannot die because they cannot live – the social beings.

As far as I can see, there is nothing but Forsyte in Galsworthy's books: Forsyte positive or Forsyte negative, Forsyte successful or Forsyte manqué. That is, every single character is determined by money: either the getting it, or the having it, or the wanting it, or the utter lacking it. Getting it are the Forsytes as such; having it are the Pendyces and patricians and Hilarys and Biancas and all that lot; wanting it are the Irenes and Bosinneys and young Jolyons; and utterly lacking it are all the charwomen and squalid poor who form the background – the shadows of the 'having' ones, as old Mr Stone says. This is the whole Galsworthy gamut, all absolutely determined by money, and not an individual soul among them. They are all fallen, all social beings, a castrated lot.

Perhaps the overwhelming numerousness of the Forsytes frightened Mr Galsworthy from utterly damning them. Or perhaps it was something else, something more serious in him. Perhaps it was his utter failure to see what you were when you weren't a Forsyte. What was there besides Forsytes in all the wide human world? Mr Galsworthy looked, and found nothing. Strictly and truly, after his frightened search, he had found nothing. But he came back with Irene and Bosinney, and offered us that. Here! he seems to say. Here is the anti-Forsyte! Here! Here you have it! Love! Pa-assion! PASSION.

We look at this love, this PASSION, and we see nothing but a doggish amorousness and a sort of anti-Forsytism. They are the anti half of the show. Runaway dogs of these Forsytes, running in the back garden and furtively and ignominiously copulating – this is the effect, on me, of Mr Galsworthy's grand love affairs, Dark Flowers or Bosinneys, or Apple Trees or George Pendyce – whatever they be. About every one of them something ignominious and doggish, like dogs copulating in the street, and looking round to see if the Forsytes are watching.

Alas! this is the Forsyte trying to be freely sensual. He can't do it; he's lost it. He can only be doggishly messy. Bosinney is not only a Forsyte, but an anti-Forsyte, with a vast grudge against property. And the thing a man has a vast grudge against is the man's determinant. Bosinney is a property hound, but he has run away from the kennels, or been born outside the kennels, so he is a rebel. So he goes sniffing round the property bitches, to get even with the successful property hounds that way. One cannot help preferring Soames Forsyte, in a choice of evils.

Just as one prefers June or any of the old aunts to Irene. Irene seems to me a sneaking, creeping, spiteful sort of bitch, an anti-Forsyte, absolutely living off the Forsytes – yes, to the very end; absolutely living off their money and trying to do them dirt. She is like Bosinney, a property mongrel doing dirt in the property kennels. But she is a real property prostitute, like the model in *Fraternity*. Only she is *anti*! It is a type recurring again and again in Galsworthy: the parasite upon the parasites, 'Big fleas have little fleas, etc.' And Bosinney and Irene, as well as the vagabond in *The Island Pharisees*, are among the little fleas. And as a tramp loves his own vermin, so the Forsytes and the Hilarys love these, their own particular body parasites, their *antis*.

It is when he comes to sex that Mr Galsworthy collapses finally. He becomes nastily sentimental. He wants to make sex important, and he only makes it repulsive. Sentimentalism is the working off on yourself of feelings you haven't really got. We all *want* to have certain feelings: feelings of love, of passionate sex, of kindliness, and so forth. Very few people really feel love, or sex passion, or kindliness, or anything else that goes at all deep. So the mass just fake these feelings inside themselves. Faked feelings! The world is all gummy with them. They are better than real feelings, because you can spit them out when you brush your teeth; and then tomorrow you can fake them afresh. . . .

Mr Galsworthy's treatment of passion is really rather shameful. The whole thing is doggy to a degree. The man has a temporary 'hunger'; he is 'on the heat' as they say of dogs. The heat passes. It's done. Trot away, if you're not tangled. Trot off, looking shamefacedly over your shoulder. People have been watching! Damn them! But never mind, it'll blow over. Thank God, the bitch is trotting in the other direction. She'll soon have another trail of dogs after her. That'll wipe out my traces. Good for that! Next time I'll get properly married and do my doggishness in my own house.

With the fall of the individual, sex falls into a dog's heat. Oh, if only Mr Galsworthy had had the strength to satirize this too, instead of pouring a sauce of sentimental savouriness over it. Of course, if he had done so he would never have been a popular writer, but he would have been a great one.

However, he chose to sentimentalize and glorify the most doggy sort of sex. Setting out to satirize the Forsytes, he glorifies the *anti*, who is one worse. While the individual remains real and unfallen, sex remains a vital and supremely important thing. But once you have the fall into social beings, sex becomes disgusting, like dogs on the heat. Dogs are social beings, with no true canine individuality. Wolves and foxes don't copulate on the pavement. Their sex is wild and in act utterly private. Howls you may hear, but you will never see anything. But the dog is tame – and he makes excrement and he copulates on the pavement, as if to spite you. He is the Forsyte *anti*.

The same with human beings. Once they become tame they become, in a measure, exhibitionists, as if to spite everything. They have no real feelings of their own. Unless somebody 'catches them at it' they don't really feel they've felt anything at all. And this is how the mob is today. It is Forsyte *anti*. It is the social being spiting society.

Oh, if only Mr Galsworthy had satirized *this* side of Forsytism, the anti-Forsyte posturing of the 'rebel', the narcissus and the exhibitionist, the dogs copulating on the pavement! Instead of that, he glorified it, to the eternal shame of English literature.

The satire, which in *The Man of Property* really had a certain noble touch, soon fizzles out, and we get that series of Galsworthian 'rebels' who are, like all the rest of the modern middle-class rebels, not in rebellion at all. They are merely social beings behaving in an anti-social manner. They worship their own class, but they pretend to go one better and sneer at it. They are Forsyte *antis*, feeling snobbish about snobbery. Nevertheless, they want to attract attention and make money. That's why they are *anti*. It is the vicious circle of Forsytism. Money means more to them than it does to a Soames Forsyte, so they pretend to go one better, and despise it, but they will do anything to have it – things which Soames Forsyte would not have done.

If there is one thing more repulsive than the social being positive, it is the social being negative, the mere *anti*. In the great debacle of decency this gentleman is the most indecent. In a subtle way Bosinney and Irene are more dishonest and more indecent than Soames and Winifred, but they are *anti*, so they are glorified. It is pretty sickening.

The introduction to *The Island Pharisees* explains the whole show: 'Each man born into the world is born to go a journey, and for the most part he is born on the high road. . . . As soon as he can toddle, he moves, by the queer instinct we call the love of life, along this road: . . . his fathers went this way before him, they made this road for him to tread, and, when they bred him, passed into his fibre the love of doing things as they themselves had done them. So he walks on and on. . . . Suddenly, one day, without intending to, he notices a path or opening in the hedge, leading to right or left, and he stands looking at the undiscovered. After that he stops at all the openings in the hedge; one day, with a beating heart, he tries one. And this is where the fun begins.' – Nine out of ten get back to the broad road again, and sidetrack no more. They snuggle down comfortably in the next inn, and think where they might have been. 'But the poor silly tenth is faring on. Nine times out of ten he goes down in a bog; the undiscovered has engulfed him.' But the tenth time he gets across, and a new road is opened to mankind.

It is a class-bound consciousness, or at least a hopeless social consciousness which sees life as a high road between two hedges. And the only way out is gaps in the hedge and excursions into naughtiness! These little *anti* excursions, from which the wayfarer slinks back to solid comfort nine times out of ten; an odd one goes down in a bog; and a very rare one finds a way across and opens out a new road.

In Mr Galsworthy's novels we see the nine, the ninety-nine, the nine hundred and ninety-nine slinking back to solid comfort; we see an odd Bosinney go under a bus, because he hadn't guts enough to do something else, the poor *anti*! but that rare figure sidetracking into the unknown we do *not* see. Because, as a matter of fact, the whole figure is faulty at that point. If life is a great highway, then it must forge on ahead into the unknown. Sidetracking gets nowhere. That is mere *anti*. The tip of the road is always unfinished, in the wilderness. If it comes to a precipice and a canon – well, then, there is need for some exploring. But we see Mr Galsworthy, after *The Country House*, very safe on the old highway, very secure in comfort, wealth, and renown. He at least has gone down in no bog, nor lost himself striking new paths. The hedges nowadays are ragged with gaps, anybody who likes strays out on the little trips of 'unconventions'. But the Forsyte road has not moved on at all. It has only become dishevelled and sordid with excursionists doing the *anti* tricks and being 'unconventional', and leaving tin cans behind.

In the three early novels, *The Island Pharisees*, *The Man of Property*, *Fraternity*, it looked as if Mr Galsworthy might break through the blind end of the highway with the dynamite of satire, and help us out on to a new lap. But the sex ingredient of his dynamite was damp and muzzy, the explosion gradually fizzled off in sentimentality, and we are left in a worse state than before. . . .

It is time somebody began to spit out the jam of sentimentalism, at least, which smothers the 'bobbing-up' philosophy. It is time we turned a straight light on this horde of rats, these younger Forsyte sentimentalists whose name is legion. It is sentimentalism which is stifling us. Let the social beings keep on bobbing up while ever they can. But it is time an effort was made to turn a hosepipe on the sentimentalism they ooze over everything. The world is one sticky mess, in which the little Forsytes indeed may keep on bobbing still, but in which an honest feeling can't breathe.

But if the sticky mess gets much deeper, even the little Forsytes won't be able to bob up any more. They'll be smothered in their own slime along with everything else. Which is a comfort.

SOURCE: extracts from 'John Galsworthy', in *Scrutinies, By Various Writers* (London,   1928);   reprinted in   *Phoenix*   (London, 1936)
pp. 539−45, 546−9, 550

Lionel Trilling

MANNERS, MORALS, AND THE NOVEL (1948)

. . . Somewhere below all the explicit statements that a people makes through its art, religion, architecture, legislation, there is a dim mental region of intention of which it is very difficult to become aware. We now and then get a strong sense of its existence when we deal with the past, not by reason of its presence in the past but by reason of its absence. As we read the great formulated monuments of the past, we notice that we are reading them without the accompaniment of something that always goes along with the great formulated monuments of the present. The voice of multifarious intention and activity is stilled, all the buzz of implication which always surrounds us in the present, coming to us from what never gets fully stated, coming in the tone of greetings and the tone of quarrels, in slang and humor and popular songs, in the way children play, in the gesture the waiter makes when he puts down the plate, in the nature of the very food we prefer.

Some of the charm of the past consists of the quiet – the great distracting buzz of implication has stopped and we are left only with what has been fully phrased and precisely stated. And part of the melancholy of the past comes from our knowledge that the huge, unrecorded hum of implication was once there and left no trace – we feel that because it is evanescent it is especially human. And we feel, too, that the truth of the great preserved monuments of the past does not fully appear without it. From letters and diaries, from the remote, unconscious corners of the great works themselves, we try to guess what the sound of the multifarious implication was and what it meant.

Or when we read the conclusions that are drawn about our own culture by some gifted foreign critic – or by some stupid native one – who is equipped only with a knowledge of our books, when we try in vain to say what is wrong, when in despair we say that he has read the books 'out of context', then we are aware of the matter I have been asked to speak about tonight.

What I understand by manners, then, is a culture's hum and buzz of implication. I mean the whole evanescent context of its explicit statements. It is that part of a culture which is made up of half-uttered or unuttered or unutterable expressions of value. They are hinted at by small actions, sometimes by the arts of dress or decoration, sometimes by tone, gesture, emphasis, or rhythm, sometimes by the words that are used with a special frequency or a special meaning. They are the things that for good or bad draw the people of a culture together and that separate them from the people of another culture. It is the part of a culture which is not art, nor religion, nor morals, nor politics, and yet it relates to all these highly formulated departments of culture. It is modified by them; it modifies them; it is generated by them; it generates them. In this part of culture assumption rules, which is often so much stronger than reason.

The right way to begin to deal with such a subject is to gather together as much of its detail as we possibly can. Only by doing so will we become fully aware of what the gifted foreign critic or the stupid native one was not aware of, that in any complex culture there is not a single system of manners but a conflicting variety of manners, and that what we mean by a culture is the adjustment of this conflict.

But the nature of our present occasion does not permit this accumulation of detail and so I shall try to drive toward a generalization and a hypothesis which, however wrong they may be, will at least permit us to circumscribe the subject. I propose to generalize the subject of American manners by talking about the attitude of Americans toward the subject of manners itself. And since in a complex culture there are, as I say, many different systems of manners and since I cannot talk about them all, I shall select the manners and the attitude toward manners of the literate, reading, responsible middle class of people who are ourselves. I specify that they be reading people because I shall draw my conclusions from the novels they read. The hypothesis I propose is that our attitude toward manners is the expression of a particular conception of reality.

All literature tends to be concerned with the question of reality – I mean quite simply the old opposition between reality and appearance, between what really is and what merely seems.

'Don't you *see?*' is the question we want to shout at Oedipus as he stands before us and before fate in the pride of his rationalism. And at the end of *Oedipus Rex* he demonstrates in a particularly direct way that he now sees what he did not see before. 'Don't you *see*?' we want to shout again at Lear and Gloucester, the two deceived, self-deceiving fathers: blindness again, resistance to the clear claims of reality, the seduction by mere appearance. The same with Othello – reality is right under your stupid nose, how *dare* you be such a gull? So with Molière's Orgon – my good man, my honest citizen, merely *look* at Tartuffe and you will know what's what. So with Milton's Eve – 'Woman, watch out! Dont' you see – anyone can see – that's a *snake*!'

The problem of reality is central, and in a special way, to the great forefather of the novel, the great book of Cervantes, whose four-hundredth birthday we celebrate this year. There are two movements of thought in *Don Quixote*, two different and opposed notions of reality. One is the movement which leads toward saying that the world of ordinary practicality *is* reality in its fullness. It is the reality of the present moment in all its powerful immediacy of hunger, cold, and pain, making the past and the future, and all ideas, of no account. When the conceptual, the ideal, and the fanciful come into conflict with this, bringing their notions of the past and the future, then disaster results. For one thing, the ordinary proper ways of life are upset – the chained prisoners are understood to be good men and are released, the whore is taken for a lady. There is general confusion. As for the ideal, the conceptual, the fanciful, or romantic – whatever you want to call it – it fares even worse: it is shown to be ridiculous.

Thus one movement of the novel. But Cervantes changed horses in mid-stream and found that he was riding Rosinante. Perhaps at first not quite consciously – although the new view is latent in the old from the very beginning – Cervantes begins to show that the world of tangible reality is not the real reality after all. The real reality is rather the wildly conceiving, the madly fantasying mind of the Don: people change, practical reality changes, when they come into its presence.

In any genre it may happen that the first great example contains the whole potentiality of the genre. It has been said that all philosophy is a footnote to Plato. It can be said that all prose fiction is a variation on the theme of *Don Quixote*. Cervantes sets for the novel the problem of appearance and reality: the shifting and conflict of social classes becomes the field of the problem which at that very moment of history is vexing the philosophers and scientists. And the poverty of the Don suggests that the novel is born with the appearance of money as a social element – money, the great solvent of the solid fabric of the old society, the great generator of illusion. Or, which is to say much the same thing, the novel is born in response to snobbery.

Snobbery is not the same thing as pride of class. Pride of class may not please us but we must at least grant that it reflects a social function. A man who exhibited class pride – in the day when it was possible to do so – may have been puffed up about what he *was*, but this ultimately depended on what he *did*. Thus, aristocratic pride was based ultimately on the ability to fight and administer. No pride is without fault, but pride of class may be thought of as today we think of pride of profession, toward which we are likely to be lenient.

Snobbery is pride in status without pride in function. And it is an uneasy pride of status. It always asks, 'Do I belong – do I really belong? And does he belong? And if I am observed talking to him, will it make me seem to belong or not to belong?' It is the peculiar vice, not of aristocratic societies, which have their own appropriate vices, but of bourgeois democratic societies. For us the legendary strongholds of snobbery are the Hollywood studios, where two thousand dollars a week dare not talk to three hundred dollars a week for fear they be taken for nothing more than fifteen hundred dollars a week. The dominant emotions of snobbery are uneasiness, self-consciousness, self-defensiveness, the sense that one is not quite real but can, in some way, acquire reality.

Money is the medium that, for good or bad, makes for a fluent society. It does not make for an equal society but for one in which there is a constant shifting of classes, a frequent change in the personnel of the dominant class. In a shifting society great emphasis is put on appearance – I am using the word now in the common meaning, as when people say that 'a good appearance is very important in getting a job'. To appear to be established is one of the ways of being established. The old notion of the solid merchant who owns far more than he shows increasingly gives way to the ideal of signalizing status by appearance, by showing more than you have: status in a democratic society is presumed to come not with power but with the tokens of power. Hence the development of what Tocqueville saw as a mark of democratic culture, what he called the 'hypocrisy of luxury' – instead of the well-made peasant article and the well-made middle-class article, we have the effort of all articles to appear as the articles of the very wealthy.

And a shifting society is bound to generate an interest in appearance in the philosophical sense. When Shakespeare lightly touched on the matter that so largely preoccupies the novelist – that is, the movement from one class to another – and created Malvolio, he immediately involved the question of social standing with the problem of appearance and reality. Malvolio's daydreams of bettering his position present themselves to him as reality and in revenge his enemies conspire to convince him that he is literally mad and that the world is not as he sees it. The predicaments of the characters in *A Midsummer Night's Dream* and of Christopher Sly seem to suggest that the intermingling of social extremes always suggested to Shakespeare's mind some doubting of the senses.

The characteristic work of the novel is to record the illusion that snobbery generates and to try to penetrate to the truth which, it assumes, lies hidden beneath all the false appearances. Money, snobbery, the ideal of status, these become in themselves the objects of fantasy, the support of the fantasies of love, freedom, charm, power, as in *Madame Bovary*, whose heroine is the sister at a three-centuries' remove of Don Quixote. The greatness of *Great Expectations* begins in its title: modern society bases itself on great expectations which, if ever they are realized, are found to exist by reason of a sordid, hidden reality. The real thing is not the gentility of Pip's life but the hulks and the murder and the rats and decay in the cellarage of the novel.

An English writer, recognizing the central concern of the novel with snobbery, recently cried out half ironically against it. 'Who cares whether Pamela finally exasperates Mr B. into marriage, whether Mr Elton is more or less than moderately genteel, whether it is sinful for Pendennis nearly to kiss the porter's daughter, whether young men from Boston can ever be as truly refined as middle-aged women in Paris, whether the District Officer's fiancée ought to see so much of Dr Aziz, whether Lady Chatterley ought to be made love to by the game-keeper, even if he was an officer during the war. Who cares?'

The novel, of course, tells us much more about life than this. It tells us about the look and feel of things, how things are done and what things are worth and what they cost and what the odds are. If the English novel in its special concern with class does not, as the same writer says, explore the deeper layers of personality, then the French novel in exploring these layers must start and end in class; and the Russian novel exploring the ultimate possibilities of spirit, does the same – every situation in Dostoevski, no matter how spiritual, starts with a point of social pride and a certain number of rubles. The great novelists knew that manners indicate the largest intentions of men's souls as well as the smallest and they are perpetually concerned to catch the meaning of every dim implicit hint.

The novel, then, is a perpetual quest for reality, the field of its research being always the social world, the material of its analysis being always manners as the indication of the direction of man's soul. One can understand the pride of profession that moved D. H. Lawrence to say, 'Being a novelist, I consider myself superior to the saint, the scientist, the philosopher and the poet. The novel is the one bright book of life.'

Now the novel as I have described it has never really established itself in America. Not that we have not had very great novels but that the novel in America diverges from its classic intention, which, as I have said, is the investigation of the problem of reality beginning in the social field. The fact is that American writers of genius have not turned their minds to society. Poe and Melville were quite apart from it; the reality they sought was only tangential to society. Hawthorne was acute when he insisted that he did not write novels but romances – he thus expressed his awareness of the lack of social texture in his work. Howells never fulfilled himself because, although he saw the social subject clearly, he would never take it with full seriousness. In the nineteenth century, Henry James was alone in knowing that to scale the moral and esthetic heights in the novel one had to use the ladder of social observation.

There is a famous passage in James' life of Hawthorne in which James enumerates the things which are lacking to give the American novel the thick social texture of the English novel – no State; barely a specific national name; no sovereign; no court; no aristocracy; no church; no clergy; no army; no diplomatic service; no country gentlemen; no palaces; no castles; no manors; no old country houses; no parsonages; no thatched cottages; no ivied ruins; no cathedrals; no great universities; no public schools; no political society; no sporting class – no Epsom, no Ascot! That is, no sufficiency of means for the display of a variety of manners, no opportunity for the novelist to do his job of searching out reality, not enough complication of appearance to make the job interesting. Another great American novelist of very different temperament had said much the same thing some decades before: James Fenimore Cooper had said that American manners were too simple and dull to nourish the novelist.

This is cogent but it does not explain the condition of the American novel at the present moment. For life in America has increasingly

thickened since the nineteenth century. It has not, to be sure, thickened
so much as to permit my students to understand the characters of
Balzac – to understand, that is, life in a crowded country where the
competitive pressures are great, forcing intense passions to express
themselves fiercely and yet within the limitations set by a strong and
complicated tradition of manners. Still, life here has become more
complex and more pressing. And even so we do not have the novel that
touches significantly on society, on manners. Whatever the virtues of
Dreiser may be, he could not report the social fact with the kind of
accuracy it needs. Sinclair Lewis is shrewd, but no one, however
charmed with him as a social satirist, can believe that he does more than
a limited job of social understanding. John Dos Passos sees much, sees it
often in the great way of Flaubert, but can never use social fact as more
than either backdrop or 'condition'. Of our novelists today perhaps only
William Faulkner deals with society as the field of tragic reality and he
has the disadvantage of being limited to a provincial scene.

It would seem that Americans have a kind of resistance to looking
closely at society. They appear to believe that to touch accurately on the
matter of class, to take full note of snobbery, is somehow demeaning. It
is as if we felt that one cannot touch pitch without being defiled – which,
of course, may possibly be the case. Americans will not deny that we
have classes and snobbery, but they seem to hold it to be indelicate to
take precise cognizance of these phenomena. Consider that Henry
James is, among a large part of our reading public, held to be to blame
for noticing society as much as he did. Consider the conversation that
has, for some interesting reason, become a part of our literary folklore.
Scott Fitzgerald said to Ernest Hemingway: 'The very rich are different
from us.' Hemingway replied, 'Yes, they have more money.' I have seen
the exchange quoted many times and always with the intention of
suggesting that Fitzgerald was infatuated by wealth and had received a
salutary rebuke from his democratic friend. But the truth is that after a
certain point quantity of money does indeed change into a quality of
personality: in an important sense the very rich *are* different from us. So
are the very powerful, the very gifted, the very poor. Fitzgerald was
right, and almost for that remark alone he has been received in Balzac's
bosom in the heaven of novelists.

And if I may bring my own experience into evidence, I can adduce
the response to a review of mine in which I praised John O'Hara's gift of
acute observation of snobbery. Friends took me seriously to task,

acquaintances greeted me coolly. It was clear to everyone that I had
said that snobbery was a good thing.

It is of course by no means true that the American reading class has
no interest in society. Its interest fails only before society as it used to be
represented by the novel. And if we look at the successful serious novels
of the last decade, we see that almost all of them have been written from
an intense social awareness – it might be said that our definition of a
serious book is one which holds before us some image of society to
consider and condemn. What is the situation of the dispossessed
Oklahoma farmer and whose fault it is, what situation the Jew finds
himself in, what it means to be a Negro, how one gets a bell for Adano,
what is the advertising business really like, what it means to be insane
and how society takes care of you or fails to do so – these are the matters
which are believed to be most fertile for the novelist and certainly they
are the subjects most favoured by our reading class.

The public is probably not deceived about the quality of most of these
books. If the question of quality is brought up, the answer is likely to be:
no, they are not great, they are not 'literature'. But there is an
unexpressed addendum: and perhaps they are all the better for
that – they are not literature, they are reality, and *in a time like this* what
we need is reality in large doses.

When, generations from now, the historian of our times undertakes to
describe the assumptions of our culture, he will surely discover that the
word *reality* is of central importance in his understanding of us. He will
observe that for some of our philosophers the meaning of the word was a
good deal in doubt, but that for our political writers, many of our
literary critics, and most of our reading public, the word did not open
discussion but, rather, closed it. Reality, as conceived by us, is whatever
is external and hard, gross, unpleasant. Involved in its meaning is the
idea of power conceived in a particular way. Some time ago I had
occasion to remark how, in the critical estimates of Theodore Dreiser, it
is always being said that Dreiser has many faults but that it cannot be
denied that he has great power. No one ever says 'a kind of power'.
Power is assumed to be always 'brute' power, crude, ugly, and
undiscriminating, the way an elephant appears to be. It is seldom
understood to be the way an elephant is, precise and discriminating; or
the way electricity is, swift and absolute and scarcely embodied.

The word *reality* is an honorific word and the future historian will
naturally try to discover our notion of its pejorative opposite, ap-

pearance, mere appearance. He will find it in our feeling about the internal: whenever we detect evidences of style and thought we suspect that reality is being a little betrayed, that 'mere subjectivity' is creeping in. There follows from this our feeling about complication, modulation, personal idiosyncrasy, and about social forms, both the great and the small.

Having gone so far, our historian is then likely to discover a puzzling contradiction. For we claim that the great advantage of reality is its hard, bedrock, concrete quality, yet everything we say about it tends toward the abstract and it almost seems that what we want to find in reality is abstraction itself. Thus we believe that one of the unpleasant bedrock facts is social class, but we become extremely impatient if ever we are told that social class is indeed so real that it produces actual differences of personality. The very people who talk most about class and its evils think that Fitzgerald was bedazzled and Hemingway right. Or again, it might be observed that in the degree that we speak in praise of the 'individual' we have contrived that our literature should have no individuals in it – no people, that is, who are shaped by our liking for the interesting and memorable and special and precious.

Here, then, is our generalization: that in proportion as we have committed ourselves to our particular idea of reality we have lost our interest in manners. For the novel this is a definitive condition because it is inescapably true that in the novel manners make men. It does not matter in what sense the word *manners* is taken – it is equally true of the sense which so much interested Proust or of the sense which interested Dickens or, indeed, of the sense which interested Homer. The Princesse de Guermantes, unable to delay departure for the Duchesse's party to receive properly from her friend Swann the news that he is dying, but able to delay to change the red slippers her husband objects to; Mr Pickwick and Sam Weller; Priam and Achilles – they exist by reason of their observed manners.

So true is this, indeed, so creative is the novelist's awareness of manners, that we may say that it is a function of his love. It is some sort of love that Fielding has for Squire Western that allows him to note the great, gross details that bring that insensitive, sentient being into existence for us. If that is true, we are forced to certain conclusions about our literature and about the particular definition of reality that has shaped it. The reality we admire tells us that the observation of manners is trivial and even malicious, that there are things much more important for the novel to consider. As a consequence our social sympathies have indeed broadened, but in proportion as they have done so we have lost something of our power of love, for our novels can never create characters who truly exist. We make public demands for love, for we know that broad social feelings should be infused with warmth, and we receive a kind of public product which we try to believe is not cold potatoes. The reviewers of Helen Howe's novel thought that its satiric first part, an excellent satire on the manners of a small but significant segment of society, was ill-natured and unsatisfactory, but they approved the second part, which is the record of the heroine's self-accusing effort to come into communication with the great soul of America. Yet it should have been clear that the satire had its source in a kind of affection, in a real community of feeling, and told the truth, while the second part, said to be so 'real', was mere abstraction, one more example of our public idea of ourselves and our national life. The novelist John Steinbeck satisfies our desire for reality the more by being an amateur scientist, and it is believed that his representations of reality are infused with warm-heartedness. In his latest novel the lower-class characters receive a doctrinaire affection in proportion to the suffering and sexuality which define their existence, while the ill-observed middle-class characters are made to submit not only to moral judgement but to the withdrawal of all fellow feeling, being mocked for their very misfortunes and almost for their susceptibility to death. Only a little thought or even less feeling is required to perceive that the basis of his creation is the coldest response to abstract ideas.

Two novelists of the older sort had a prevision of our present situation. In Henry James' *The Princess Casamassima* there is a scene in which the heroine is told about the existence of a conspiratorial group of revolutionaries pledged to the destruction of all existing society. She has for some time been drawn by a desire for social responsibility; she has wanted to help 'the people', she has longed to discover just such a group as she now hears about, and she exclaims in joy, 'Then it's real, it's solid!' We are intended to hear the Princess' glad cry with the knowledge that she is a woman who despises herself, 'that in the darkest hour of her life she sold herself for a title and a fortune. She regards her doing so as such a terrible piece of frivolity that she can never for the rest of her days be serious enough to make up for it.' She seeks out poverty, suffering, sacrifice, and death because she believes that these things alone are real; she increasingly believes that art is contemptible; she more and more withdraws her awareness and love from the one person of her acquaintance who most deserves her awareness and love and she increasingly scorns all that suggests variety and modulation and is dissatisfied with the humanity of the present in her longing for the more perfect humanity of the future. It is one of the great points the novel makes that with each step that she takes toward the real, the solid, she in fact moves farther away from it.

In E. M. Forster's *The Longest Journey* there is a young man named Stephen Wonham who, although a gentleman born, has been carelessly brought up and has no real notion of the responsibilities of his class. He has a friend, a country laborer, a shepherd, and on two occasions he outrages the feelings of certain intelligent, liberal, democratic people in the book by his treatment of this friend. Once, when the shepherd reneges on a bargain, Stephen quarrels with him and knocks him down; and in the matter of the loan of a few shillings he insists that the money be paid back to the last farthing. The intelligent, liberal, democratic people know that this is not the way to act to the poor. But Stephen cannot think of the shepherd as the poor, nor, although he is a country laborer, as an object of research by J. L. and Barbara Hammond; he is rather a reciprocating subject in a relationship of affection – as we say, a friend – and therefore liable to anger and required to pay his debts. But this view is held to be deficient in intelligence, liberalism, and democracy.

In these two incidents we have the premonition of our present cultural and social situation, the passionate self-reproachful addiction to a 'strong' reality which must limit its purview to maintain its strength, the replacement with abstraction of natural, direct human feeling.

It is worth noting, by the way, how clear is the line by which the two novels descend from *Don Quixote* – how their young heroes come into life with large preconceived ideas and are knocked about in consequence; how both are concerned with the problem of appearance and reality, *The Longest Journey* quite explicitly, *The Princess Casamassima* by indirection; how both evoke the question of the nature of reality by contriving a meeting and conflict of diverse social classes and take great note of the differences of manners. Both have as their leading characters people who are specifically and passionately concerned with social injustice and both agree in saying that to act against social injustice is right and noble but that to choose to act so does not settle all moral problems but, on the contrary, generates new ones of an especially difficult sort.

I have elsewhere given the name of moral realism to the perception of the dangers of the moral life itself. Perhaps at no other time has the enterprise of moral realism ever been so much needed, for at no other time have so many people committed themselves to moral righteousness. We have the books that point out the bad conditions, that praise us for taking progressive attitudes. We have no books that raise questions in our minds not only about conditions but about ourselves, that lead us to refine our motives and ask what might lie behind our good impulses.

There is nothing so very terrible in discovering that something does lie behind. Nor does it need a Freud to make the discovery. Here is a publicity release sent out by one of our oldest and most respectable publishing houses. It bears the heading: 'What Makes Books Sell?' 'Blank & Company reports the current interest in horror stories has attracted a great number of readers to John Dash's novel . . . because of its depiction of Nazi brutality. Critics and readers alike have commented on the stark realism of Dash's handling of the torture scenes in the book. The publishers originally envisaged a woman's market because of the love story, now find men reading the book because of the other angle.' This does not suggest a more than usual depravity in the male reader, for 'the other angle' has always had a fascination, no doubt a bad one, even for those who would not themselves commit or actually witness an act of torture. I cite the extreme example only to suggest that something may indeed lie behind our sober intelligent interest in moral politics. In this instance the pleasure in the cruelty is protected and licensed by moral indignation. In other instances moral indignation, which has been said to be the favorite emotion of the middle class, may be in itself an exquisite pleasure. To understand this does not invalidate moral indignation but only sets up the conditions on which it ought to be entertained, only says when it is legitimate and when not.

But, the answer comes, however important it may be for moral realism to raise questions in our minds about our motives, is it not at best a matter of secondary importance? Is it not of the first importance that we be given a direct and immediate report on the reality that is daily being brought to dreadful birth? The novels that have done this have effected much practical good, bringing to consciousness the latent feelings of many people, making it harder for them to be unaware or indifferent, creating an atmosphere in which injustice finds it harder to thrive. To speak of moral realism is all very well. But it is an elaborate, even fancy, phrase and it is to be suspected of having the intention of sophisticating the simple reality that is easily to be conceived. Life presses us so hard, time is so short, the suffering of the world is so huge, simple, unendurable – anything that complicates our moral fervor in dealing with reality as we immediately see it and wish to drive headlong upon it, must be regarded with some impatience.

True enough: and therefore any defense of what I have called moral realism must be made not in the name of some highflown fineness of feeling but in the name of simple social practicality. There is a simple social fact to which moral realism has a simple practical relevance, but it is a fact very difficult for us to perceive. It is that the moral passions are even more willful and imperious and impatient than the self-seeking passions. All history is at one in telling us that their tendency is to be not only liberating but restrictive.

It is probable that at this time we are about to make great changes in our social system. The world is ripe for such changes, and if they are not made in the direction of greater social liberality, the direction forward, they will, almost of necessity, be made in the direction backward, of a terrible social niggardliness. We all know which of these two directions we want. But it is not enough to want it, not even enough to work for it – we must want it and work for it with intelligence. Which means that we must be aware of the dangers which lie in our most generous wishes. Some paradox of our natures leads us, when once we have made our fellow men the objects of our enlightened interest, to go on to make them the objects of our pity, then of our superior wisdom, ultimately of our coercion. It is to prevent this corruption, the most ironic and tragic that man knows, that we stand in need of the moral realism which is the product of the free play of the moral imagination.

For our time the most effective agent of the moral imagination has been the novel of the last two hundred years. It was never, either esthetically or morally, a perfect form and its faults and failures can be quickly enumerated. But its greatness and its practical usefulness lay in its unremitting work of involving the reader himself in the moral life, inviting him to put his own motives under examination, suggesting that reality is not as he sees it. It taught us, as no other genre ever did, the extent of human variety and the value of variety. It was the literary form to which the emotions of understanding and forgiveness were indigenous, as if by the definition of the form itself. At the moment its impulse does not seem strong, for there never was a time when the virtues of its greatness were so likely to be thought of as weaknesses. Yet there never was a time when its particular activity was so much needed, was of so much practical, political, and social use – so much so that if its impulse does not respond to the need, we can be sad not only over a waning form of art but also over a waning freedom.

SOURCE: *Kenyon Review*, X I (Winter, 1948) 11–27, based on a paper prepared for the Second Kenyon College Conference on the Heritage of English Speaking Peoples and Their Responsibility (September 1947). Reprinted in *Beyond Culture* (London, 1951).

F. R. Leavis

1. THE NOVEL AS DRAMATIC POEM: *ST. MAWR* (1950)

St. Mawr, I suppose, would commonly be described as a long short-story – a *nouvelle*, rather than a novel. Actually, that description, with its limiting effect, has a marked infelicity. It certainly doesn't suggest the nature or weight of the astonishing work of genius that Lawrence's 'dramatic poem' is. *St. Mawr* seems to me to present a creative and technical originality not less remarkable than that of 'The Waste Land', and to be, more unquestionably than that poem, completely achieved, a full and self-sufficient creation. It can hardly strike the admirer as anything but major.

The comparative reference isn't random: *St. Mawr*, too, has the Waste Land for theme. To say this is to suggest scope as well as intensity, and the suggestion isn't idle. There are, besides the horse and the two grooms, only three main actors, but, at the end of the hundred and eighty odd pages, it is as if we had had a representative view of the civilized world. Lawrence's art, then, commands a pregnancy and a concentrated force not suggested by 'tale' or '*nouvelle*'. Yet what strikes us in the opening of *St. Mawr* is not a portentousness or any kind of tension, but a freedom – something extraordinarily like careless ease:

Lou Witt had had her own way so long, that by the age of twenty-five she didn't know where she was. Having one's way landed one completely at sea.
To be sure for a while she had failed in her grand love affair with Rico. And then she had had something really to despair about. But even that had worked out as she wanted. Rico had come back to her, and was dutifully married to her. And now, when she was twenty-five and he was three months older, they were a charming married couple. He flirted with other women still, to be sure. He wouldn't be the handsome Rico if he didn't. But she had 'got' him Oh yes! You had only to see the uneasy backward glance at her, from his big blue eyes: just like a horse that is edging away from its master: to know how completely he was mastered.
She, with her odd little *museau*, not exactly pretty, but very attractive; and her

quaint air of playing at being well-bred, in a sort of charade game; and her
queer familiarity with foreign cities and foreign languages; and the lurking sense
of being an outsider everywhere, like a sort of gipsy, who is at home anywhere
and nowhere: all this made up her charm and her failure. She didn't quite
belong.

Of course she was American: Louisiana family, moved down to Texas. And
she was moderately rich, with no close relation except her mother. But she had
been sent to school in France when she was twelve, and since she had finished
school, she had drifted from Paris to Palermo, Biarritz to Vienna and back via
Munich to London, then down again to Rome. Only fleeting trips to her
America.

So what sort of American was she, after all?

And what sort of European was she either? She didn't 'belong' anywhere.
Perhaps most of all in Rome, among the artists and the Embassy people.

It was in Rome she had met Rico. He was an Australian, son of a government
official in Melbourne, who had been made a baronet. So one day Rico would be
Sir Henry, as he was the only son. Meanwhile, he floated round Europe on a
very small allowance – his father wasn't rich in capital – and was being an
artist.

The economy of those opening pages, establishing the present from
which the drama starts, is very remarkable. For what looks like
carelessness – the relaxed, idiomatic and even slangy familiarity – is
actually precision and vivid firsthandness. And we soon discover that
there is no limit to the power of easy and inevitable transitions. For
Lawrence writes out of the full living language with a flexibility and a
creative freedom for which I can think of no parallel in modern times.
His writing seems to have the careless ease of extraordinarily fluent and
racy speech; but you see, if you stop to cast a critical eye back over the
page, that everything is precisely and easily *right* – the slangy colloquialism, the flippant cliché given an emotional intensity, the
'placing' sardonic touch, and, when it comes (as it so marvellously can
at any moment), the free play of poetic imagery and imaginative
evocation, sensuous and focally suggestive. 'Il écrit extrêmement mal': I
remember my surprise at coming on that about Lawrence in *La Nouvelle
Revue Française*, years ago, above Mr Eliot's name. It is true that
Lawrence wasn't interested in style; no great writer could be less like
Flaubert – he is as unlike Flaubert as Shakespeare is. But he does
precisely what he wants to do, or, rather, what the grasped, the realized
theme that possesses him demands.

The opening pages are sardonic comedy, and it looks as if we are
going to have merely a variant of that admirable short story, 'Mother

and Daughter'. Rico and Lou, though 'they reacted badly on each other's nerves,' and he 'couldn't stand Mrs Witt, and Mrs Witt couldn't stand him',

. . . couldn't get away from one another, even though in the course of their rather restrained correspondence he informed her that he was 'probably' marrying a very dear girl, friend of his childhood, only daughter of one of the oldest families in Victoria. Not saying much.

He didn't commit the probability, but reappeared in Paris, wanting to paint his head off, terribly inspired by Cézanne and by old Renoir. He dined at the Rotonde with Lou and Mrs Witt, who, with her queer democratic New Orleans sort of conceit looked round the drinking-hall with savage contempt, and at Rico as part of the show. 'Certainly', she said, 'when these people here have got any money, they fall in love on a full stomach. And when they've got no money they fall in love with a full pocket. I never was in a more disgusting place. They take their love like some people take after-dinner pills.'

She would watch with her arching, full, strong grey eyes, sitting there erect and silent in her well-bought American clothes. And then she would deliver some such charge of grape-shot. Rico always writhed.

Mrs Witt hated Paris: 'this sordid, unlucky city', she called it. 'Something unlucky is bound to happen to me in this sinister, unclean town', she said. 'I feel *contagion* in the air of this place. For heaven's sake, Louise, let us go to Morocco or somewhere.'

'No mother dear, I can't now. Rico has proposed to me, and I have accepted him. Let us think about a wedding, shall we?'

'There!' said Mrs Witt. 'I said it was an unlucky city!'

The marriage is not a success – as Mrs Witt, 'watching as it were from outside the fence, like a potent well-dressed demon, full of uncanny energy and a shattering sort of sense', realizes almost immediately. And we note with what easy economy the different values of the main actors in the drama are established: Rico, representative of modern civilized 'life'; the formidable Mrs Witt, who hardly disguises her contempt for him; and Lou, who can't happily accept either what Rico *is* or her mother's satisfaction in mere destructive negativity. Lou's sense of the nature of the unsuccess of her marriage is brought to full consciousness by the stallion, St Mawr, and we note how we are sensitized beforehand to take his significance as soon as he makes his entrance. An instance occurred in the opening passage quoted above: 'You had only to see the uneasy backward glance at her, from his big blue eyes: just like a horse that is edging away from its master: to know how completely he was mastered.' And here is the consequence of Mrs. Witt's will to ride in the

Park, where Lou, 'for very decency's sake' ('Mrs Witt was *so* like a
smooth, levelled, gun-metal pistol, Lou had to be a sort of sheath'), must
ride with her:

> 'Rico dear, you must get a horse.'
> The tone was soft and southern and drawling, but the overtone had a decisive
> finality. In vain Rico squirmed – he had a way of writhing and squirming which
> perhaps he had caught at Oxford. In vain he protested that he couldn't ride,
> and that he didn't care for riding. He got quite angry, and his handsome arched
> nose tilted and his upper lip lifted from his teeth, like a dog that is going to bite.
> Yet daren't quite bite.
> And that was Rico. He daren't quite bite. Not that he was really afraid of the
> others. He was afraid of himself, once he let himself go. He might rip up in an
> eruption of life-long anger all this pretty-pretty picture of a charming young
> wife and a delightful little home and a fascinating success as a painter of
> fashionable, and at the same time 'great' portraits: with colour, wonderful
> colour, and at the same time form, marvellous form. He had composed this little
> *tableau vivant* with great effort. He didn't want to erupt like some suddenly
> wicked horse – Rico was really more like a horse than a dog, a horse that might
> go nasty any moment. For the time, he was good, very good, dangerously good.

Rico is the antithesis of St Mawr; he represents the irremediable defeat
of all that St Mawr stands for. Nevertheless, as the passage just quoted
conveys, the frustrated drives of life are still there, down below, always
threatening trouble in Rico, and making security and satisfaction
impossible. He's always in danger of 'making a break' of the kind for
which St Mawr becomes notorious.

And, we are told, Rico 'was being an artist'. As that way of putting it
conveys, he's *not*, in Lawrence's sense, an artist: his 'being' an artist is
simply a manifestation of his inability to be anything but superficial; to
see anything except out of his superficially and deceptively 'conscious'
'personality'. Introduced to the stallion that has had so profound an
effect on Lou, he can only say:

> 'Yes, dear, he certainly *is* beautiful! such a marvellous colour! Almost orange!
> But rather large, I should say, to ride in the Park.'
> 'No, for you he's perfect. You are so tall.'
> 'He'd be marvellous in a composition. That colour!' And all Rico could do
> was to gaze with the artist's eye at the horse, with a glance at the groom.

This comes just after the rendering of the first impact of St Mawr on
Lou. She had found herself slipping away at every opportunity from the

charming little house in Westminster to the mews where her sorrel mare Poppy is kept: 'Whatever it was, her life with Rico in the elegant little house, and all her social engagements, seemed like a dream, the substantial reality of which was those mews in Westminster, her sorrel mare, the owner of the mews, Mr Saintsbury, and the grooms he employed.' Then she is shown St Mawr:

> The wild, brilliant, alert head of St Mawr seemed to look at her out of another world. It was as if she had had a vision, as if the walls of her own world had suddenly melted away, leaving her in a great darkness, in the midst of which the large, brilliant eyes of that horse looked at her with demonish question, while his naked ears stood up like daggers from the naked lines of his inhuman head, and his great body glowed red with power.
> What was it? Almost like a god looking at her terribly out of the everlasting dark, she had felt the eyes of that horse; great, glowing, fearsome eyes, arched with a question, and containing a white blade of light like a thread. What was his non-human question, and his uncanny threat? She didn't know.

By now it is plain that we have to do with much more than sardonic comedy. To call St Mawr a poetic symbol doesn't help much. To call him a sexual symbol is positively misleading. In fact, this 'story about a stallion' refutes in the most irrefutable of ways, for those who take what it offers, the common notion that Lawrence is obsessed with sex, or preaches some religion of sex, or is more preoccupied with sex than the T. S. Eliot of 'The Waste Land'. The marriage between Lou and Rico, this 'attachment of the will and the nerves', does indeed, the datum is given us, fail at the level of sex, in becoming 'more like a friendship, Platonic'; but the failure there is the index of a transcending failure.

St Mawr seemed to look at Lou 'out of another world': this kind of suggestion in Lawrence, irresistibly (one would have thought) as his art conveys it, is often dismissed as 'romantic – that is, as an indulgence of imagination or fancy that cannot, by the mature, be credited with any real significance or taken seriously. The reader who is inclined to 'place' so the rendering, quoted from above, of the first effect of St Mawr on Lou should pay heed to what follows – to the account of the immediate consequence for Lou's relations with Rico. 'No matter where she was, what she was doing, at the back of her consciousness loomed a great, over-aweing figure out of a dark background', and Rico senses something unusual:

'You are thinking about something, Lou dear!' Rico said to her that evening.

He was so quick and sensitive to detect her moods – so exciting in this respect. And his big, slightly prominent blue eyes, with the whites a little bloodshot, glanced at her quickly, with searching, and anxiety, and a touch of fear, as if his conscience were always uneasy. He, too, was rather like a horse – but forever quivering with a sort of cold, dangerous mistrust, which he covered with anxious love.

At the middle of his eyes was a central powerlessness, that left him anxious. It used to touch her to pity, that central look of powerlessness in him. But now, since she had seen the full, dark, passionate blaze of power and of different life in the eyes of the thwarted horse, the anxious powerlessness of the man drove her mad. Rico was so handsome, and he was so self-controlled, he had a gallant sort of kindness and a real worldly shrewdness. One had to admire him: at least *she* had to.

But after all, and after all, it was bluff, an attitude. He kept it all working in himself, deliberately. It was an attitude. She read psychologists who said that everything was an attitude. Even the best of everything. But now she realized that, with men and women, everything is an attitude only when something else is lacking. Something is lacking and they are thrown back on their own devices. That black fiery flow in the eyes of the horse was not 'attitude'. It was something much more terrifying, and real, the only thing that was real. Gushing from the darkness in menace and question, and blazing out in the splendid body of the horse.

There we have it, the preoccupation that, in Lou Carrington (and in Lawrence) so far transcends sex; 'real' – the something other than attitude; the *real* that, surely, we should be able to oppose to the attitudes, to distinguish *them* for what they are. 'Attitudes' belong to the 'personality', the life of 'ideas' and will and nerves. What else is there? Lawrence believes – knows – that there is, or should be, something else – he believes that 'sincerity' can have a meaning; and if this conviction, which carries with it a belief that irreverence, and an incapacity for awed wonder in the face of life, are deathly, is 'romantic', then Lawrence deserves to be called that.

There is a passage in 'Apropos of *Lady Chatterley's Lover*' that comes in aptly here; it might have been written by way of helping us to give an adequate account of the stallion and of the significance that he focusses:

The body's life is the life of sensations and emotions. The body feels real hunger, real thirst, real joy in the sun or the snow, real pleasure in the smell of roses or the look of a lilac bush; real anger, real sorrow, real love, real tenderness, real warmth, real passion, real hate, real grief. All the emotions belong to the body, and are only recognized by the mind. We may hear the most sorrowful piece of news, and only feel a mental excitement. Then, hours after, perhaps in sleep, the awareness may reach the bodily centres, and true grief wrings the heart.

How different they are, mental feelings and real feelings. Today, many people live and die without having had any real feelings – though they have had a 'rich emotional life' apparently, having showed strong mental feeling. But it is all counterfeit. In magic, one of the so-called 'occult' pictures represents a man standing, apparently, before a flat table mirror, which reflects him from the waist to the head, so that you have the man from head to waist, then his reflection downwards from waist to head again. And whatever it may mean in magic, it means what we are today, creatures whose active emotional self has no real existence, but is all reflected downwards from the mind. Our education from the start has *taught* us a certain range of emotions, what to feel and what not to feel, and how to feel the feelings we allow ourselves to feel. All the rest is just non-existent. . . . The higher emotions are strictly dead. They have to be faked.

And by higher emotions we mean love in all its manifestations, from genuine desire to tender love, love of our fellowmen, and love of God: we mean love, joy, delight, hope, true indignant anger, passionate sense of justice and injustice, truth and untruth, honour and dishonour, and real belief in *anything*: for belief is a profound emotion that has the mind's connivance.

By 'body', then, Lawrence means all that deep spontaneous life which is not at the beck and call of the conscious and willing mind, and so in that sense cannot be controlled by it, though it can be thwarted and defeated. St Mawr, the stallion, *is* that life. And in presenting the drama in which the stallion figures so centrally Lawrence leaves us unable to doubt that his essential – and triumphant – concern is to vindicate 'love, joy, delight, hope, true indignant anger, passionate sense of justice and injustice, truth and untruth, honour and dishonour', and the capacity for real belief. It is an astonishing triumph of the highest creative art.

As we have seen, the significance of St Mawr is first imparted to us through Lou's sense of it. It is developed and enforced by a wealth of poetic and dramatic means. We may take for illustration the way in which Rico is played off against Lewis, the Welsh groom.

He peered straight at her from under his overhanging black hair. He had pale grey eyes, that looked phosphorescent, and suggested the eyes of a wild cat peering intent from under the darkness of some bush where it lies unseen. Lou, with her brown, unmatched, oddly perplexed eyes, felt herself found out. 'He's a common little fellow', she thought to herself. 'But he knows a woman and a horse, at sight.' Aloud she said, in her southern drawl:
'How do you think he'd be with Sir Henry?'

Lewis turned his remote, coldly watchful eyes on the young baronet. Rico was tall and handsome, and balanced on his hips. His face was long and well-defined, and with the hair taken straight back from the brow. It seemed as well-made as his clothing, and as perpetually presentable. You could not imagine his face dirty, or scrubby and unshaven, or bearded, or even moustached. It was perfectly prepared for social purposes. If his head had been cut off, like John the Baptist's, it would have been a thing complete in itself, would not have missed the body in the least. The body was perfectly tailored. The head was one of the famous 'talking heads' of modern youth, with eyebrows a trifle Mephistophelian, large blue eyes a trifle bold, and curved mouth thrilling to death to kiss.

The force of this needs no explaining. 'If his head had been cut off . . . it would have been a thing complete in itself, it would not have missed the body in the least' – all the same, Rico has a strong desire to own and to ride St Mawr, till he finds him too dangerous: he cannot be happy in his deficiency. Lewis, of course, 'the little aboriginal Lewis', gets on perfectly well with St Mawr – 'he goes with the horse'. ('When I speak to him', says Mrs Witt, 'I never know whether I'm speaking to a man or a horse.') He has what Rico lacks – or *is* what Rico is not. He explains the case of his own relations with the stallion, whom the gentlemen have found too much for them, by saying that, like Phoenix the other groom, he is 'different'.

Mrs Witt, with her conscious mind, sees the difference as simple inferiority. After the sardonic comedy of the episode in which she cuts his hair, we have this (a passage that, coming where it does, illustrates the delicacy and range of Lawrence's poetic method):

'It is extraordinary what hair that man has!' Said Mrs Witt. 'Did I tell you when I was in Paris, I saw a woman's face in the hotel that I thought I knew? I couldn't place her, till she was coming towards me. *Aren't you Rachel Fannière?* she said. *Aren't you Janette Leroy?* We hadn't seen each other since we were girls of twelve and thirteen at school in New Orleans. *Oh!* she said to me. *Is every illusion doomed to perish? You had such wonderful golden curls! All my life I've said, Oh, if only I had such lovely hair as Rachel Fannière! I've seen those beautiful golden curls of yours all my life. And now I meet you, you're grey!* Wasn't that terrible, Louise? Well, that man's hair made me think of it – so thick and curious. It's strange, what a difference there is in hair; I suppose it's because he's just an animal – no mind! There's nothing I admire in a man like a good *mind*. Your father was a very clever man, and all the men I've admired have been clever. But isn't it curious now, I've never cared much to touch their hair. How strange life is! If it gives one thing, it takes away another.'

As this passage shows, she has actually been affected, in the depths of

herself by something other than 'mind' in Lewis. The discussion that
follows between her and her daughter offers a good example of a
method that, as part of the complex process of establishing his values
and significances, Lawrence can use with great delicacy. They discuss
what may be called his central theme, and while doing so in a wholly
dramatic way, bring to the point of explicitness the essential work of
implicit definition that has been done by image, action and symbolic
presentation. By the end of the exchange certain possibilities of
misunderstanding have been eliminated.

'Why, mother!' said Lou impatiently. 'I think one gets so tired of your men
with mind, as you call it. There are so many of that sort of clever men. And there
are lots of men who aren't very clever, but are rather nice: and lots are stupid. It
seems to me there's something else besides mind and cleverness, or niceness or
cleanness. Perhaps it is the animal. Just think of St Mawr! I've thought so much
about him. We call him an animal, but we never know what it means. He seems
a far greater mystery to me than a clever man. He's a horse. Why can't one say
in the same way, of a man: *He's a man*? There seems no mystery in being a man.
But there's a terrible mystery in St Mawr.'
    Mrs Witt watched her daughter quizzically.
    'Louise', she said, 'you won't tell me that the mere animal is all that counts in
a man. I will never believe it. Man is wonderful because he is able to *think*.'
    'But is he?' cried Lou, with sudden exasperation. 'Their thinking seems to me
all so childish: like stringing the same beads over and over again. Ah, men! They
and their thinking are all so *paltry*. How can you be impressed?'
    Mrs Witt raised her eyebrows sardonically.
    'Perhaps I'm not – any more', she said with a grim smile.

As the conversation proceeds, Lou makes it plain that neither St Mawr
nor Lewis represents all that she would wish to find in a man. She
doesn't dispute that Lewis 'is a servant', and though she says he has 'far
more real mind than . . . any of the clever men', 'he has a good intuitive
mind, he knows things without thinking them', she is far from
suggesting that the ideal man wouldn't be able to think. She repudiates
any backing of 'blood' and 'instinct' against intelligence, and she
repudiates any primitivistic leaning.

'Don't be silly, mother. That's much more your subconscious line, you
admirer of Mind. – I don't consider the cave man is a real human animal at all.
He's brute, a degenerate.'

What she wants, in fact, is the real intelligence, the power of really thinking, that the clever men seem to her not to have:

> 'I don't know one single man who is a proud living animal. I know they've left off really thinking. But then men always do leave off really thinking, when the last bit of wild animal dies in them.
> 'Because we have minds.'
> 'We have no minds once we are tame, mother. Men are all women, knitting and crochetting words together.'
> 'He stands where one can't get at him. And he burns with life. And where does his life come from, to him? That's the mystery. That great burning life in him, that never is dead. Most men have a deadness in them, that frightens me so because of my own deadness. Why can't men get their life straight, like St Mawr, and then think? Why can't they think quick, mother: quick as a woman: only farther than we do? Why isn't men's thinking quick like fire, mother? Why is it so slow, so dead, so deadly dull?'

The kind of intelligence, 'burning like a flame fed straight from underneath', that Lou postulates – the intelligence of a full thinking man who, more than merely intuitive, can sit the stallion as Lewis does – doesn't prove its possibility by being presented in any character: Lou, at the close, has little hope of meeting the man she would care to mate with. But it *is*, nevertheless, irresistibly present in *St Mawr* the dramatic poem; it is no mere abstract postulate. It is present as the marvellous creative intelligence of the author.

For creative genius (and can it ever be other than intelligent?) manifests itself as supreme intelligence in Lawrence – even though writers in the intellecutal weeklies and the Sunday papers can still compare him to Carlyle, and we still find the attitude persisting that, while conceding 'genius' to Lawrence (a kind of genius not very interesting to intellectuals, one gathers), used to send one for intelligence to Aldous Huxley. What is it but intelligence that we have in that deep insight into human nature; that clairvoyant understanding of so wide a range of types and of social milieux; that generalizing power which never leaves the concrete – the power of exposing the movement of civilization in the malady of the individual psyche? It is the same intelligence as that which functions, unmistakably as *that*, one would have thought (but is Lawrence known as a great critic?) in *Phoenix*, the volume of literary criticism, and (for all the lapses) in *Studies in Classic American Literature*.

Formidably critical though it may be, it is the expression of triumphant creativity, and the associate of reverence and wonder. In the conversation with her mother quoted from above, Lou claims:

'Ah no, mother, I want the wonder back again, or I shall die. I don't want to be like you, just criticizing and annihilating these dreary people and enjoying it.'

Lawrence can make 'wonder', as an answer to the potent actuality of Mrs Witt, seem so much more than a vaguely recoiling romanticism because for him it is so much more. He can affirm with a power not given to poor Lou, who is not a genius, and there is nothing of the merely postulated about the positives that he affirms.

The power of the affirmation lies, not in any insistence or assertion or argument, but in the creative fact, his art; it is that which bears irrefutable witness. What his art *does* is beyond argument or doubt. It is not a question of metaphysics or theology – though no doubt there are questions presented for the metaphysician and the theologian. Great art, something created and *there*, is what Lawrence gives us. And there we undeniably *have* a world of wonder and reverence, where life wells up from mysterious springs. It is no merely imagined world; what the creative imagination of the artist makes us contemplate bears an unanswerable testimony.

The witness, the affirmation, is there in the very presentment of this 'cardboard world', so desolating to Lou Carrington, of 'personality' and petty will and 'lots of fun', the world of mechanical repetition: the disgust, the exposure and the rejection are utterly different from what one finds in Aldous Huxley: one can never be unaware of the affirmation, the positive, that gives them their force. The sardonic comedy of Mrs Witt, for instance, turns into something poignant. As the destructive negation, the spirit of rejection and disgust, she 'places' herself.

After the scene, the fiasco, with St Mawr in Rotten Row – provoked by Mrs Witt, he misbehaves – they all go down to spend the summer on the Welsh border:

So down went Lou and Rico, Lewis, Poppy and St Mawr, to Shrewsbury, then out into the country. Mrs Witt's 'cottage' was a tall red-brick Georgian house looking straight on to the churchyard, and the dark, looming big Church.
'I never knew what a comfort it would be', said Mrs Witt, 'to have grave-stones under my drawing-room, and funerals for lunch.'
She really did take a strange pleasure in sitting in her panelled room, that was

painted grey, and watching the Dean or one of the curates officiating at the graveside, among a group of black country mourners, with black-bordered handkerchiefs luxuriantly in use.

'Mother!', said Lou, 'I think it's gruesome!'

Mrs Witt's note is not so merely light as it sounds. The churchyard, with its funerals, becomes an insistent theme. It isn't, for Mrs Witt, an obsession with death as the terrifying and inescapable reality, but a fear that death will prove unreal. Reported in this way, the case may not seem to promise much in the way of convincing poignancy. But this is what we are actually given; the thing is *done*, in its inevitability an astonising triumph of genius; and since the success – the convincing transmutation, in Mrs Witt, of hard-boiled ironic destructiveness into agonized despair – is crucial to the success of the whole, a long quotation may be in place:

In the morning she found her mother sitting at a window watching a funeral. It was raining heavily, so that some of the mourners even wore mackintosh coats. The funeral was in the poorer corner of the churchyard, where another new grave was covered with wreaths of sodden, shrivelling flowers. The yellowish coffin stood on the wet earth, in the rain; the curate held his hat, in a sort of permanent salute, above his head, like a little umbrella, as he hastened on with the service. The people seemed too wet to weep more wet.

It was a long coffin.

'Mother, do you really *like* watching?' asked Lou irritably, as Mrs Witt sat in complete absorption.

'I do, Louise, I really enjoy it.'

'Enjoy, mother!' Lou was almost disgusted.

'I'll tell you why. I imagine I'm the one in the coffin – this is a girl of eighteen, who died of consumption – and those are my relatives, and I'm watching them put me away. And you know, Louise, I've come to the conclusion that hardly anybody in the world really lives, and so hardly anybody really dies. They may well say *Oh Death, where is thy sting-a-ling-a-ling?* Even Death can't sting those that have never really lived. I always used to want that – to die without death stinging me. And I'm sure that girl in the coffin is saying to herself. *Fancy Aunt Emma putting on a drab slicker, and wearing it while they bury me. Doesn't show much respect. But then my mother's family always were common!* I feel there should be a solemn burial of a roll of newspapers containing the account of the death and funeral, next week. It would be just as serious: the grave of all the world's remarks – '

'I don't want to think about it, mother. One ought to be able to laugh at it. I want to laugh at it.'

'Well, Louise, I think it's just as great a mistake to laugh at everything as to cry at everything. Laughter's not the one panacea, either. I should *really* like, before I do come to be buried in a box, to know where I am. That young girl in that coffin never was anywhere – any more than the newspaper remarks on her death and burial. And I begin to wonder if I've ever been anywhere. I seem to have been a daily sequence of newspaper remarks, myself. I'm sure I never really conceived you and gave you birth. It all happened in newspaper notices. It's a newspaper fact that you are my child, and that's about all there is to it.'

Lou smiled as she listened.

'I always knew you were philosophic, mother. But I never dreamed it would come to elegies in a country churchyard, written to your motherhood.'

'*Exactly*, Louise! Here I sit and sing the elegy to my own motherhood. I never had any motherhood, except in newspaper fact. I never was a wife, except in newspaper notices. I never was a young girl, except in newspaper remarks. Bury everything I ever said or that was said about me, and you've buried *me*. But since Kind Words Can Never Die, I can't be buried, and death has no sting-a-ling-a-ling for me! Now listen to me, Louise: I want death to be real to me – not as it was to that young girl. I *want* it to hurt me, Louise. If it hurts me enough, I shall know I was alive.'

These exchanges, intimately *tête-à-tête*, between Lou and her mother are marvellous in their range and suppleness, their harmonic richness, and the sureness of their inflexion, which, since the surface, belonging to the conversational everyday world, is always kept in touch with the depths, can blend in one utterance the hard-boiled sardonic with the poignant. It is astonishing what Lawrence can do, in dialogue, with complete convincingness; dialogue that starts from, and, when it likes, lapses back into, slangy colloquialism, yet, invoking the essential resources of poetic expression, can hazard the most intense emotional and imaginative heightening. One would have said that the kind of thing hadn't been done, and couldn't be done, outside Shakespearean dramatic poetry – which has the advantage of the formal, and explicitly poetic, verse mode.

The note of comedy – sardonic comedy – is always within call. It prevails, magnificently, in the scene that immediately precedes the *tête-à-tête* just quoted from; the scene presenting the consequences of the stallion's crowning misbehaviour. During a riding-party over the moors, St Mawr 'makes a break'; he rears, and is pulled over backwards by Rico, whom he lames. He also kicks another young man in the face, and spoils his beauty. Local society – County – represented by Dean and Mrs Vyner, and the Manbys of Corrabach Hall, are determined now, quite resolutely, that this vicious and dangerous horse shall be 'put away'.

Well, St Mawr *is* a vicious and dangerous horse: he had killed two

men, 'accidentally', before Lou brought him for Rico. What we have to
note is the way in which he is made for us something more than,
something decidedly other than, a vicious horse. It's largely the way in
which we see him through Lou's eyes, so that he is invested for us with
the significance he has for her. We are really made to feel – and it is an
extraordinary creative triumph of the poet – that he represents deep
forces of life that are thwarted in the modern world; to feel, on the plane
of the outward drama, that he has been provoked and outraged by his
human master, so that his 'break' isn't mere viciousness, but a protest of
life.

   This effect, by which we are made to take our stand with the horse, is
also largely got by the way in which the insistence on his being
destroyed is brought home to us as both spiteful and mean – as a
spiteful, mean and deadly hatred of the really (as opposed to the
mechanically and repetitively) living; or, what amounts to the same
thing, a determination to eliminate every element of danger from life.
And *this* effect is got by what might seem to fall within the ordinary
conception of the novelist's art. (For Lawrence is a consummate
novelist.) It is got in a subtle and vivid rendering of personality,
dramatically evoked in a lively comedy.

   It is during this journey that Mrs Witt makes a proposal of marriage
to Lewis. The journey forms a kind of enchanted interlude; but the
convincingness of the episode is not a matter of mere enchantment. We
are made to realize at the setting-out than Mrs Witt has with her
another travelling-companion, a terrible despair, the graveyard mood
become extreme: the odd circumstances leave her, but for Lewis, alone
with this, in the prolonged lull after her latest triumph of 'annihilating
dreary people'. The interlude is one for inescapable meditation:

   Almost she was tempted in her heart to cry: 'Conquer me, oh God, before I
die!' – But then she had a terrible contempt for the God that was supposed to
rule this universe. She felt she could made *Him* kiss her hand. Here she was a
woman of fifty-one, past the change of life. And her great dread was to die an
empty, barren death. Oh, if only Death might open dark wings of mystery and
consolation. To die an easy, barren death. To pass out as she had passed in,
without mystery or the rustling of darkness! That was her last, final, ashy dread.
   'Old' she said to herself. 'I am not *old*! I have lived many years, that is all. But
I am as timeless as an hour-glass that turns morning and night, and spills the
hours of sleep one way, the hours of consciousness the other way, without itself
being affected. Nothing in all my life has ever truly affected me – I believe

Cleopatra only tried the asp, as she tried her pearls in wine, to see if it would really, really have any effect on her. Nothing had ever really had any effect on her, neither Cæsar nor Antony nor any of them. Never once had she really been lost, lost to herself. Then try death, see if that trick would work. If she would lose herself to herself that way. – Ah, death!'

But Mrs Witt mistrusted death too. She felt she might pass out as a bed of asters passes out in autumn, to mere nothingness. – And something in her longed to die, at least, *positively.*

Out of this distress she contemplates Lewis, who may have 'no mind', and be 'strictly a nonentity', but who yet ('what made him perhaps the only real entity to her') seems 'to inhabit another world from hers'. It emphasizes the irony of the situation that the groom, in a moment of confidential unselfconsciousness, breaks out into a long fantasia of folk-beliefs ('A man's mind has to be full of something, so I keep to what we used to think as lads'). It is immediately on this that the admirer of 'mind' and of 'clever men' makes her proposal – to be coldly rejected.

The novelist who can bring off this strange country interlude with complete success can then give us (Mrs Witt having arrived at her destination) the comedy of Lou's letters from Shropshire, which describes with a perfectly got feminine edge and vivacity the convalescent Rico's flirtations with Flora Manby, his devoted nurse.

The 'drama' in the ordinary sense is now virtually over. For if *St. Mawr* deserves to be called a dramatic poem, it is not because it comes to what would ordinarily be called a dramatic close. The burden that represents its essential inspiration demands something quite other. And the actual close seems to me as consummately right, and as clear a proof of genius, as anything else about the work.

Taking a kind of indefinite leave of Rico, Lou decides to go back with her mother to America: Mrs Witt can't stand England, and Lou can't stand the bright young people. I have remarked already on the way in which the little drama of three main actors, a horse and two grooms, is given an inclusive effect and a representative significance. We seem to have presented to us the case of modern civilisation in general. The journey back to Texas and then up into the mountains illustrates some of the workings of this generalizing process.

They are at sea:

By mid-afternoon it was blue summer, on the blue, running waters of the

Channel. And soon, the ship steering for Santander, there was the coast of France; the rocks twinkling like some magic world.

The magic world! And back of it, that post-war Paris, which Lou knew only too well, and which depressed her so thoroughly. Or that post-war Monte Carlo, the Riviera still more depressing even than Paris. No, no one must land, even on magic coasts. Else you found yourself in a railway station and a 'centre of civilization' in five minutes.

They arrive at Havana, and find 'the green leaf of American prosperity shedding itself recklessly, from every roaming sprig of a tourist, over this city of sunshine and alcohol'. As for Texas:

> It left Lou blank with wonder. And in the face of this strange cheerful living in the mirror – a rather cheap mirror at that – England began to seem real to her again.
> Then she had to remember herself back in England. And no, oh God, England was not real either, except poisonously.
> What was real? What under heaven was real?

Out of this they flee north to Santa Fé, and then into the mountain country, the scale and beauty of which are marvellously evoked. The wild, overwhelming, inhuman beauty has its place in the total significance. There's an obvious contrast with the squalor, meanness and pettiness of human life. But that's not all; it's not so simple as that. There's no defeatism in Lawrence, and no resting in any opposition of loathsome men to beautiful nature. He is very unlike Mrs Witt in his radical attitudes: all his negatives and his critical valuations have their significance in relation to a positive – and that is not of the order of 'Back to Nature'. The total effect of *St. Mawr* (as of any characteristic work of Lawrence's) is an affirmation – if that is not a misleading word; for it is the 'tale' we think of as affirming, not the 'artist'. ('Never trust the artist; trust the tale.') There is nothing willed about it.

It's partly a matter of the way in which the nullities and the negative in the drama – Rico and his friends on the one hand, and Mrs Witt on the other – are placed: the positive is powerfully present by implication. And it's there in the extraordinary vitality everywhere of Lawrence's art. The intensity is not an intensity of repulsion and rejection; it is patently and essentially creative, a marvellous and triumphant expression of the creative force of life, in its very nature an affirmation.

And take the concluding pages of *St. Mawr*, superficially so incon-

sequent and tailing-off, essentially so germane, so *belonging* to the
significance. The stallion himself and Lewis have been left behind in
Texas, and we hear no more of them. Lou buys a ranch, high up in the
mountains, in a miraculously beautiful place with a vast outlook over
the desert below. The ranch has a history, which is given us in vivid
epitome – a history of defeat. But 'defeat' is not the word on which the
emphasis rests – the emphasis as conveyed by Lawrence's art. The
series of pioneering efforts are evoked with poignant sympathy. You're
not at all inclined to any smile of superiority when the little New
England wife of the pioneer finally has the mountain water flowing
through the bright taps in her kitchen in the log-built farmhouse. You
feel it as a real triumph; the triumph of civilization is a triumph of the
spirit, though upon exhausting effort and ultimate fatigue defeat
ensures, and then decay. On this, Lou supervenes, to make a fresh start.
And here is the comment:

> Every new stroke of civilization has cost the lives of countless brave men, who
> have fallen defeated by the 'dragon', in their effort to win the apples of the
> Hesperides, or the fleece of gold. Fallen in their efforts to overcome the old, half-
> sordid savagery of the lower stages of creation, and win to the next stage.
>
> For all savagery is half-sordid. And man is only himself when he is fighting on
> and on, to overcome the sordidness.
>
> And every civilization, when it loses its inward vision and its cleaner energy,
> falls into a new sort of sordidness, more vast and more stupendous than the old
> savage sort. An Augean stables on metallic filth.
>
> And all the time, man has to rouse himself afresh, to cleanse the new
> accumulation of refuse. To win from the crude wild nature of victory and the
> power to make another start, and to cleanse behind him the century-deep
> deposits of layer upon layer of refuse: even of tin cans.

Lawrence can allow himself this because the affirmation merely brings
to explicitness what his art has affirmed pervasively and cumulatively.
And, with his easy sureness of poise, he can allow the ironical Mrs Witt
the closing note.

Source: *Scrutiny*, xvii (1950) 38–53; reprinted with minor
changes in F. R. Leavis, *D. H. Lawrence: Novelist* (London, 1955).
The original *Scrutiny* version is reproduced here.

2. 'CONRAD'S PROSE' (1975)

.... my avowed undertaking... in one of its aspects, is to bring out the force of my contention that the intelligent study of creative literature entails the study of language in its fullest use, the conceptual implications of the word 'linguistic' as used in general by philosophers being disastrously misleading. I have explained why it is peculiarly difficult in an argument such as mine to enforce it by adducing representative pieces of prose, so that one has to rely mainly on formally poetic uses of language for what I may perhaps call one's concrete terms of discourse. But it remains necessary to make it plain that the argument doesn't involve any naïve assumptions about the difference between 'prose' and 'poetry'. For one thing, I have in mind the need to insist that, in spite of the ways in which the 'positive civilization' denounced by Blake with such strong reason affected the literature of the English language in the eighteenth century, the subsequent literary achievement made the nineteenth century one of the greatest creative ages in human history.

I will, then... clinch the suggestive reminder of what we might relevantly and abundantly, and in great variety, adduce under 'prose' by adding one critical commentary on a passage. Actually, what I select as appropriate for the purpose I found in a proposed comparative exercise on an examination paper, but it will be plain at once that one of the passages serves merely as a foil to the other.

(a) We sat down by the side of the road to continue the argument begun half a mile or so before. I am certain it was an argument because I remember perfectly how my tutor argued and how without the power of reply I listened with my eyes fixed obstinately on the ground. A stir on the road made me look up – and then I saw my unforgettable Englishman. There are acquaintances of later years, familiars, shipmates, whom I remember less clearly. He marched rapidly towards the east (attended by a hang-dog Swiss guide) with the mien of an ardent and fearless traveller. He was clad in a knicker-bocker suit, but as at the same time he wore short socks under his laced boots, for reasons which, whether hygienic or conscientious, were surely imaginative, his calves, exposed to the public gaze and to the tonic air of high altitudes, dazzled the beholder by the splendour of their marble-like condition and their rich tone of young ivory. He was the leader of a small caravan. The light of a headlong, exalted satisfaction with the world of men and the scenery of mountains illumined his clean-cut, very red face, his short, silver-white whiskers, his innocently eager and triumphant eyes. In passing he cast a glance of kindly curiosity and a friendly gleam of big, sound, shiny teeth towards the man and the boy sitting like dusty tramps by the roadside, with a modest knapsack lying at their feet. His white calves twinkled sturdily, the uncouth Swiss guide with a surly mouth stalked like an unwilling bear at his elbow; a small train of three mules followed in single file the lead of this inspiring enthusiast. Two ladies rode past one behind the other, but from the way they sat I only saw their calm, uniform backs, and the long ends of blue veils hanging behind far down over their identical hat-brims. His two daughters, surely. An industrious luggage mule, with unstarched ears and guarded by a slouching, sallow driver, brought up the rear. My tutor, after pausing for a look and a faint smile, resumed his earnest argument.

(b) There's a certain sort of man whose doom in the world is dis-appointment – who excels in it – and whose luckless triumphs in his meek career of life, I have often thought, must be regarded by the kind eyes above with as much favour as the splendid successes and achievements of coarser and more prosperous men. As I sat with the lieutenant upon deck, his telescope laid over his lean legs and he looking at the sunset with a pleased, withered old face, he gave me a little account of his history. I take it he is in nowise disinclined to talk about it, simple as it is: he has been seven-and-thirty years in the navy, being somewhat more mature in the service than Lieutenant Peel, Rear-Admiral Prince de Joinville, and other commanders who need not be mentioned. He is a very well-educated man, and reads prodigiously – travels, histories, lives of eminent worthies and heroes, in his simple way. He is not in the least angry at his want of luck in the profession. 'Were I a boy tomorrow,' he said, 'I would begin it again; and when I see my schoolfellows, and how they have got on in life, if some are better off than I am, I find many are worse, and have no call to be discontented.' So he carries her Majesty's mails meekly through this world, waits upon port-admirals and captains in his old glazed hat, and is as proud of the pennon at the bow of his little boat, as if it were flying from the mainmast of a thundering man-of-war. He gets two hundred a year for his services, and has an old mother and a sister living in England somewhere, who I will wager (though he never, I swear, said a word about it) have a good portion of this princely income.

What the two passages may be said to have in common is the aim to present a character the contemplation of whom evokes both amusement and sympathetic respect. A preliminary glance at them leaves one with the certainty that (b) is the foil, and couldn't be anything else. It has, of its nature, a design on the reader, and the design is so crude and so obvious as to be insulting – at least, that would be one's comment if one had been expected to take the passage seriously. In fact, the design is virtually explicit: the first sentence announces it with the 'meek' (incontinently repeated and reinforced) and the 'coarser and more prosperous men', and what ensues as the filling-out of the human case, or situation, that the writer offers to present is all cliché – down to the old mother and the sister who live on his pay.

This is all that need be said about (*b*), except in so far as, in its quality as foil, it helps with the commentary on (*a*). But we didn't need the contrast to be struck by the distinction of the passage that comes first: it is unmistakably by a great master. The contrast prompts us to describe what produces that conviction as an astonishing specificity. There is in the whole paragraph nothing approaching cliché in any sense the term might carry. The 'unforgettable Englishman' might in another context have seemed to invite the adverse characterization in the most obvious sense, but here the whole actual context evokes in compelling concreteness what it is that makes the Englishman unforgettable; the adjective has nothing of the reach-me-down about it; we are beyond questioning, when we come to it, that it is on the way to being completely validated – to receiving its full charge of particularizing force. We are beyond questioning because the evocative process by which statement and the general are transcended has, in the very few preceding lines, worked on us so potently:

> We sat down by the side of the road to continue the argument begun half a mile before. I am certain it was an argument because I remember perfectly how my tutor argued and how without the power of reply I listened with my eyes fixed obstinately on the ground. A stir on the road made me look up – and then . . . .

Creative art here is an exercise in the achieving of precision (a process that is at the same time the achieving of complete sincerity – the elimination of ego-interested distortion and all impure motives) in the recovery of a memory now implicitly judged – implicitly, for actual judgment can't be stated – to be, in a specific life, of high significance. The evocation of concrete thisness begins in terms of the disciplined act of remembering, which, of course, is selective, and, in its re-creativity, creative, as all our achieved apprehension of the real must be. The recovered memory is the remembered, implicitly, in the re-creating evocation, valued and placed: it is to be noted that the unforgettable vision is enclosed organically in a vision of the writer's own impressed young self – the attitude towards the Englishman goes with an attitude towards Conrad's youth. For it is, of course, Conrad; I saw at once that it could be no other; I couldn't, however, recall any novel or tale in which the passage could have come. Then I realized that it is Conrad's account of his conceiving the ambition to become a British master mariner, which I had read in *A Personal Record* on the appearance of this in the nineteen-twenties. (The other piece I guess to be by Marryat.)

The highly Conradian passage offers us a study of the difference between mere itemizing description and the evoked specificity that a great writer effects with his distinctive use of the English language – distinctive and unique, yet generating a vital something in which minds can meet, and in this sense real.

There are acquaintances of later years, familiars, shipmates, whom I remember less clearly. He marched rapidly towards the east (attended by a hang-dog Swiss guide) with the mien of an ardent and fearless traveller.

These coupled sentences enforce, as the whole paragraph, with its diverse wealth of unforeseeable felicities does marvellously in sum, the truth that it is the creative writer who maintains the life and potentiality of the language. The first of the sentences might have been written in a letter. The contrasting second, its exalted dignity enhanced by the parenthetic 'hang-dog' guide, suggests Gibbon describing the advance of a Roman conqueror. It is not parody, though it registers the element of amusement in the mature Conrad's sense of the unforgettable – a prompting, this critical perception, to reflect on the essential part played by the opening two sentences in the subtlety (which, for the reader, is life, vividness and reality) of the whole.

But what I meant to call attention to immediately was the pregnant and diversely manifested truth that, for Conrad, a great writer of our century, to compose in the living English of our time was to use freely and flexibly the resources of a language that had a literature behind it – a great literature still (to creative writers) relevantly native. For Conrad (and it is equally true of Lawrence and of Eliot) to write out of the present is to write out of a present that is with an immensely fuller realization on his part the present of the past than is represented even by the most cultivated contemporary speech. This goes with the general truth that, in his artist's rightness, precision and freedom from affectation, he is in the good sense of the word (as both Lawrence and Eliot the major poet are) sophisticated – a truth the force of which is exemplified in the sentence that follows the pair just quoted:

He was clad in a knicker-bocker suit, but as at the same time he wore short socks under his laced boots, for reasons which, whether hygienic or conscientious, were surely imaginative, his calves, exposed to the public gaze and to the tonic air of high altitudes, dazzled the beholder by the splendour of their marble-like condition and their rich tone of young ivory.

The sophistication – the implicit presence of a cultural background transcending what 'vernacular' suggests – can be pointed to at once in 'the tonic air of high altitudes' and 'their marble-like condition and their rich tone of young ivory.' But of course that is very far from all coming under that head, as we can, with great readiness to particularize, say if we use the couple of opening sentences as giving a norm of modern 'ordinary' prose. It is unnecessary to proceed by offering to substantiate the 'readiness'. Instead, I will emphasize that the paragraph is all of a piece – as a poem is: it imposes itself, in its idiosyncratic livingness, as natural and unaffected modern English. What in it is most vividly idiosyncratic, in fact, may itself be felt to refer us implicitly to the cultural heritage; it is unmistakably and inimitably Conrad, but a Conrad for whom the English language that had adopted and naturalized him was the language not only of Shakespeare, but, in the not distant past, of Dickens. What we have everywhere is the antithesis of cliché; it is, given us in the words which it has unerringly found and seems to replace, perceived specificity – the Conradian perception. 'His white calves twinkled sturdily' – a characteristically unprecedented collocation of words that we feel to have achieved itself instantaneously, with such inevitability does it make us see, and, in an implicitly evaluative way, realize and respond in a given total effect. It is everywhere so in the paragraph; 'their calm uniform backs', 'an industrious luggage mule, with unstarched ears' – but further instancing is unnecessary. It remains to note that the final sentence completes the enclosing 'frame' that is in and of the memory, being essential to its subtlety – that *is* the livingness.

The passage compares with the speech from *Macbeth* as a creative use of language of a closely related order. We have left the words 'image' and 'imagery' behind, and there is no sharp provocation to use them here; yet the process and the effect are of the kind in which 'imagery' was observed to play a major part: this is prose, but what it achieves is presentment with its concrete specificity, as opposed to the mode of 'taking about' which we call 'description' (I haven't discussed, not thinking it necessary, the expressive play in it of 'movement').

It is prose, and prose – unlike what can be found in *Ulysses*, for instance – in an obvious way that signifies a clear continuity with the 'modern' discursive prose that was established in the great seventeenth-century change. . . .

SOURCE: extract from *The Living Principle* (London, 1975) pp. 139–44.

PART TWO

The Art of Fiction

Barbara Hardy

'THE AUTHOR'S VOICE USED DRAMATICALLY: GEORGE ELIOT' (1959)

. . . The narrative medium is composed of many voices. There is the direct speech of the author's pity, both for her own creatures and extending in generalization to lament and admiration for all humanity. There is the more detached voice of irony and analysis. There is the omniscient warning, veiled and unveiled, working in the interests of aesthetic unity and dramatic irony. At times – though I believe these occasions to be rare – we may resent the absence of dramatic isolation and feel, as some readers certainly have in the case of Dorothea, that the author's solicitude stands between us and the character, blurring the sharp edges of the clear portrait, softening, idealizing, or sentimentalizing. But such blurred effects are not the consequence of the author's inability to withdraw her own commentary. There are some very powerful instances of her sense of a dramatic decorum which demands just such a withdrawal, and both the voice of maternal pity, and the voice of ironical wisdom, can be stilled in favour of a dramatic method which presents the character in its nakedness. When this happens the very change in convention has its own effect of isolation and constriction. This is what happens as early as *Adam Bede*, in the section describing Hetty's flight from Hayslope, her search for Arthur, and her terror and panic which ends – though not for the direct view of the reader – in the birth of her child and its murder. This account, though grammatically presented in *oratio obliqua*, is restricted to Hetty's sensibility and experience. It is as if George Eliot had expended both pity and irony and, at the moment of crisis, let the character present itself.

This account begins with the author's point of view. George Eliot comments on Hetty's sorrow and fear and the uncaring natural beauty around her:

A long, lonely journey, with sadness in the heart; away from the familiar to the strange: that is a hard and dreary thing even to the rich, the strong, the instructed: a hard thing, even when we are called by duty, not urged by dread.   Ch. 36.).

This is gradually converted into an ungeneralized and unreflective commentary which is in all essentials – vocabulary, syntax and re-ference, in fact everything except the third-person form – the flight as it is experienced by Hetty. There is little or no margin for the author's sensibility. The words are short and simple, the sentences short and broken, there are many questions and repetitions. If we compare this episode with the first-person account given by Hetty to Dinah in prison there is little difference. The first-person account is ungrammatical, and the extracts below are a kind of linguistic compromise: grammatical accuracy alone gives the superficial adherence to the third-person narration, but the sophisticated narrator is, to all intents and purposes, absent:

What *could* she do? She would go away from Windsor – travel again as she had done the last week, and get among the flat green fields with the high hedges round them, where nobody could see her or know her; and there, perhaps, when there was nothing else she could do, she should get courage to drown herself in some pond like that in the Scantlands. . . .   (Ch. 37.)

Later in the same chapter:

The pool had its wintry depth now: by the time it got shallow, as she remembered the pools did at Hayslope, in the summer, no one could find out that it was her body. But then there was her basket – she must hide that too: she must throw it into the water – make it heavy with stones first, and then throw it in. She got up to look about for stones, and soon brought five or six, which she laid down beside her basket, and then sat down again. There was no need to hurry – there was all the night to drown herself in. She sat leaning her elbow on the basket. She was weary, hungry. There were some buns in her basket – three, which she had supplied herself with at the place where she ate her dinner. She took them out now, and ate them eagerly, and then sat still, looking at the pool.   (Ch. 37.)

Compare this with Hetty's direct statement:

And I walked on and on, and I hardly felt the ground I trod on; and it got lighter, for there came the moon – O Dinah, it frightened me when it first looked at me out o' the clouds – it never looked so before; and I turned o' the roads into the fields, for I was afraid o' meeting anybody with the moon shining on me. And I came to a haystack, where I thought I could lie down and keep myself warm all night.   (Ch. 45.)

This goes on for more than six pages of faltering simplicity. The similarities between it and the account of the journey are striking: *oratio recta* and *oratio obliqua* alike have the same simplicity of words and sentences: there is no periodic elaboration or surview, but a sentence-by-sentence, step-by-step absorption in the present. The style is abrupt and jerky, and the details are given flatly, with an extraordinary impression of practical and precise care. It is a childlike practical absorption which makes a terrifying impression in the moments of crisis: the very absence of emotional language and the presence of practical detail is almost unbearable when Hetty is planning her suicide, thinking of the discovery of her body, or covering up her baby in the wood. It is dramatic narrative reminiscent of the naïve practical detail of 'The Ancient Mariner' or 'The Idiot Boy'. The pointed exclusion of the author's sensibility has its own kind of heightening effect, in no way dependent on heightened language or generalization. Indeed, all generalization is shut off here: Hetty is incapable of it. We are face to face with her 'narrow imagination' which cannot anticipate. She plans unemotionally, and only recoils from death when she is about to jump into the pond. Instead of imagination we have the flat references to her actual experience – to the woman and baby who came to Hayslope, nearly dead with cold and hunger, to the pond in the Scantlands: this is the unimaginative mind which thought of Arthur's love in terms of finery. George Eliot speaks of 'the narrow circle of her imagination' and this is exactly demonstrated in the account of her flight. It is done in terms of sensation not of sensibility, of practical memory not of generalization, of careful matter-of-fact planning not of terrified anticipation.

   This is perhaps the most striking example of the dramatic ability to present a limited consciousness, and it is sustained, in the account of Hetty's flight, for many pages. But there are many other examples of George Eliot's refusal to present character in the frame of her own thought and feeling: there is the presentation of Tito's process of rational argument, limiting his sensibility as it accelerates. There is the account of Casaubon's surprise at the disappointing quality of his own

ardour. There is the elated description of Will's walk across the fields to
see Dorothea at church, blinkered by love and sunlight. There is the
survey of Gwendolen, oscillating between intention and desire.

> Quick, quick, like pictures in a book beaten open with a sense of hurry, came
> back vividly, yet in fragments, all that she had gone through in relation to
> Grandcourt – the allurements, the vacillations, the resolve to accede, the final
> repulsion; the incisive face of that dark-eyed lady with the lovely boy; her own
> pledge (was it a pledge not to marry him?) – the new disbelief in the worth of
> men and things for which that scene of disclosure had become a symbol. That
> unalterable experience made a vision at which in the first agitated moment,
> before tempering reflections could suggest themselves, her native terror shrank.
> Where was the good of choice coming again? What did she wish? Anything
> different? No! and yet in the dark seed-growths of consciousness a new wish was
> forming itself – 'I wish I had never known it!'   (Ch. 26.)

It was perhaps this dramatic immediacy which the reviewer of *Felix Holt*
in *The Westminster Review*, July 1866, had in mind when he made this not
altogether fair contrast of Jane Austen with George Eliot:

> Whilst Miss Austen makes you feel that you are in the next room to the speakers,
> and can overhear them, George Eliot, that you are in the room with them. Jane
> Austen gives you the idea that her characters are all members of the Established
> Church, George Eliot, that they have souls.

There are some occasions when the dramatic presentation depends on a
slightly different version of this absence of comment. The crudest
example is the account of Dunsey Cass on the night of his death when he
robs Silas Marner. We do not know what has happened to Dunsey until
Raveloe knows, but if we look back we find that George Eliot has played
fair. The last word about Dunsey is ambiguous: 'So he stepped forward
into the darkness.' It is, in one sense, the last word that can be said about
him, and the withdrawal from his narrative, essential for the plot, has a
literal necessity.

In *Romola* there is something similar. It also involves a refusal to use
the omniscient commentary; it interrupts George Eliot's normal
method and makes a kind of hiatus in time. To begin with, we do not
know much about Tito, except that he has a special sensibility to certain
references:

> 'Anybody might say the saints had sent *you* a dead body; but if you took the

jewels, I hope you buried him – and you can afford a mass or two for him into the bargain.'   (Ch. 1.)

'Young man, I am painting a picture of Sinon deceiving old Priam, and I should be glad of your face for my Sinon, if you'd give me a sitting.'   (Ch. 4.)

'Ah, then, they are fine intagli,' said Bardo. 'Five hundred ducats! Ah, more than a man's ransom!' (Ch. 6.)

There is also the deliberate question accompanying Tito, as it introduces Gwendolen at the beginning of the novel. Bratti scents a mystery:

'I picked up a stranger this morning as I was coming in from Rovezzano, and I can spell him out no better than I can the letters on that scarf I bought from the French cavalier.'

'But the riddle about him is –'   (Ch. 1.)

But there is the deliberate refusal either to describe Tito's character or to reveal his secret in any other way until chapter 9. Then we return to the phrase Bardo used in innocence, and at last Tito's inner conflict appears, together with the guilty secret of his abandoned foster-father:

'A man's ransom!' – who was it that had said five hundred florins was more than a man's ransom? If now, under this mid-day sun, on some hot coast far away, a man somewhat stricken in years – a man not without high thoughts and with the most passionate heart – a man who long years ago had rescued a little boy from a life of beggary, filth, and cruel wrong, had reared him tenderly, and had been to him as a father – if that man were now under this summer sun toiling as a slave, hewing wood and drawing water, perhaps being smitten and buffeted because he was not deft and active?   (Ch. 9.)

This suspension may seem at first to be a mere device for creating mystery and tension at the beginning, but it is an unusually long mystery for George Eliot, who usually gives the necessary data about her characters at an early stage in the process of introduction. A little later we are given the reason:

This was his first real colloquy with himself: he had gone on following the impulses of the moment, and one of those impulses had been to conceal half the fact; he had never considered this part of his conduct long enough to face the consciousness of his motives for the concealment.

George Eliot has moved a long way from her affectionate exposition of character in *Scenes of Clerical Life* and *Adam Bede* – here she fits exposition to character, and Tito's past is withheld from us until he ceases to withhold it from his own consciousness. It is a decorous subduing of author's commentary to the process of character, so that the two seem to move together.

There is something like this in the portrayal of Bulstrode in *Middlemarch*, where once more there is the question of facing the problem within the mind. Bulstrode is at first presented externally, almost flatly, like Raffles or Rigg. Then George Eliot, refusing to make flat characters, explores his consciousness, and once more we see villainy from the inside.

This inside view of egoism often shows a terrifying and unexpected innocence. We turn back to Bulstrode's past rather as we might in a play by Ibsen, because we are forced to, because the fuse laid in the past has led to the explosion in the present:

> Even without memory, the life is bound into one by a zone of dependence in growth and decay; but intense memory forces a man to open his own blameworthy past. With memory set smarting like a reopened wound, a man's past is not simply a dead history, an outworn preparation of the present: it is not a repented error shaken loose from the past: it is a still quivering part of himself, bringing shudders and bitter flavours and the tinglings of merited shame.
>
> Into this second life Bulstrode's past had now risen, only the pleasures of it seeming to have lost their quality. Night and day, without interruption save of brief sleep which only wove retrospect and fear into a fantastic present, he felt the scenes of his earlier life coming between him and everything else, as obstinately as, when we look through the window from a lighted room, the objects we turn our backs on are still before us, instead of the grass and the trees. . . .
>
> Once more he saw himself the young banker's clerk. . . . (ch. 61.)

He does not turn back, we do not turn back, until memory has been 'set smarting like a reopened wound' by Raffles's threats. He faces the past only when he is forced to, and it is not until then that the reader moves back in time with him.

Bulstrode, like Casaubon, is trapped by necessity, but in his case the process from bad to worse took place in the past. It is presented, necessarily and organically, as past haunts present, in retrospect. It may look like the haunting of guilt, and yet it presents a kind of innocence. What is innocent is Bulstrode's fear – he is afraid of the past only as something which might be discovered. Set in counterpoint against

George Eliot's insistence that he is what the past has made him, is his hope that he is free, except from being found out.

There is another dramatic evasion of this kind, this time not leading up to disclosure. On the night of Raffles's death, there is Bulstrode's version of Tito's refusal to face his consciousness, shown in the conflict of words and images. This is the hypocrite at prayer:

Whatever prayers he might lift up, whatever statements he might inwardly make of this man's wretched spiritual condition, and the duty he himself was under to submit to the punishment divinely appointed for him rather than to wish for evil to another – through all this effort to condense words into a solid mental state, there pierced and spread with irresistible vividness the images of the events he desired.   (Ch. 70.)

There is no account of the moment of decision. We are given the process, the sleight-of-hand which Bulstrode performs in his 'indirect' and verbally innocuous prayers, and then comes Mrs Abel's fatal suggestion of brandy. This is dealt with from her point of view – like her, the reader is outside Bulstrode's door, only hearing the silences and the husky voice. Bulstrode gives her the key of the wine-cooler. This is George Eliot's comment:

Early in the morning – about six – Mr Bulstrode rose and spent some time in prayer. Does any one suppose that private prayer is necessarily candid – necessarily goes to the roots of action? Private prayer is inaudible speech, and speech is representative: who can represent himself just as he is, even in his own reflections? Bulstrode had not yet unravelled in his thought the confused promptings of the last four-and-twenty hours.

When we are expecting her to continue her commentary on what goes on in Bulstrode, she withdraws. There is a gap in explanation because there is a gap in the consciousness. Bulstrode, like Tito, is withdrawn from our view, and the convention of omniscience suspended. The voice is as expressive in its absence as in its presence.

SOURCE   : Extract from chapter 8 of *The Novels of George Eliot*
(London, 1959; revised edition 1963) pp. 177–84.

Wayne Booth

'TELLING AS SHOWING: FIELDING AS NARRATOR' (1961)

What is the context into which Fielding's narrator intrudes, at the end of *Joseph Andrews*, to say of Fanny, 'How, reader, shall I give thee an adequate idea of this lovely young creature! . . . to comprehend her entirely, conceive youth, health, bloom, beauty, neatness, and innocence, in her bridal bed; conceive all these in their utmost perfection, and you may place the charming Fanny's picture before your eyes'? His earlier comments obviously provide part of the context. But if this is so, how does this new context, itself made up of 'intrusions', relate to the whole story? And what of that still larger context, the author's and reader's experience with previous fiction?

Obviously the notion of function with which we have been working so far must be enlarged. Though commentary has served in the ways outlined above, and though no other device could have served most of them as well, it is also true that to look at these functions is only a first step in explaining the power of the great commentators. In *Don Quixote*, for example, our delight in the comments by various narrators obviously is not fully explained by showing that such commentary serves to heighten the effect of the knight's adventures. Though Cid Hamete Benengeli's farewell to his pen parallels in comic style Don Quixote's farewell to his books and to life itself, such a parallel fails to explain the full delight of the passage. 'Here shalt thou remain, hung upon this rack by this brass wire. I know not if thou beest well cut or not, O pen of mine, but here thou shalt live for long ages to come, unless some presumptuous and scoundrelly historians should take thee down to profane thee. . . . For me alone Don Quixote was born and I for him; it was for him to act, for me to write, and we two are one in spite of that Tordesillesque pretender who had, and may have, the audacity to write with a coarse and ill-trimmed ostrich quill of the deeds of my valiant knight. . . .'[1]

The effect here is made up of many elements. There is pleasure in mere ornament: the history of intruding narrators is full of sheer overflowing narrative exuberance, as if the story itself, good as it is, did not provide adequate scope for the author's genius. There is parody of previous fiction: the laying down of swords, flutes, horns, and other romantic objects was part of the tradition ridiculed in *Don Quixote*. But quite obviously the most important quality here is something else entirely: the narrator has made of himself a dramatized character to whom we react as we react to other characters.

Narrators like Cid Hamete, who can speak for the norms on which the action is based, can become companions and guides quite distinct from the wonders they have to show. Our admiration or affection or sympathy or fascination or awe – no two of these narrators affect us in precisely the same way – is more intense just because it has been made personal; the telling is itself a dramatic rendering of a relationship with the author's 'second self' which in strictly impersonal fiction is often less lively because only implicit.

There has been very little critical discussion of this relationship. But it is not hard to find confessions to its effect. At the beginning of *The Catcher in the Rye* (1951), J. D. Salinger's adolescent hero says, 'What really knocks me out is a book that, when you're all done reading it, you wish the author that wrote it was a terrific friend of yours and you could call him up on the phone whenever you felt like it'. Many more mature readers have found themselves feeling the same way. Even Henry James, in spite of his mistrust of the author's voice, cannot resist the appeal of a great loquacious author like Fielding. After describing the deficiencies of Tom Jones's mind and the partial compensation of his vitality, James says, 'Besides which his author – *he* handsomely possessed of a mind – has such an amplitude of reflexion for him and round him that we see him through the mellow air of Fielding's fine old moralism, fine old humour and fine old style, which somehow enlarge, make every one and every thing important.'[2]

It may be extreme to call this relationship one of identification, as do Paul Goodman and H. W. Leggett,[3] but there are times when we do surrender ourselves to the great authors and allow our judgments to merge completely with theirs. Our surrender need not be dramatized by giving open voice to the narrator, but it is in its service that many comments find their major justification. Much commentary that seems excessive if judged by narrow standards of function is wholly defensible when seen as contributing to our sense of traveling with a trustworthy companion, an author who is sincerely battling to do justice to his materials. George Eliot, for example, involves us constantly in her battle to deal with the truth, even at the expense of beauty or pleasure. '"This Rector of Broxton is little better than a pagan!" I hear one of my readers exclaim. "How much more edifying it would have been if you had made him give Arthur some truly spiritual advice! You might have put into his mouth the most beautiful things – quite as good as reading a sermon."' The story of *Adam Bede* (1859) stops for several pages while she gives her answer to 'my fair critic'. 'Certainly I could, if I held it the highest vocation of the novelist to represent things as they never have been and never will be.' But her 'strongest effort is to avoid any such arbitrary picture, and to give a faithful account of men and things as they have mirrored themselves in my mind'. Even if the mirror is 'defective', she feels herself 'as much bound to tell you as precisely as I can what that reflection is, as if I were in the witness-box narrating my experience on oath'. Out of context such talk may sound overdone, even boastful. But in context it can be convincing. 'So I am content to tell my simple story, without trying to make things seem better than they were; dreading nothing, indeed, but falsity, which, in spite of one's best efforts, there is reason to dread. Falsehood is so easy, truth so difficult.'[4] Obviously, one effect of this passage is to remind us that the Rector *is* more convincing than an idealized portrait would be. But a more important effect is to involve us on the side of the honest, perceptive, perhaps somewhat inept, but certainly uncompromising author in the almost overwhelming effort to avoid falsehood.

Even the most clumsily worded intrusion can redeem itself by conveying this sense of how deeply the narrator cares about what he is doing. The graceless conclusion of Melville's *Billy Budd*, for example, serves to remind us of the author's very real problems and thus to make us forgive every seeming fault. 'The symmetry of form attainable in pure fiction cannot so readily be achieved in a narration essentially having less to do with fable than with fact. Truth uncompromisingly told will always have its ragged edges. . . . Though properly the story ends with his life something in way of sequel will not be amiss. Three brief chapters will suffice' (p. 274, ch. 29).

Dostoevski is frequently masterful in making his narration seem to be a part of the battle. When he says that he does 'not feel very competent' to the tremendous task before him, the effect is never to make us doubt his competence. His tendency to identify himself and his weaknesses with his hero's is especially effective. In *The Double* there is a fine satirical passage about the futility of the author's desire to portray the glorious world into which his hero desires, with equal futility, to rise.[5]

'FIELDING' IN 'TOM JONES'

It is frustrating to try to deal critically with such effects, because they can in no way be demonstrated to the reader who has not experienced them. No amount of quotation, no amount of plot summary, can possibly show how fully the implied author's character dominates our reactions to the whole. About all we can do is to look closely at one work, *Tom Jones*, analyzing in static terms what in any successful reading is as sequential and dynamic as the action itself.

Though the dramatized Fielding does serve to pull together many parts of *Tom Jones* that might otherwise seem disconnected, and though he serves dozens of other functions, from the standpoint of strict function he goes too far: much of his commentary relates to nothing but the reader and himself. If we really want to defend the book as art, we must somehow account for these 'extraneous' elements. It is not difficult to do so, however, once we think of the effect of our intimacy on our attitude toward the book as a whole. If we read straight through all of the seemingly gratuitous appearances by the narrator, leaving out the story of Tom, we discover a running account of growing intimacy between the narrator and the reader, an account with a kind of plot of its own and a separate denouement. In the prefatory chapter to his final volume, the narrator makes this denouement explicit, suggesting a distinct interest in the 'story' of his relationship with the reader. This interest certainly requires some explanation if we wish to claim that *Tom Jones* is a unified work of art and not half-novel, half-essay.

We are now, reader, arrived at the last stage of our long journey. As we have, therefore, travelled together through so many pages, let us behave to one another like fellow-travellers in a stagecoach, who have passed several days in the company of each other; and who, notwithstanding any bickerings or little animosities which may have occurred on the road, generally make all up at last, and mount, for the last time, into their vehicle with cheerfulness and good-humour.

The farewell goes on for several paragraphs, and at times the bantering tone of much of the work is entirely abandoned. 'And now, my friend, I take this opportunity (as I shall have no other) of heartily wishing thee well. If I have been an entertaining companion to thee, I promise thee it is what I have desired. If in anything I have offended, it was really without any intention.'

It may be extravagant to use the term 'subplot' for the story of our relationship with this narrator. Certainly the narrator's 'life' and Tom Jone's life are much less closely parallel than we expect in most plots and subplots. In *Lear*, Gloucester's fate parallels and reinforces Lear's. In *Tom Jones*, the 'plot' of our relationship with Fielding-as-narrator has no similarity to the story of Tom. There is no complication, not even any sequence except for the gradually increasing familiarity and intimacy leading to farewell. And much of what we admire or enjoy in the narrator is in most respects quite different from what we like or enjoy in his hero.

Yet somehow a genuine harmony of the two dramatized elements is produced. It is from the narrator's norms that Tom departs when he gets himself into trouble, yet Tom is always in harmony with his most important norms. Not only does he reassure us constantly that Tom's heart is always in the right place, his presence reassures us of both the moral and the literary rightness of Tom's existence. As we move through the novel under his guidance, watching Tom sink to the depths, losing, as it appears, Allworthy's protection, Sophia's love, and his own shaky hold on decency, we experience for him what R. S. Crane has called the 'comic analogue of fear'.[6] And our growing intimacy with Fielding's dramatic version of himself produces a kind of comic analogue of the true believer's reliance on a benign providence in real life. It is not just that he promises a happy ending. In a fictional world that offers no single character who is both wise and good – even Allworthy, though all worthy, is no model of perspicacity – the author is always there on his platform to remind us, through his wisdom and benevolence, of what human life ought to be and might be. What is more, his self-portrait is of a life enriched by a vast knowledge of literary culture and of a mind of great creative power – qualities which could never be so fully conveyed through simply exercising them without comment on the dramatic materials of Tom's story.

For the reader who becomes too much aware of the author's claim to superlative virtues, the effect may fail. He may seem merely to be posing. For the reader with his mind on the main business, however, the narrator becomes a rich and provocative chorus. It is his wisdom and learning and benevolence that permeate the world of the book, set its comic tone between the extremes of sentimental indulgence and scornful indignation, and in a sense redeem Tom's world of hypocrites and fools.

One can imagine, perhaps, a higher standard of virtue, wisdom, or learning than the narrator's. But for most of us he succeeds in being the highest possible in his world – and, at least for the nonce, in ours. He is not trying to write for any other world, but for *this* one he strikes the precise medium between too much and too little piety, benevolence, learning, and worldly wisdom.[7] When he draws to the end of his farewell, then, at the time when we know we are to lose him, and uses terms which inevitably move us across the barrier to death itself, we find, lying beneath our amusement at his playful mode of farewell, something of the same feeling we have when we lose a close friend, a friend who has given us a gift which we can never repay. The gift he leaves – his book – is himself, precisely himself. The author has created this self as he has written the book. The book and the friend are one. 'For however short the period may be of my own performances, they will most probably outlive their own infirm author, and the weakly productions of his abusive contemporaries.' Was Fielding literally infirm as he wrote that sentence? It matters not in the least. It is not Fielding we care about, but the narrator created to speak in his name

SOURCE: extract from chapter 8 of *The Rhetoric of Fiction* (Chicago, 1961) pp. 211–18.

NOTES

1. Samuel Putnam translation (New York, 1949).
2. Preface to *The Princess Casamassima*, p. 68.
3. 'In novels we identify with the omniscient narrator' – Goodman, *Structure of Literature* (Chicago, 1954) p. 153. 'It is indeed true that the reader of fiction identifies himself with the author of a story rather than with the characters of the story – H. W. Leggett, *The Idea in Fiction* (London, 1934) p. 188.
4. *Adam Bede*, Book II, ch. 17, 'In Which the Story Pauses a Little'.
5. *The Short Novels of Dostoievsky*, trans. Constance Garnett (New York, 1945), ch. 4, p. 501.
6. *Critics and Criticism*, ed. R. S. Crane (Chicago, 1952) p. 637.
7. Ibid., p. 642. William Empson gives a lively and convincing defense of

Fielding's code and of the moral stature of *Tom Jones* in '*Tom Jones*', *Kenyon Review*, XX (Spring 1958) 217–49. Though Empson mars his case a bit by arriving 'circuitously at what Fielding tells us plainly enough' (C. J. Rawson, 'Professor Empson's *Tom Jones*', *Notes and Queries*, new ser., VI (Nov 1959) 400), his statement is a valuable antidote to the oversimplifications which have been used in dismissing Fielding and his commentary.

Robert Scholes

THE REVIVAL OF ROMANCE: LAWRENCE DURRELL 1967

Once upon a time the first words of a story used to be 'Once upon a time'. But these are the last words, or almost the last words, of Lawrence Durrell's *Alexandria Quartet*. Which suggests that we may have come to the end of a literary cycle, or rather to the beginning of a new loop in the spiral of literary history. You remember the passage which closes *Clea*, the last volume of the *Quartet*:

> Yes, one day I found myself writing down with trembling fingers the four words (four letters! four faces!) with which every story teller since the world began has staked his slender claim to the attention of his fellow men. Words which presage simply the old story of an artist coming of age. I wrote: 'Once upon a time . . .'
> And I felt as if the whole universe had given me a nudge!

In reading the passage we feel very strongly a kind of duality which pervades Durrell's work: we are pulled toward the primitive by those four magical words and by the description of the artist as a mere story-teller, but we are also made aware of the modernity of the work; we are pulled toward the sophisticated by the preoccupation of the passage with the art of story-telling. Like so many modern works, this is a portrait of the artist, a *Künstlerroman*, about a character in a book who is writing a book in which he is a character. And the shades of Proust and Gide, among others, hover between our eyes and the page. What is new in Durrell, however, is neither the primitive nor the sophisticated but his peculiar combination of the two.

Take, for example, the scene in which Pursewarden and Justine visit the house of the child prostitutes. The two visitors are surrounded by these terrible children, who in another scene nearly drive Mountolive out of his wits as they attempt to capture him in the manner of the Lilliputians against Gulliver. Pursewarden describes the way Justine tames the little creatures:

And when the light was brought she suddenly turned herself, crossed her legs under her, and in the ringing words of the street story-teller she intoned: 'Now gather about me, all ye blessed of Allah, and hear the wonder of the story, I shall tell you...'

It was a wild sort of poetry for the place and the time – the little circle of wizened faces, the divan, the flopping light; and the strangely captivating lilt of the Arabic with its heavy damascened imagery, the thick brocade of alliterative repetitions, the nasal twanging accents, gave it a Laic splendour which brought tears to my eyes – gluttonous tears! It was such a rich diet for the soul! It made me aware how thin the fare is which we moderns supply to our hungry readers. The epic contours, that is what her story had. I was envious. How rich those beggar children were. And I was envious too of her audience. Talk of suspended judgment! They sank into the imagery of her story like plummets.

This scene is typical of the book. It is wild, exotic, romantic. Yet its main interest is not life, but art. It is really a little essay in esthetics, presented in the form of a dramatic scene. It reminds us of the moments in *Don Quixote* when there is pause in the adventures of the Knight of the Mournful Countenance to allow for a literary discussion involving the Bachelor and the Curate or some passing stranger. And the resemblance is not a chance one. Cervantes's work was written as an anti-romance, and became, via Fielding and Smollett in English tradition, a major ancestor of a new literary form – the novel. Durrell's work, as the passage quoted above indicates, is an anti-novel in the same sense as Cervantes's work was an anti-romance. Both men were faced with a constricting literary tradition and revolted against it.

Of course, Pursewarden's point about the thinness of modern literary fare is not meant to be mere literary discussion in a vacuum, any more than the similar discussions in *Don Quixote*. We are meant to apply Pursewarden's theory to Durrell's practice. To do so we must look back, as Pursewarden suggests, to an older literary tradition than the novel. And so we shall. But before we do so we must observe that Durrell's revolt is not an isolated and magnificent gesture of defiance against an entrenched and flourishing literary tradition. The tradition he finds thin and constricting is the very one started by Cervantes – the tradition which begins as anti-romance and gradually insists on more and more scientific treatment of life: the empirical tradition which in its theoretical formulations calls itself first realism and finally naturalism.

The naturalism to which Durrell is reacting is, of course, about as feeble now as the romances were in the time of Cervantes, and the new revolutionary is no more alone in his revolt than the old. A James Joyce can adapt naturalism to allegorical purposes as well as an Edmund Spenser could adapt romance. And a Marcel Proust can destroy empirical notions of characterization as thoroughly as Cervantes himself could destroy the romantic heroes. Just as Samuel Beckett is the heir of Joyce – a somewhat rebellious heir, producing anti-naturalistic anti-allegories – Lawrence Durrell is the heir of Proust. For it is Proust who explodes the empirical notions of characterization so essential to realistic and naturalistic fiction, by demonstrating the artificiality of the real and the reality of artificial. 'Even in the most insignificant details of our daily life,' the narrator of *Swann's Way* tells us,

none of us can be said to constitute a material whole, which is identical for everyone, and need only be turned up like a page in an account book or the record of a will; our social personality is created by the thoughts of other people. Even the simple act which we describe as 'seeing someone we know' is, to some extent, an intellectual process. We pack the physical outline of the creature we see with all the ideas we have already formed about him . . . so that each time we see the face or hear the voice it is our own ideas of him which we recognize and to which we listen.

Proust emphasizes here the artificiality of reality. We do not see our friends, only our ideas of them. In another passage he develops this paradox further, illustrating the converse principle, the reality of artifice:

None of the feelings which the joys or misfortunes of a 'real' person awaken in us can be awakened except through a mental picture of those joys or misfortunes; and the ingenuity of the first novelist lay in his understanding that, as the picture was the one essential element in the complicated structure of our emotions, so, that simplification of it which consisted in suppression, pure and simple, of 'real' people would be a decided improvement. A real person, profoundly as we may sympathize with him, is in great measure perceptible only through our senses, that is to say, he remains opaque, offers a dead weight which our sensibilities have not the strength to lift. . . . The novelist's happy discovery was to think of substituting for those opaque sections, impenetrable by the human spirit, their equivalent in immaterial sections, things, that is, which the spirit can assimilate to itself.

Proust's brilliant exposition of the paradoxical notion that we can truly

experience life only through art is the death knell of the
realistic – naturalistic movement in fiction, though even today, forty
years afterward, neo-naturalists like James Jones continue to write
frantically, headless chickens unaware of the decapitating axe. For
Durrell, however, Proust's new esthetic is a release and an inspiration.
In the following passages from *Justine*, we can observe him adapting the
Proustian view to his own purposes. In the first we find the narrator,
Darley, examining Arnauti's diary, *Moeurs*, in which Justine is a
character called Claudia:

Nor can it be said that the author's intentions are not full of interest. He
maintains for example that real people can only exist in the imagination of an
artist strong enough to contain them and give them form. 'Life, the raw
material, is only lived *in potentia* until the artist deploys it in his work. Would that
I could do this service for poor Justine.'

Like Pursewarden, Arnauti longs for a different kind of fiction. He
wishes to set his ideal book 'free to dream'. His view is different from
Pursewarden's but complementary, not contradictory; and Durrell's
novel embodies both views. Darley finds Arnauti's diary so vivid that he
feels at times like some paper character out of *Moeurs*. And after
Pursewarden's death he writes of him,

How much of him can I claim to know? I realize that each person can only claim
one aspect of our character as part of his knowledge. To every one we turn a
different face of the prism. Over and over again I have found myself surprised by
observations which brought this home to me. . . . And as for Pursewarden, I
remember, too, that in the very act of speaking . . . he straightened himself and
caught sight of his pale reflection in the mirror. The glass was raised to his lips,
and now, turning his head he squirted out upon his own glittering reflection a
mouthful of the drink. That remains clearly in my mind: a reflection liquifying
in the mirror of that shabby, expensive room which seems now so appropriate a
place for the scene which must have followed later that night.

The *Alexandria Quartet* is alive with mirrors. The prismatic facets of
character glitter, unreconciled, in our imaginations. Appearance and
reality are continually confused, and the line between life and art
continually blurred. Darley feels like a character out of *Moeurs*. But
Darley *is* a character in Durrell's novel. What we took for fact in one
volume is exposed as false in another, and the exposé itself is proved
incorrect in the third. Stendhal could compare his story to a mirror,

strolling down a lane, reflecting the sky and the mud. But for Durrell fiction is a whirling prism reflected in a liquifying mirror. In the scene quoted at the beginning of this chapter, in which Justine tells the child prostitutes a story in Arabic, Pursewarden longs for the opportunity to tell a story of Laic splendor to an audience which is really able to suspend its disbelief. Since the modern reader cannot recapture the esthetic innocence of Justine's audience, Durrell attempts on the one hand to establish in the reader's mind his version of the new, Proustian esthetic, and on the other to blur the line between the real and the artificial in order to make it harder for the reader to begin applying his disbelief, even if he refuses to suspend it. Durrell seeks to confuse and bewilder the reader, to separate him from his habitual reliance on probability and verisimilitude, so as to offer him something better. *Behold*, he as much as tells us, *you thought you could not walk without that crutch of realism. I tell you you can fly*! And he nearly convinces us that we can. Using the modern esthetic of Proust, and a narrative technique which, with its multiple narrators and dislocations of time, seems also typically modern, Durrell takes us on a journey – a magic carpet ride not only through space but through time as well – a return to Alexandria.

For, though Pursewarden says he longs for the old 'epic contours', what Durrell gives us is – appropriately enough – more Alexandrian than Attic. As Moses Hadas has observed in his introduction to *Three Greek Romances*, ' "Once upon a time" is not the way the classical Greeks opened a work of literature.' But 'Once upon a time' does reflect the spirit of Alexandrian literature and of the romances written in the Greek language all over the Mediterranean world in post-Alexandrian times. Alexandria was a Greek city on Egyptian soil. In it the East and West met as they rarely have elsewhere. The old joke has it that when Greek meets Greek, they open a restaurant. But when Greek met Egyptian in ancient Alexandria, they opened a library. From this meeting of cultures developed the first literary critics and a new kind of literature. E. M. Forster has described this literature for us in his *Alexandria, a History and a Guide* – a book Lawrence Durrell frequently alludes to in the *Alexandria Quartet*. Forster points out that the distinguishing characteristic of the new literature was its emphasis on love:

Ancient Greece had also sung of love, but with restraint, regarding it as one activity among many. The Alexandrians seldom sang of anything else: their

epigrams, their elegies and their idylls, their one great epic, all turn on the
tender passion, and celebrate it in ways that previous ages had never
known. . . .

> Who sculptured love and set him by the pool,
> Thinking with water such a fire to cool?

runs a couplet ascribed to one of the early Librarians, and containing in brief
the characteristics of the school – decorative method, mythological allusiveness,
and the theme of love.

How appropriate, too, that in the twentieth century Durrell's anti-
novel should be set in this romantic spot. It is clear that Durrell's
Alexandria is as much a country of the mind as Poe's Virginia or
Kafka's Germany. Some of the place-names are real, but beyond that
there is little resemblance between the fictional Alexandria of Durrell
and the geographical one. Yet Durrell's work is completely faithful to
the ancient spirit of the place.

As Forster points out, the literature of Alexandria was, unlike the
literature of Greece itself, a literature of love. It was in Alexandria that
love made its way into epic poetry: in the *Argonautica* of the librarian
Apollonius the love of Medea for Jason was presented so dramatically
that it left an indelible mark on poetic fiction. Vergil's Dido and many
of Ovid's love-stricken females are directly derived from this Alexandrian epic. And the prose romances that were written in Greek around
the Mediterranean in the second and third centuries A.D. of which
Heliodorus' *Ethiopica* and Longus' *Daphnis and Chloe* are the best known
examples) are also derived, apparently, from the Alexandrian combination of Greek and Oriental literary traditions. A papyrus dating
from the second century B.C. and called 'The Alexandrian Erotic
Fragment' was described by its last editor as being written in Greek
prose similar to the ornate rhyming prose of Arabic narrative. In its
combination of erotic subject matter and rich prose it also exemplifies
the characteristic qualities of Durrell's work, written over two millennia
later.

The *Ethiopica*, richest and most elaborate of the Greek romances,
stands very much in the same relation to the Homeric epics as Durrell's
Quartet does to such great realistic novels of the nineteenth century as
Anna Karenina and *Middlemarch*. Both the epics and the great realistic
novels present events as ordered by an omniscient narrator whose
controlling mind not only shapes the events but colors them and

comments on them. But in Heliodorus much of the narrative is conveyed to us directly by characters in the story. Furthermore, Heliodorus is not content simply to imitate the *Odyssey* and have one man narrate much of his own tale. In the *Ethiopica* we have as many narrators as in the *Alexandria Quartet*. Indeed, one of the first stories we are told, a brief résumé of her life by the heroine, turns out to be â tissue of falsehoods designed to deceive her captors (and also the reader, who only afterwards learns the truth). In the hands of Heliodorus the romance is characterized by a multiplicity of narrators and tales within tales like a sequence of Chinese boxes; by a consequent dislocation of the time scheme, as the narrative moves backwards and forwards from its beginning in what George Saintsbury has called a 'sort of cat's cradle manner'; and by a fondness for elaborate set pieces of a spectacular nature, involving such things as battles, rituals, necromancy, and celebrations.

Though the general resemblance of the *Alexandria Quartet* to the *Ethiopica* is obvious (some of the action of the ancient story even takes place on the shores of Durrell's beloved Lake Mareotis), the point is not that the resemblance indicates any direct indebtedness; rather, it is that the two works are so similar in spirit. Durrell is not so much a descendant of Heliodorus as a reincarnation of him in the twentieth century. When Durrell speaks of his characters in an interview as 'puppets', he reminds us of the way in which Heliodorus manipulates his characters in a virtuoso display of sustained and integrated form. And form, for Durrell, is nearly everything. His early novel, *The Black Book*, displays many of the characteristics of his later work – everything, almost, except form. *The Black Book* was written when Durrell was very much under the influence of D. H. Lawrence and Henry Miller, writers who tend to disdain form, to think of it as a way of distorting reality. In the recently published correspondence between Durrell and Miller we can see him gradually becoming more critical of Miller's work on the grounds of its formlessness. Though traces of Lawrence and Miller remain in Durrell's mature work, there can be little doubt that the spirit which presides over the *Alexandria Quartet* is Proust's. And in turning to Proust, Durrell brought himself into contact with a tradition of sustained form which was fundamentally opposed to the 'slice of life' technique characteristic of empirically oriented mimetic fiction. The tradition of elaborate form in fiction leads back through the romances of the seventeenth century to the European rediscovery of Heliodorus in

the sixteenth, whose influence on the subsequent development of prose
fiction can hardly be exaggerated.

The purely melodramatic side of the Greek romance has, of course,
been greatly modified in its modern reincarnation. In the old romances
the characters were mainly highly stylized extremes of virtue and vice,
and the plot was always subservient to the decorum of poetic justice. In
the *Alexandria Quartet* the characters and the prevailing ethos are as
elaborate and complicated as the plot and the setting. The thinness of
characterization which, for the modern reader, relegates the *Ethiopica* to
that secondary level of works whose influence surpasses their interest
would be inexcusable in a modern work of serious intent. But even
richness of characterization, which we think of as a peculiarly modern
attribute of fiction, has its roots in Alexandria. The Alexandrians and
their followers, especially Ovid and the Greek romancers, introduced
the arts of rhetoric into narrative literature. The combination of
psychology and rhetoric, which characterizes the crucial monologue of
Medea in the Third Book of the *Argonautica*, works through Dido and
the Ovidian lovers into the mainstream of narrative literature.
Lawrence Durrell's rhetoric, rich and evocative as it is, has been
roundly criticized by the English press as some sort of wild Celtic
aberration – not (in the phrase of Mr. Podsnap) English, and hardly
appropriate for a novel. But one of the glories of our resurgent narrative
art has been the rhetoric of Joyce, of Faulkner, of Conrad, and of Proust;
though none of them are (alas) English, either. The flat prose of
sociological fiction is being abandoned to the sociologists, who, God
knows, have need of it; and the rich rhetoric of the Alexandrians, of
Ovid and the Greek romancers, is beginning once again to return
narrative literature to the domain of art. The novel may indeed be
dying, but we need not fear for the future. Durrell and others are
generating a renaissance of romance. The return to Alexandria should
be almost as exciting a voyage as the one described by the city's greatest
story-teller, Apollonius; for, like the voyage of the Argo, it will be an
enchanted one. And already, like the laggard Argonauts on one
occasion, we can hear our vehicle itself admonishing us:

From Pelian Argo herself came a voice, bidding hasten away:
For within her a beam divine had been laid, which Athena brought
From the oak Dodonaean and into the midst of her stem it was wrought.

WHAT GOOD IS PURE ROMANCE?

A fair question, apparently. Plato asked it and nobody has answered it. Maybe it isn't as fair as it looks: what the question actually meant to him requires a bit of explanation. As I understand it, however, we can approximate Plato's intention by breaking the question into two parts: (*a*) What good effect will listening to stories have on our understanding of the world?, and (*b*) what good effect will listening to stories have on our behavior in the world? Like the good philosopher he was, Plato discovered that philosophy could do both (*a*) and (*b*) better than fiction could. That is, philosophy could tell us more truly both the nature of the cosmos and the attributes of right action. All those apologists for poetry who have accepted Plato's gambit have been reduced to presenting fiction either as sugar coating for the pill of philosophy, or as a handy and accurate short-hand notation of reality – that is, as allegory or as realism.

What Plato was really asking was 'What good is poetry *as philosophy*?' – since for him philosophy already had a monopoly on both truth and goodness. Now that science owns truth and goodness knows where goodness went (religion had it last but seems to have mislaid it), Plato's question has shifted its meaning so far as to expose its underpinnings. Zola tried to answer the question, 'What good is fiction *as science*?' and worked himself into the absurd corner of the 'experimental' novel, a notion he seems to have had the good sense not to believe but merely to use as journalistic puffery for his own productions, much as his heirs are now crying 'phenomenological' novel for similar reasons. Matthew Arnold tried to answer the question, 'What good is fiction *as religion*?', and twisted himself around to the point where he could see literature replacing dogma. Now the Marxist asks, 'What good is fiction *as politics*?', and the Freudian asks, 'What good is fiction *as psychology*?', and so on. But the real question, the one that Plato pretended to be asking, has got lost. Probably Plato could not see it himself. Since literary criticism started as a branch of philosophy, it was doubtless necessary to see Plato's question in terms of metaphysics and ethics. Even Aristotle succeeded only in adding a psychological concept, *katharsis*, to his notion of literature, and then returned quickly to its philosophical value as 'imitation'. But now that we can see criticism as a branch of literature itself, we should be able to set Plato's question in its proper context and make it mean what it should mean: What are the special qualities of fiction for which we value it? In other words, 'What good is fiction *as fiction*?'

Not as the 'representation of an action' but as an imaginative construct. Not in terms of what it tells us about, even including the imagination itself, but in terms of what makes our experience of fiction a good experience. The Aristotle of *katharsis* is much closer to the mark than the Aristotle of *mimesis*. The students of sleep have discovered that dreaming is necessary to the well-being of the human organism, and perhaps to the higher animals as well. It is not that our dreams teach us anything; they are simply a means of expression for us, a nightly cinema in which we are producer, director, all the actors, and all the audience. And if we are cheated of this imaginative performance in our sleep, we suffer for it during our waking existence in ways still not entirely understood.

I do not think fiction is a substitute for dream, but I think it must work for us in a similar way. It must provide us with an imaginative experience which is necessary to our imaginative well-being. And that is quite enough justification for it. We need all the imagination we have, and we need it exercised and in good condition. The simplest kind of fabling will do this for us to some extent, as long as we can respond to it fully, as long as it can engage our imagination totally. But as our imagination stretches and as we grow more serious (this combination of processes being what we mean, ideally, by the verb 'to mature'), we require not fabling but fabulation. Pure romance must be enriched, like skim milk, if it is to sustain a full imaginative life. Allegory is one way of enriching pure romance. . . . There is a shadowy allegorical dimension to the *Alexandria Quartet* (an esthetic allegory, mainly, about ways of story-telling), and . . . this dimension is, in fact, part of the story.

But once this is said, it should be qualified by observing that Durrell's story is remarkably independent of its allegorical dimension. It is to the author's credit, I think, that he manages to be so engaging while keeping his narrative so squarely in the tradition of pure romance. He seems to have preserved enough from the tradition of the novel – to have learned enough from Lawrence, Proust, and others – to manage a revival of romance with a minimal amount of allegorizing. This is one important dimension of modern fabulation. In a way it is the simplest: the direct plunge back into the tide of story which rolls through all narrative art. Such a return to story for renewed vigor is a characteristic of the modern fabulators. . . . Without [story], the blood of narrative ceases to flow. The humors atrophy, the brain shrivels, and finally the soul itself departs.

Source: extract from chapter 2 of *The Fabulators* (New York, 1967) pp. 17–31

David Lodge

SAMUEL BECKETT: SOME PING UNDERSTOOD (1968)

The enigma of Samuel Beckett's 'Ping' (*Encounter*, February 1967) derives a special interest from the context of debate, initiated in the same journal by Frank Kermode (March – April 1966) and carried on by Ihab Hassan (January 1967) and Bernard Bergonzi (May 1967) concerning the contemporary *avant-garde*. Whether fortuitously or not, 'Ping' seems a timely illustrative or testing 'case' for such critical speculation.

The speculation is, I take it, concerned basically with such questions as: is contemporary *avant-garde* literature, in common with experimental art in other media, making a much more radical break with 'tradition' than did the literature and art of what Kermode calls 'paleomodernism'? Is it, in effect, seeking the extinction of literary culture by denying from within the epistemological function of the literary medium itself (i. e. language)? Is it, not literature at all, but 'anti-literature'? Is it immune to conventional criticism; and if so, does this demonstrate criticism's impotence, or its own?

Of the three critics mentioned above, the one who answers these questions in a spirit most sympathetic to radical discontinuity with tradition is Ihab Hassan. The essential argument of his article 'The Literature of Silence' is that today, 'Literature, turning against itself, aspires to silence, leaving us with uneasy intimations of outrage and apocalypse. If there is an *avant-garde* in our time, it is probably bent on discovery through suicide.' Beckett is one of Hassan's chief examples:

Writing for Beckett is absurd play. In a certain sense, all his works may be thought of as a parody of Wittgenstein's notion that language is a set of games, akin to the arithmetic of primitive tribes. Beckett's parodies, which are full of self-spite, designate a general tendency in anti-literature. Hugh Kenner brilliantly describes this tendency when he states: 'The dominant intellectual analogy of the present age is drawn not from biology, not from psychology . . .

but from general number theory.' Art in a closed field thus becomes an absurd game of permutations, like Molloy sucking stones at the beach; and 'the retreat from the word' (the phrase is George Steiner's) reduces language to pure ratio.

Beckett . . . comes close to reducing literature to a mathematical tautology. The syllogism of Beckett assumes that history has spent itself; we are merely playing an end game. . . . Language has become void; therefore words can only demonstrate their emptiness. . . . Thus literature becomes the inaudible game of a solipsist.

Professor Hassan must have been gratified by the appearance of 'Ping' in the very next issue of *Encounter*, for one of its key-words is *silence*, and in other ways it appears to confirm his description of Beckett's art. 'Permutation', for instance, seems an appropriate description of the way language is used in 'Ping': that is, an unusually limited number of words are repeated to an unusual extent in various combinations. (By 'unusual' I mean unusual for a piece of literary prose of this length.) There are only a few words that occur only once in 'Ping': *brief, hair, nails, scars, torn, henceforth, unlustrous*. Other words are used at least twice, and most words are used more than twice. The word *white*, which seems to be the most frequently recurring word, is used more than ninety times. Many phrases or word groups are repeated, but rarely an entire sentence. Thus, if the first sentence is divided up into the following word groups:

All known/all white/bare white body fixed/one yard/legs joined like sewn.

each word group recurs later in the piece, but never with all the others in the same order in a single sentence – always with some modification or addition. Typical variations are:

Bare white body fixed one yard ping fixed elsewhere.   (15)[1]
Bare white body fixed one yard ping fixed elsewhere white on white invisible heart breath no sound. (40/42)
Bare white one yard fixed ping fixed elsewhere no sound legs joined like sewn heels together right angle hands hanging palms front. (66/68)

It is this kind of repetition with variation that makes 'Ping' so difficult to read, and the label 'anti-literature' a plausible one. Repetition is often a key to meaning in literary discourse, but repetition on this scale tends to defeat the pursuit of meaning. That is, a familiar critical strategy in dealing with narrative prose is to look for some significant pattern of repetition hidden in the variegated texture of the discourse: the variegated texture, by which 'solidity of specification' is achieved, is woven in a logical, temporal progression, while the pattern of repetition holds the work together in a kind of spatial order and suggests the nature of the overall theme. But in 'Ping' this relationship is inverted: the repetition is far from hidden – it overwhelms the reader in its profusion and disrupts the sense of specificity and of logical, temporal progression. It is extraordinarily difficult to read through the entire piece, short as it is, with sustained concentration. After about forty or fifty lines the words begin to slide and blur before the eyes, and to echo bewilderingly in the ear. This is caused not merely by the elaborate repetition, but also by the meagreness of explicit syntax, the drastic reduction of such aids to communication as punctuation, finite verbs, conjunctions, articles, prepositions and subordination.

All this, then, goes to confirm Hassan's comments; and as a general account of what Beckett is up to they are no doubt fair enough. But I must confess to finding something unsatisfactory about this kind of critical response. I don't see, for instance, how it could help us to distinguish between one piece by Beckett and another, except as progressive – or regressive – steps towards silence. If the sole object of the game is to expose the limitations of language by a bewildering permutation of words, it wouldn't matter what particular words were used, or what their referential content was. But I think that the more closely acquainted we become with 'Ping' the more certain we become that it does matter what words are used, and that they refer to something more specific than the futility of life or the futility of art. Beckett is telling us 'about' something; and if the telling is extraordinarily difficult to follow this is not simply because all experience is difficult to communicate (though this is true) but because this experience is difficult to communicate in *this* particular way.

It would be dishonest to make this assertion without going on to suggest what 'Ping' is about. What follows doesn't pretend to be a definitive or exclusive reading, but its tentativeness differs only in degree from the tentativeness imposed on the critic by any complex literary work.

I suggest that 'Ping' is the rendering of the consciousness of a person confined in a small, bare, white room, a person who is evidently under extreme duress, and probably at the last gasp of life. He has no freedom of movement: his body is 'fixed', the legs are joined together, the heels turning at right angles, the hands hanging palms front; the 'heart breath' makes 'no sound' (43). 'Only the eyes only just . . . ' – can we say, *move?* (4). There are parts of the room he cannot see, and he evidently can't move his head to see them, though he thinks there is 'perhaps a way out' there (25 and 50).

The first words of the piece are 'all known', and this phrase recurs (11, 21, 30/1 etc.). But the 'all' that is 'known' is severely limited and yields 'no meaning' (7/8 and *passim*) though the narrator is reluctant to admit this: 'perhaps a meaning (32). 'Ping' seems to record the struggles of an expiring consciousness to find some meaning in a situation which offers no purchase to the mind or to sensation. The consciousness makes repeated, feeble efforts to assert the possibility of colour, movement, sound, memory, another person's presence, only to fall back hopelessly into the recognition of colourlessness, paralysis, silence, oblivion, solitude. This rhythm of tentative assertion and collapse is marked by the frequently recurring collocation 'only just almost never' (11 and *passim*).

By colourlessness I mean the predominance of white, which is no colour, or at least the 'last colour' (74). The shining white planes of walls, floor and ceiling, the whiteness of his own body, make it difficult for the person to see more than 'traces, blurs, signs' (7 and *passim*). The attempt to assert colour – black, rose, light blue, light grey – nearly always fades into an admission that it is really 'almost white', 'white on white', is 'invisible', has 'no meaning':

Traces blurs light grey almost white on white.   (4/5)
Traces blurs signs no meaning light grey almost white.   (7/8)
Traces alone unover given black light grey almost white on white.   (13/14)
Traces alone unover given black grey blurs signs no meaning light grey almost white always the same.   (51/53)

Aural experience is equally meagre. There is 'silence within' (10). These words are followed by 'Brief murmurs'; but the murmurs are immediately qualified by 'only just almost never' (10/11). However, the next 'murmur' is associated with the speculation 'perhaps not alone' (19). A little later there is another *perhaps*-phrase, again associated with murmur':

Ping murmur perhaps a nature one second almost never that much memory almost never.   (28/29)

This is a particularly interesting and tantalizing sentence. What does 'a nature' mean? A human nature? His own, or another's? It seems to be associated with memory, anyway, and memory with meaning, for a few lines later we get: 'Ping murmur only just almost never one second perhaps a meaning that much memory almost never' (31/34):

Towards the close of the piece I think there are more definite indications that the character's search for meaning and grasp on life are connected with some effort of memory, some effort to recall a human image, and thus break out of total impotence and solitude:

Ping perhaps not alone one second with image same time a little less dim eye black and white half closed long lashes imploring that much memory almost never. (70/72)

'Long lashes imploring' is the most human touch, the most emotive phrase, in the entire piece. It deviates sharply from the linguistic norms which have been set up, and which project a generally de-humanized version of experience. It therefore has a strong impact, and this is reinforced by other features of the sentence. The 'image' is 'a little less dim'. We have met the phrase 'a little less' before (e. g. 54 and 63), but not with 'dim' – it is as if only now can the consciousness complete the phrase it has been struggling to formulate. The eye is 'black and white' – it is not black fading into light grey, into almost white, into white on white.

This sentence, then, seems to mark the apex of the character's effort at memory. It is 'Afar flash of time', but short-lived: almost immediately it is swamped by the despairing sequence:

all white all over all of old ping flash white walls shining white no trace eyes holes light blue almost white last colour ping white over. (72/74)

The next two sentences also end with the word *over*, as does the whole piece. *Over*, which makes its first appearance in line 56, seems to echo the curious nonce-word *unover* (13, 18, 37, 43, etc.) which presumably means 'not over', and is invariably preceded by the word *alone*, for example: 'Traces alone unover given black light grey almost white on white' (13/14). Such sentences, which occur mainly in the first half of the text, seem to define the very limited sense in which experience is on-going, 'not over'; but after the vision or image of the eye with 'long lashes imploring' the emphasis shifts to the idea that experience is finished, over. The formula 'that much memory almost never' is changed to 'that much memory *henceforth* never' in line 82. The image of the eye recurs unexpectedly in the last two lines of the piece, with the addition of the word *unlustrous* – a word rather striking in itself, and notable for occurring only this once in 'Ping', thus giving a further specificity to the 'eye black and white half-closed long lashes imploring'. But this seems to be the last effort of the consciousness – the sentence continues and ends, 'ping silence ping over'. The image or vision is over, consciousness is over, the story is over.

I have implied that the black and white eye (singular) is not one of the character's own eyes, which are, I think, the ones referred to throughout the passage (in the plural) as being light blue or grey, tending to the overall condition of whiteness. This black eye with the lashes is, I suggest, someone else's eye, part of some emotional and human connection which the character is struggling to recall through memory. The effort to do so is only successful to a very limited extent, and exhausts him, perhaps kills him: 'ping silence ping over'.

I can't offer any confident explanation of the word *ping* itself. On the referential level it might denote the noise emitted by some piece of apparatus, perhaps marking the passage of time (there are repeated references to 'one second', though the *pings* do not occur at regular intervals). On the level of connotation, *ping* is a feeble, pathetic, unresonant, irritating, even maddening sound, making it an appropriate enough title for this piece, which it punctuates like the striking of a triangle at intervals in the course of a complicated fugue.

The above commentary is based on some introductory remarks made by the present writer to a discussion of 'Ping' by some members of the English Department at Birmingham University. My remarks were followed by the independently prepared comments of a linguist, whose descriptive analysis of the structure of the piece was in general accord with my own (though it corrected some rash assertions I had made). I shall try to do justice to the main points of this linguistic commentary in a general account of the discussion as a whole.

In this discussion there was inevitably a good deal of conflict, but on the whole the measure of agreement was more striking. A minority of the participants were inclined to think that 'Ping' was indeed a language game, a verbal construct cunningly devised to yield an infinite number of interpretations – and therefore, in effect, resistant to interpretation. It could be about a man having a bath or a shower or a man under rifle fire or a man being tortured; *ping* might be the sound of a bullet ricocheting, or the sound of water dripping or the sound of a bell, and the bell might be a bicycle bell or a sanctus bell or a typewriter bell (perhaps the writer's own typewriter bell). But the majority were disposed to find 'Ping' more specifically meaningful, to see it as the rendering of a certain kind of experience, and as having a perceptible design. While it might not be possible to agree on a formulation of the experience more precise than the effort of a consciousness to assert its identity in the teeth of the void, the verbal medium was operating selectively to induce a much more finely discriminated range of effects than that formulation suggested. Considered as a whole, in isolation, the piece satisfied the traditional aesthetic criteria of *integritas*, *consonantia*, and *claritas*. At the same time it had an obvious continuity with the rest of Beckett's work, and to consider it in relation to his whole *œuvre* would be the next logical step in interpretation.

The two main points of dispute, and the ones where I feel my own reading of 'Ping' to have been most inadequate, concerned the possibility of some allusion to Christ, and the significance of the word *ping* itself.

As to the first, it was pointed out that there are a number of words and phrases reminiscent of the passion and death of Christ: 'legs joined like sewn', 'hands hanging palms front' are vaguely evocative of the Crucifixion; 'seam like sewn invisible' suggests the cloak without a seam. More striking is this passage:

Given rose only just nails fallen white over. Long hair fallen white invisible over. White scars invisible same white as flesh torn of old given rose only just. (55/57)

The words *nails*, *hair*, *scars*, *flesh*, *torn*, belong to that (in 'Ping') rare class that occur only once, and their clustering together here might well be designed to alert us to an interpretative clue. For a dizzy moment we entertained the possibility that the whole piece might be a bleakly anti-metaphysical rendering of the consciousness of the dying Christ – Christ in the tomb rather than Christ on the Cross (hence the cramped, cell-like room) – in short, Beckett's version of *The Man Who Died*. But this reading seemed not only to leave much unexplained, but to be impoverishing; for the piece doesn't read like a riddle to which there is a single answer. However, the possibility of some allusion to Christ cannot, I think, be discounted.

Discussion about the significance of the word *ping* polarized around those who like myself, regarded it as a noise external to the discourse, which it punctuated at arbitrary intervals, a noise so meaningless as not to enter into the murmur/silence dichotomy, the most meaningless item, in fact, in the character's field of perception; and on the other hand those who regarded it as part of the discourse, as having some conceptual content or as being an ironic, or movingly pathetic; substitute or code-word for some concept that cannot be fully and openly entertained, such as God (cf. 'Godot'). Thus the sentence 'Ping elsewhere always there only known not' (36/37) becomes almost lucid if you replace *Ping* with *God*; and it is interesting to note that this is one of the rare sentences that recur in exactly the same form (69).

Strengthening this case that *ping* is part of the discourse, or stream of consciousness, rather than an arbitrary intrusion from outside, is the fact that it is associated with a selective number of other words and phrases. Thus, going through the piece and noting the words which immediately follow the word *ping*, we get the following pattern:

ping fixed elsewhere
ping fixed elsewhere
ping fixed elsewhere
Ping murmur
ping murmur
ping silence
Ping murmur
Ping murmur
ping elsewhere
Ping elsewhere
ping murmur
ping fixed elsewhere
Ping murmurs
Ping perhaps a nature
ping perhaps way out
ping silence
Ping perhaps not alone
ping silence
Ping image
Ping a nature
ping a meaning
ping silence
ping fixed elsewhere
Ping elsewhere

Ping perhaps not alone
ping flash
ping white over
Ping fixed last elsewhere
ping of old
Ping of old
ping last murmur
ping silence
ping over.

This doesn't look like randon occurrence. *Ping* tends to be followed by words or phrases which suggest the possibility of some other presence or place: *fixed elsewhere, murmur, image, perhaps a nature, perhaps a way out, perhaps not alone,* etc. It is natural, I think, to look first at the words and phrases which follow *ping,* for if it has a quasigrammatical status it would appear to be that of a subject – it is, for instance, often the first word of a sentence. If we look at the words and phrases which immediately precede *ping* we get, in fact, a 'sequence which is no less patterned, but it is interesting that these words and phrases are mostly of a quite different order; they tend to stress the bleak limitations of the character's situation and field of perceptions: *bare white body fixed, invisible, never seen, almost never,* are among the most frequently recurring. We might suggest that *ping* marks the intervals between the oscillating movements of the character's consciousness from dull despair to tentative hope; though this leaves open the question of whether it is part of the discourse, or an intrusion from outside which stimulates thought in a mechanical and arbitrary way.

I should note, finally, the ingenious suggestion that *ping* alludes to the parlour game 'Ping Pong' which assumes that all words and concepts can be placed in one of two great categories, 'Ping' and 'Pong'. Thus, for example, *white* is Ping and *black* is Pong; and Beckett's piece is the account of a man inhabiting a Ping world, struggling feebly to reach out to or recover a Pong world.

The above discussion, needless to say, leaves much unexplained or in doubt (a phrase which particularly puzzles me is 'blue and white in the wind' 49, 58, 64, 81). But it does suggest, I think, that 'Ping' is not, as it appears at first sight, totally impenetrable and meaningless. The important point was made in the course of our discussion that the piece *has* got a syntax: it is rudimentary, but it does control the possible range of meaning. It would be perverse, for instance, to read the first sentence grouping the words in this way:

All/known all white bare/white body fixed one/yard legs/joined like/ sewn.

The piece draws on the principles of a shared language, especially the principle of word order. (Ping itself is the most ambiguous word in the text precisely because it is the one least defined by any referential or structural function in ordinary usage.) Though these principles are drastically modified, they are never abandoned. A good deal of logical organization persists, as can be demonstrated by reading the text backwards and measuring the loss of sense.

If Beckett were really writing anti-literature, it wouldn't matter whether we read the text backwards or forwards, from left to right or from right to left. Of course, terms like 'anti-literature' and 'literature of silence' are rhetorical paradoxes aimed to suggest a radical degree of innovation: they are not to be taken literally. But they can have the effect of deterring us from engaging closely with a text like 'Ping'. To confirm Professor Hassan's comments on Beckett, it is not necessary to give 'Ping' more than a quick, superficial glance. If the object of the exercise is merely to baffle our intelligences and cheat our conventional expectations, why should we bother to do more? But if we do bother to do more, the rewards are surprisingly great. 'Ping' proves, after all, not to be totally resistant to methods of critical reading derived from conventional literature. Its language is not void; its words do not merely demonstrate their emptiness. It is, like any literary artefact, a marriage of form and meaning.

PING

All known all white bare white body fixed one yard legs joined like sewn. Light heat white floor one square yard never seen. White walls one yard by two white ceiling one square yard never seen. Bare white body fixed only the eyes only just. Traces blurs light
5 grey almost white on white. Hands hanging palms front white feet heels together right angle. Light heat white planes shining white bare white body fixed ping fixed elsewhere. Traces blurs signs no

meaning light grey almost white. Bare white body fixed white on
white invisible. Only the eyes only just light blue almost white.
10 Head haught eyes light blue almost white silence within. Brief
murmurs only just almost never all known. Traces blurs signs no
meaning light grey almost white. Legs joined like sewn heels
together right angle. Traces alone unover given black light grey
almost white on white. Light heat white walls shining white one
15 yard by two. Bare white body fixed one yard ping fixed elsewhere.
Traces blurs signs no meaning light grey almost white. White feet
toes joined like sewn heels together right angle invisible. Eyes
alone unover given blue light blue almost white. Murmur only just
almost never one second perhaps not alone. Given rose only just
20 bare white body fixed one yard white on white invisible. All white
all known murmurs only just almost never always the same all
known. Light heat hands hanging palms front white on white
invisible. Bare white body fixed ping fixed elsewhere. Only the
eyes only just light blue almost white fixed front. Ping murmur
25 only just almost never one second perhaps a way out. Head haught
eyes light blue almost white fixed front ping murmur ping silence.
Eyes holes light blue almost white mouth white seam like sewn
invisible. Ping murmur perhaps a nature one second almost never
that much memory almost never. White walls each its trace grey
30 blur signs no meaning light grey almost white. Light heat all
known all white planes meeting invisible. Ping murmur only just
almost never one second perhaps a meaning that much memory
almost never. White feet does joining like sewn heels together
right angle ping elsewhere no sound. Hands hanging palms front
35 legs joined like sewn. Head haught eyes holes light blue almost
white fixed front silence within. Ping elsewhere always there only
known not. Eyes holes light blue alone unover given blue light
blue almost white only colour fixed front. All white all known
white planes shining white ping murmur only just almost never
40 one second light time that much memory almost never. Bare white
body fixed one yard ping fixed elsewhere white on white invisible
heart breath no sound. Only the eyes given blue light blue almost
white fixed front only colour alone unover. Planes meeting
invisible only one shining white infinitely only known not. Nose
45 ears white holes mouth white seam like sewn invisible. Ping
murmurs only just almost never one second always the same all

known. Given rose only just bare white body fixed one yard invisible all known without within. Ping perhaps a nature one second
with image same time a little less blue and white in the wind. White
50 ceiling shining white one square yard never seen ping perhaps way
out there one second ping silence. Traces alone unover given black
grey blurs signs no meaning light grey almost white always the
same. Ping perhaps not alone one second with image always the
same time a little less that much memory almost never ping
55 silence. .Given rose only just nails fallen white over. Long hair
fallen white invisible over. White scars invisible same white as
flesh torn of old given rose only just. Ping image only just almost
never one second light time blue and white in the wind. Head
haught nose ears white holes mouth white seam like sewn invisible
60 over. Only the eyes given blue fixed front light blue almost white
only colour alone unover. Light heat white planes shining white
on only shining white infinite only known not. Ping a nature only
just almost never one second with image same time a little less blue
and white in the wind. Traces blurs light grey eyes holes light
65 blue almost white fixed front ping a meaning only just almost never
ping silence. Bare white one yard fixed ping fixed elsewhere no
sound legs joined like sewn heels together right angle hands hanging
palms front. Head haught eyes holes light blue almost white fixed
front silence within. Ping elsewhere always there only known not.
70 Ping perhaps not alone one second with image same time a little
less dim eye black and white half closed long lashes imploring that
much memory almost never. Afar flash of time all white all over all
of old ping flash white walls shining white no trace eyes holes light
blue almost white last colour ping white over. Ping fixed last else-
75 where legs joined like sewn heels together right angle hands
hanging palms front head haught eyes white invisible fixed front
over. Given rose only just one yard invisible bare white all known
without within over. White ceiling never seen ping of old only
just almost never one second light time white floor never seen
80 ping of old perhaps there. Ping of old only just perhaps a meaning
a nature one second almost never blue and white in the wind that
much memory henceforth never. White planes no trace shining
white one only shining white infinite only known not. Light heat
all known all white heart breath no sound. Head haught eyes white
85 fixed front old ping last murmur one second perhaps not only eye

unlustrous black and white half closed long lashes imploring ping
silence ping over.

Translated from the French by the author

SOURCE: *Encounter*, February 1968; reprinted in David Lodge,
The Novelist at the Crossroads (London, 1971) pp. 172–83.

NOTE

1. Line references are to the text printed in *Encounter*, February 1967, 25–6,
reprinted at the end of this essay.

PART THREE

Fiction and Reality

Frank Kermode

ON WILLIAM GOLDING   (1962)

The critical reception of Mr. Golding's fourth novel, *Free Fall* (1959) was on the whole hostile; that of its predecessor (*Pincher Martin*, 1956) uncomprehending. Not since his first, *Lord of the Flies* (1954) has he enjoyed general acclaim; yet the opinion that he is the most important practising novelist in English has, over this period of five or six years, become almost commonplace. One reason for this apparent paradox is that Golding's books do not (if only because each is extremely original in construction) yield themselves at one reading: *The Inheritors* (1955) and *Pincher Martin* have been better understood with the passing of time, and the same will be true of *Free Fall*. This suggests that Golding is a difficult writer; and it would not be strange if this were true. We have become accustomed, for intelligible historical reasons, to the idea that significant works of art are necessarily obscure.

It is, however, true only in a limited sense. We may note at once that despite the roar of baffled critics Mr. Golding's intentions are always simple. Of *Pincher Martin* he says 'I fell over backwards in making that novel explicit. I said to myself, "Now here is going to be a novel, it's going to be a blow on behalf of the ordinary universe, which I think on the whole likely to be the right one, and I'm going to write it so vividly and accurately and with such an exact programme that nobody can possibly mistake exactly what I mean." '[1] But he goes on to admit that his handling of the story was 'unspecific'; he did not actually *tell* the reader that Martin drowns on page 2; the evidence that he did so is oblique, and is completed only by the last sentence of the book. Golding is unlike many modern writers in his willingness to state the 'programme' of his book (and also in denying the reader much liberty of interpretation); but he does not pretend that what seems to him simple must be so explicitly and directly set down that the reader will not have to work. In short, his simplicity is a quality best understood as intellectual economy. His theme takes the simplest available way to full embodiment. But embodiment is not explanation; and all that can be guaranteed the reader is that there is no *unnecessary* difficulty, nothing to make the business of explaining and understanding more difficult than, in the nature of the case, it has to be.

The best course for sympathetic critics is to be a shade more explicit, to do what the novelist himself perhaps cannot do without injury to the books, which grow according to imaginative laws, and cannot be adjusted to the extravagant needs of readers. If critics have any reason for existence, this is it; to give assurances of value, and to provide, somehow – perhaps anyhow – the means by which readers may be put in possession of the valuable book.

It is worth notice that Golding is to a marked degree isolated from intellectual fashion: 'I think that my novels have very little genesis outside myself. That to a large extent I've cut myself off from contemporary literary life, and gained in one sense by it, though I may have lost in another.' He is more interested in Greek than in modern literature. Thus there are in his books preoccupations one would not expect in a highbrow modern novelist – that Ballantyne was wrong about the behaviour of English boys on a desert island, or H. G. Wells about the virtue of Neanderthal men, are not opinions many would care to dispute, but few would find in them points of departure for passionate and involved fictions. In the same way Mr. Golding, though he is in some degree an allegorical writer, is entirely free of Kafka's influence, which makes him very unlike Rex Warner, with whom he is sometimes implausibly compared. His technical equipment is as sophisticated as Conrad's; yet like Conrad be begins each new book as if it were his first, as if the germination of the new theme entailed the creation of its own incomparable form. (There are, however, some habitual devices – the sudden shift of viewpoint at the end of the first three novels, for instance.) Perhaps the resemblance to Conrad could be developed: an isolated indeed exiled sensibility, a preoccupation with guilt, desperate technical resource. Sometimes this last power re-invests what others have done before, old devices labelled in text-books: stream of consciousness, changing point of view, time-shifts. There was a time according to the author himself, when he wrote novels intended to meet the requirements of the public, as far as he could guess them; but these novels failed, were never even published. Then, with *Lord of the Flies*, he saw that it was himself he had to satisfy; he planned it in very great detail, and wrote it as if tracing over words already on the page. How, in pleasing his own isolated taste, and doing it in these essentially unmodish and rather private ways, has he come to represent to so many the best in modern English writing?

The answer to this is necessarily involved, though the situation is in itself simple enough. One thinks of Mr. Golding's world: he sees it swinging through its space, its wet or rocky surfaces lifting under the pull of the moon; its inhabitants, locked on to it by gravity, walking upright, containing floating brains, peristaltic entrails, secreting seed at the base of the spine, somehow free and somehow guilty. Golding once called himself 'a propagandist for Neanderthal man'; his way of looking at the world has something of the candour of Lascaux. In *The Inheritors* Neanderthal man is superseded by *homo sapiens*, who has a better brain, and weapons; but it is the innocence of the doomed predecessor that we see enacted, for, until the last pages, we see the activities of the new man, intelligent and so capable of evil, through the bewildered eyes of the old. And Golding, though he admits that we belong with the new man, supposes that we could not recapture that innocence, that natural awe for Oa, the mother-goddess, had not something of it survived in us.

I am groping for an answer to the question, how such a writer can strike us as profoundly attuned to contemporary sensibility? It seems to be that in his own way, and short-circuiting a great deal of fashionable and sophisticated mythologizing, Golding gives remarkably full expression to a profound modern need, the need for reassurance in terms of the primitive; the longing to know somehow of a possible humanity that lived equably in the whole world; the need for myths of total and satisfactory explanation. Our developed consciousness, our accumulated knowledge are marks of guilt; the fragmentary nature of our experience is the theme of our artists. To discover again the undifferentiated-myth, is to return to Eden or to Neanderthal man – or indeed to the primary germ-cell the splitting of which is the beginning of guilt: that is to find innocence and wisdom.

Golding has been called a writer of 'fables'; 'what I would regard as a tremendous compliment to myself', he says, 'would be if someone would substitute the word "myth" for "fable" . . . I do feel fable as being an invented thing on the surface whereas myth is something which comes out from the roots of things in the ancient sense of being the key to existence, the whole meaning of life, and experience as a whole'. And he accepts the description, 'myths of total explanation' for his works. The genesis of these myths is naturally obscure. They do not much resemble the myths of Joyce or those of Mr. Eliot or Mr. David Jones; yet they are related to the same Symbolist aspirations towards prelogical primitive images which animate all these authors. The differences are attributable to Mr. Golding's relative isolation from any mainstream of speculation. To put it too simply: he sees a world enormously altered by new knowledge. He understands the strong reaction against this new knowledge which is characteristic of modern art, an art in love with the primitive; also the patterns of human behaviour are now very generally explained by reference to psychic residua or infantile guilt. It is a world you can blame 'science' for if you like, a world in which the myth of progress has failed; but the rival myth of necessary evil and universal guilt has come back without bringing God with it. He looks at this world understanding what it contains, as the painters at Lascaux understood theirs. He thinks of the books of his childhood – *Coral Island*, Wells's *Outline of History* – and observes that they are wrong about the world, because they thought cannibals more wicked than white men and Neanderthal man less worthy than his conqueror. These books have, in his own figure, rotted to compost in his mind; and in that compost the new myth puts down roots. When it grows it explains the ancient situation to which our anxieties recall us: loss of innocence, the guilt and ignominy of consciousness, the need for pardon. Mr. Golding owns that he is a religious man. He believes that some people are saints: in *Lord of the Flies* Simon is a saint, and this is why, he says, literary people have found Simon incomprehensible; 'but he *is* comprehensible to the illiterate person . . . The illiterate person believes in saints and sanctity.' (This is not the first time a modern artist has found his allies among the illiterate – Yeats and Eliot have made similar declarations.) Golding believes in human guilt and the human sense of paradise lost; he also believes in divine mercy.

The evidence for holiness lies scattered among the fragments of our world, and those fragments are represented in Golding's books; they form part of the whole. But this whole is a world of imagination, where everything is related, everything counts, and truth is accessible; the world of myth. For Golding's own term is the right one; out of the single small seed grows this instrument 'for controlling . . . ordering . . . giving a shape and significance to the immense paradox of futility and anarchy which is contemporary history'. These are Mr. Eliot's words on Joyce's myth; but they will serve for Golding. Art, says Cassirer, requires a step back into mythical thinking; perhaps this has always been so since mythical thinking became obsolete, but never has the step back been more consciously taken than in our times. And in the contrast between our consciousness of this, and the momentary forgetfulness of our Darwinian grandfathers, Golding found the theme of his first novel.

Lord of the Flies has 'a pretty big connexion' with Ballantyne. In *The Coral Island* Ralph, Jack and Peterkin are cast away on a desert island, where they live active, civilized, and civlizing lives. Practical difficulties are easily surmounted; they light fires with bowstrings and spyglasses, hunt pigs for food, and kill them with much ease and a total absence of guilt – indeed of bloodshed. They are all Britons – a term they use to compliment each other – all brave, obedient and honourable. There is much useful information conveyed concerning tropical islands, including field-workers' reporting of the conduct of cannibals: but anthropology is something nasty that clears up on the arrival of a missionary and Jack himself prevents an act of cannibalism by telling the flatnoses not to be such blockheads and presenting them with six newly slaughtered pigs. The parallel between the island and the Earthly Paradise causes a trace of literary sophistication: 'Meat and drink on the same tree! My dear boys, we're set up for life: it must be the ancient paradise – hurrah! . . . We afterwards found, however, that these lovely islands were very unlike Paradise in many things.' But these 'things' are non-Christian natives and, later, pirates; the boys themselves are cleanly (cold baths recommended) and godly – regenerate, empire-building boys, who know by instinct how to turn paradise into a British protectorate.

The Coral Island (1858) could be used as a document in the history of ideas; it belongs inseparably to the period when boys were sent out of Arnoldian schools certified free of Original Sin. Golding takes Ralph, Jack and Peterkin (altering this name to Simon, 'called Peter') and studies them against an altered moral landscape. He is a schoolmaster, and knows boys well enough to make their collapse into savagery plausible, to see *them* as the cannibals; the authority of the grown-ups is all there is to prevent savagery. If you dropped these boys into an Earthly Paradise 'they would not behave like God-fearing English gentlemen' but 'as like as not . . . find savages who were kindly and uncomplicated. . . . The devil would rise out of the intellectual complications of the three white men.' Golding leaves the noble savages out of *Lord of the Flies* but this remark is worth quoting because it states the intellectual position in its basic simplicity. It is the civilized who are corrupt, out of phase with natural rhythm. Their guilt is the price of evolutionary success; and our awareness of this fact can be understood by duplicating Ballantyne's situation, borrowing his island, and letting his theme develop in this new and more substantial context. Once more every prospect pleases; but the vileness proceeds, not from cannibals, but from the boys, though Man is not so much vile as 'heroic and sick'. Unlike Ballantyne's boys, these are dirty and inefficient; they have some notion of order, symbolized by the beautiful conch which heralds formal meetings; but when uncongenial effort is required to maintain it, order disappears. The shelters are inadequate, the signal fire goes out at the very moment when Jack first succeeds in killing a pig. Intelligence fades; irrational taboos and blood-rituals make hopeless the task of the practical but partial intellect of Piggy; his glasses, the firemakers, are smashed and stolen, and in the end he himself is broken to pieces as he holds the conch. When civilized conditioning fades – how tedious Piggy's appeal to what adults might do or think! – the children are capable of neither savage nor civil gentleness. Always a little nearer to raw humanity than adults, they slip into a condition of animality depraved by mind, into the cruelty of hunters with their devil-liturgies and torture: they make an unnecessary, evil fortress, they steal, they abandon all operations aimed at restoring them to civility. Evil is the natural product of their consciousness. First the smallest boys create a beastie, a snake – 'as if it wasn't a good island'. Then a beast is created in good earnest, and defined in a wonderful narrative sequence. The emblem of this evil society is the head of a dead pig, fixed, as a sacrifice, on the end of a stick and animated by flies and by the imagination of the *voyant*, Simon.

Simon is Golding's first 'saint, and a most important figure'. He is 'for the illiterate a proof of the existence of God' because the illiterate (to whom we are tacitly but unmistakably expected to attribute a correct insight here) will say, 'Well, a person like this cannot exist without a good God.' For Simon 'voluntarily embraces the beast . . . and tries to get rid of him'. What he understands – and this is wisdom Golding treats with awe – is that evil is 'only us'. He climbs up to where the dead fire is dominated by the beast, a dead airman in a parachute, discovers what this terrible thing really is, and rushes off with the good news to the beach, where the maddened boys at their beast-slaying ritual mistake

Simon himself for the beast and kill him. As Piggy, the dull practical intelligence, is reduced to blindness and futility, so Simon, the visionary, is murdered before he can communicate his comfortable knowledge. Finally, the whole Paradise is destroyed under the puzzled eyes of an adult observer. Boys will be boys.

The difference of this world from Ballantyne's simpler construction from similar materials is not merely a matter of incomparability of the two talents at work; our minds have, in general, darker needs and obscurer comforts. It would be absurd to suppose that the change has impoverished us; but it has seemed to divide our world into 'two cultures' – the followers of Jack and the admirers of Simon, those who build fortresses and those who want to name the beast.

Lord of the Flies was 'worked out carefully in every possible way', and its author holds that the 'programme' of the book *is* its meaning. He rejects Lawrence's doctrine, 'Never trust the artist, trust the tale' and its consequence, 'the proper function of the critic is to save the tale from the artist'. He is wrong, I think: in so far as the book differs from its programme there is, as a matter of common sense, material over which the writer has no absolute authority. This means not only that there are possible readings which he cannot veto, but even that some of his own views on the book may be in a sense wrong. The interpretation of the dead parachutist is an example. This began in the 'programme' as straight allegory; Golding says that this dead man 'is' History. 'All that we can give our children' in their trouble is this monstrous dead adult, who's 'dead, but won't lie down'; an ugly emblem of war and decay that broods over the paradise and provides the only objective equivalent for the beast the boys imagine. Now this limited allegory (I may even have expanded it in the telling) seems to me not to have got out of the 'programme' into the book; what does get in is more valuable because more like myth – capable, that is, of more various interpretation than the rigidity of Golding's scheme allows. And in writing of this kind all depends upon the author's mythopoeic power to transcend the 'programme'. Golding has this poetic power, and nowhere is it more impressively used than in his second book, *The Inheritors*.

Prefixed to *The Inheritors* is a passage from Wells's *Outline of History*, and this serves the same purpose as Ballantyne's novel in the genesis of the earlier book; it sets off an antithetical argument. 'Wells's *Outline* played a great part in my life because my father was a rationalist, and the *Outline* was something he took neat. It is the rationalist gospel *in excelsis*. . . . By and by it seemed to me not to be large enough . . . too neat and too slick. And when I re-read it as an adult I came across his picture of Neanderthal man, our immediate predecessors, as being these gross, brutal creatures who were possibly the basis of the mythological bad man . . . I thought to myself that this is just absurd. . . .' The difference between Golding and the Wells of the *Outline* is simple; to Wells the success of the high-foreheaded, weapon-bearing, carnivorous *homo sapiens* was progress, but to Golding it was the defeat of innocence, the sin of Adam in terms of a new kind of history.

Golding's real power, the true nature of his mythopoeic obsession, became evident only with the publication of this second book. This root-idea is, as I have suggested, a variant of the Fall, transplanted from theology. Golding is fascinated by the evidence – in the nature of the case ubiquitous – that human consciousness is a biological asset purchased at a price; the price is the knowledge of evil. This evil emanates from the human mind, a product of its action upon the environment. *The Inheritors* is about the accumulation of guilt that necessarily attended the historical success of *homo sapiens*; the intellectual superiority of Man over his simian victims is precisely measured by the cruelty and guilt which dominate his life and are relatively absent from his predecessor's. The creatures to be exterminated are almost innocent, as near it as we can imagine; they practise no deceit, have an obscure sense of life as a mystery, understand wickedness as killing, but their lives are controlled by the seasons, by inhibiting fears of water, above all by a physiological equipment excellent in its way but prohibiting intellect. They know the world with senses like an animal's; they depend much upon involuntary reflexes – keen scent, night vision, acuteness of ear; they are not men at all, and that is why they are innocent. Only after prolonged observations of the new men can Lok associate sex with cruelty, derange his senses with alcohol, offer violence to a friend, or even think of one thing or process as 'like' another. Not to know evil is, in a sense, to know nothing. The new men sail away, successful and guilty, leaving Lok with the doll-goddess which is his only image of the intelligent and creative mind. Clutching this toy, he who had known useful fear is now the prey of useless terror as well as of his animal enemies; they, the real creators, plan a bloody and intelligent future.

Technically *The Inheritors* attempts a little less than *Pincher Martin*, but has fewer flaws. The natural setting, of obvious importance, needed to be wonderfully done and is. Above all, the feat of recording observations of the activities of *homo sapiens* made with the sensory equipment of Lok is of astonishing virtuosity. We are constantly reminded of the involuntary powers that sustain him; his ears speak to him even if he will not listen, small areas of skin react with useful knowledge, the nose marvellously distinguishes and identifies. We can always see, too, that the extinction of this animal is *necessary*, as in the passage where he observes a new man aiming at him with a bow and can no more conceive of what the man is doing than he can impute enmity to so similar a being or explain his tall face — his senses simply report a series of inexplicable events. In the heart of the book there is a remarkable passage of some fifty pages in which Lok and the female Fa observe the communal activities of the new people from a vantage-point in a tree. This is carried out with a fierce imaginative power that is not in the least inconsistent with a very minute attention to the complicated effect to be communicated. What we have to be shown is that although we are experiencing these events innocently, by way of the passive, vegetarian, inhuman senses of Lok, we *belong* down below in the clearing, corrupt and intelligent. And at the end we abruptly leave Lok; suddenly, with a loss of sympathy, observe him with our normal sight, joining the new men, our own sort. With these anxious and responsible technicians we sail away, with only a last glimpse of superseded innocence stumbling about on the shore of a dead world. *The Inheritors* does not, like *Lord of the Flies*, qualify as a spanking good tale, and with its publication Golding met for the first time that uncomprehending reception with which he is now so familiar. The book was written, presumably at white-heat, in a few weeks. It has not been surpassed. . . .

(For reasons of space I have here omitted Professor Kermode's discussion of *Pincher Martin* – Ed.)

Of *Free Fall*, Golding's fourth and perhaps his most ambitious book, I must say that although I do not feel that I have yet got to know it well I have no expectation that it can ever possess my mind as the others have done. It should be remembered that Golding asks a lot of his critics — this is a matter, I think, of emphasis, of his not saying 'The first page and the last page are crucial'. He does not say so because it seems to him self-evident.[2] It is not in such reticences that Mr. Golding fails (if he does fail); for in everything related to the shape of this myth his skill is all that it was in *Pincher Martin*. Technically *Free Fall* (which depends

upon a system of 'time-shifts' devised to expose the religious significance
of a man's experience) is at least accomplished as any of the others. It is
a mark of Golding's integrity that in every book he employs technical
devices of remarkable ingenuity but never indulges his skill; it is never a
hair's-breadth in excess of what the moral occasion demands. One's
coolness towards the book has other causes.

The myth of *Free Fall* is, basically, that of all Golding's books: the Fall
of Man, the expulsion from Paradise, erected wit and infected will. It is
a myth which has accumulated an enormous and various theology,
which does not matter until the novelist turns theologian himself.
Golding's hero is examining his life (made typical life by many
allegorical devices) with a view to discovering a pattern, some
connexion between his two worlds of experience, one deterministic, the
world of empirical observation, the other a world in which the burning
bush is not consumed, a world of horror and glory, heaven and hell.
Sammy's conclusion (which is not the conclusion of the novel) is that
'there is no bridge'. In his brooding over different episodes in his life,
Sammy Mountjoy is necessarily theologizing; in other words, there is
within the book continuous comment – admittedly not directly
vouched for by the author – on the myth. I do not think that this works;
there is an unwonted hollowness in these passages, the shabbiness of a
do-it-yourself theology; and the book at moments lies open to the
Coleridgean charge of mental bombast – 'thoughts and images too
great for the subject' – the subject being not the Fall but a *commentary*
upon it. In Golding's earlier books – and this is unique in modern
fiction – guilt, unconscious innocence, the taste of isolation, good and
evil, are made actual, like vomit in the mouth. It is this actuality that is
lacking in *Free Fall*; its absence takes the nature out of Golding's prose, it
takes the plasticity out of the narrative. The crucial episode, a
nightmare experience in a prison-cell, calls for, and is not provided
with, the savage compassion which went into the writing of *Pincher
Martin*. Yet it is in a way wonderfully composed, passionate and
cunning; there is no question of a failure of power or of nerve, only – to
be bold – of a flaw in the original conception.

This flaw is one to which Mr. Golding's gifts render him peculiarly
liable. Myths of total explanation are religious; comment upon them is
theology. *Free Fall*, like *Paradise Lost*, is about *everything*; the author
knows this, devises his narrative and even names his characters
accordingly. Samuel Mountjoy at first misunderstands his vocation

(like Samuel in the Bible) and is as a child in his slum an inhabitant of Paradise (Mountjoy). As he writes, he lives on Paradise Hill, 'thirty seconds from the shop and the local'. A central event of his life is the recognition of the beauty of a girl called Beatrice; later, by a positive act of will, he rejects the possibility of living by this vision, and subjects her to his lust. The two worlds between which his life is suspended (in a condition of 'free fall' as understood in science fiction) are represented by a religious schoolmistress and a science master called Nick. The child does not have to choose; in childhood the two worlds interlock. He chooses, as a young man, to desecrate Beatrice. The other world he finds again in a prison-camp, where he is subjected by a German officer named Halde[3] to an interrogation modelled on that of Christ in the desert. Will he reject the 'world'? Is he a son of God? He does not know enough to betray his comrades, and Halde sends him to a cell which he peoples with his own egotistical terrors; at the height of his agony he bursts out (or is let out) of the cell, forgiven. He walks into the world of vision: 'The power of gravity, dimension and space, the movement of the earth and sun and unseen stars, these made what might be called music and I heard it.' Beatrice has been reduced (and this passage is as fine as anything in Golding) to an incontinent idiot in an asylum; but Sammy still finds himself called to Paradise. He cannot reconcile the two worlds but the novelist, on the last page, builds a kind of bridge between them.

That it is mythologically substantial, this bridge, I do not doubt; but I do not understand it. The novel is about delivery from the body of this death; not only about the Fall but also about regeneration. This account of it is too scanty to be fair even to my imperfect understanding of the book, but it may be enough to help me make my point: that it is not the religious but the theological element that limits the imaginative scope, and brings into the writing a kind of dry heat, a brittleness, absent before. I ought to say that Messrs. Gregor and Kinkead-Weekes, in the intelligent article I have already quoted, find the theology satisfactory, and indeed orthodox. But Mr. Golding is not orthodox. He has done what writers in the Romantic tradition have done before – as Mallarmé discovered Nirvana without knowing Buddhism, or as Yeats dwelt, though heretically, on the Annunciation, he has found in experience and embodied in his own myths the truths that inform all others. But to provide accounts of mystical experience is one thing – admittedly a difficult thing, if only because of the qualitative differences between St. John of the Cross and a mescalin addict; to invent a mystical theology is another. The first is work for a genius, the second for a church. Not to see this is the flaw of all the Romantic and Symbolist writers who lapsed into the pseudo-theologies of occultism.

A final word on 'simplicity'. Golding's novels are simple in so far as they deal in the primordial patterns of human experience and in so far as they have skeletons of parable. On these simple bones the flesh of narrative can take extremely complex forms. This makes for difficulty, but of the most acceptable kind, the difficulty that attends the expression of what is profoundly simple. For all that I have said against *Free Fall* it is this kind of book, like the others a work of genius by a writer from whom we can hope for much more, since he is in superbly full possession of his great powers.

> SOURCE: extracts from chapter 22 of *Puzzles and Epiphanies* (London, 1962) pp. 198–207, 210–13. The chapter itself is Frank Kermode's collation of two earlier essays (1958, 1960) on Golding.

NOTES

1. This and several other remarks attributed to Mr. Golding in this article are derived from a transcript of a B.B.C. discussion programme.

2. There is a perceptive study of the opening and the conclusion of *Free Fall* in an article by Ian Gregor and M. Kinkead-Weekes called 'Mr. Golding and his Critics' (*Twentieth Century*, Feb 1960).

3. It has been pointed out that *Halde* means 'slope', and that this name is also allegorical, since Halde is the agent by which Sammy moves into the gravitational field of his spiritual work. Mr. Golding tells me he did not think of this. It is allegorist's luck.

Norman Holland

STYLE AND THE MAN:
JOSEPH CONRAD (1968)

Comparing two or more works by one person, be he seventeenth-century lyricist or twentieth-century film-maker, inevitably raises the question of style. 'The style', critics say, 'is the man', and though we would be hard put to define either the subject or the predicate, the two do seem to have a natural affinity. We speak of works as Miltonic or Flaubertian or Kafkaesque or Kingsley Amish. From the opposite end of the sentence, the psychoanalyst, speaking of a man, will often talk of his 'life style'. That usage suggests that the literary critic might find a useful model for his concept of style in the psychoanalyst's concept of character, particularly when he is puzzled about a writer's style, as when a novel like *The Secret Agent* seems sharply marked off from the rest of Conrad's work, and yet, in some half-understood way, deeply Conradian.

In 'style', the literary critic seems to include three things. First, and most obviously, he means a writer's way with words: Shavian wit or Joycean puns or Shakespearean quibbles. Second, he seems to include a writer's choice of material and his characteristic form for handling it: it would be hard, for example, to think of anything but social comedy that could be said to be 'in the style of Congreve', and it is hard to think of Conrad's political novels as from the same pen as his sea stories. Third, critics seem to include in the notion of style a writer's way of dealing with his audience: the snigger of a Sterne, the stage-managing of a Thackeray, the allegorizing of a Melville.

A psychoanalyst defines 'character' (the classic statement is Fenichel's) as the 'the habitual mode of bringing into harmony the tasks presented by internal demands and by the external world'.[1] There is a certain rough correspondence between the elements the literary critic includes in style and the three terms the psychoanalyst includes in character. That is, the 'internal demands' are the *Triebe*, the drives, that might lead a writer to a certain kind of material. The 'habitual mode of bringing into harmony' refers to a man's defenses; they in turn correspond to a writer's ways of dealing with his material – form and structure on the large scale, sentence or verse manner on the small. Finally, the 'external world' for a writer is his reader. Naturally, in a man, as in a work of literature, these three things interact and modify one another, but we can, I think, set up a kind of rough comparison: content is to drive as form is to defense as style is to character (defined as the habitual interactions of drive, defense, and external reality).

By these criteria, *The Secret Agent* does not seem particularly Conradian. In terms of form, we miss the usual Conradian narrator. At the sentence level, instead of the allegorical and symbolic overtones spelled out in the language of, say, 'Heart of Darkness', we have a heavily ironic and dry verbal style.[2] As for content, we do not have man pitting his own flawed self against nature, but rather a political story: anarchists, Verloc as *agent provocateur*, the Professor with his bombs; also the story of a marriage, Verloc and Winnie who married him to provide for Stevie, the idiot boy. Yet some of the incidents show Conrad's preoccupations, though deviously, in the manner of parody: the fatally significant lapse, here, Verloc's using Stevie to try to blow up the Greenwich Observatory and Stevie's consequent fragmentation; the secret, both the motive and identity of the bombers and Verloc's hoard of payments from the ministry he serves; the self-sacrificing woman – Winnie and her mother. In some sense, then, the novel is 'Conradian', but in what sense? Only a psychological concept of style, I think, can tell us.

Anarchic in form as well as content, *The Secret Agent* leaves us with the persistent question of the Professor, 'unsuspected and deadly', just as the opening line has posed us Mr. Verloc, also unsuspected, also (in the event) deadly. Those first and last lines offer a clue to the informing principle about which the novel finds its shape and inner logic: the unsuspected – a sense throughout the book that each character has a doubleness or tripleness, a secret self. Verloc, for example – one side is the anarchist, another the bourgeois family man dealing in pornography, a third, the protector of property and servant of embassies. The late Baron Stott-Wartenheim was clever indeed to designate him $\triangle$. The three anarchists are fat or impotent or helplessly and grossly dependent on some woman. The Professor is 'frail, insignificant, shabby, miserable' – but explosive.

The police, too, share this many-sidedness, for 'The terrorist and the policeman both come from the same basket' (p. 68).[3] Chief Inspector Heat must mediate between the anarchists under his jurisdiction ('our lot') and the Assistant Commissioner, who in turn feels 'himself dependent on too many subordinates and too many masters'. He must deal on one side with Heat and on another with his wife's friend, Michaelis's patroness, and on still a third, Sir Ethelred, himself torn between the Assistant Commissioner's discoveries and the Fisheries Bill.

Stevie has the same dualistic quality: immoderate compassion matched by pitiless rage. Stevie's mother mediates between the idiot boy and his enraged father, just as Winnie herself adopts a mother's role between Stevie and Verloc: ' "Might be father and son", she said to herself ', as, unknown to her, Verloc leads Stevie to his doom. And at the moment she kills, just as she has torn Heat's pink racing form in two, 'Her personality seemed to have been torn into two pieces, whose mental operations did not adjust themselves very well to each other' (p. 209).

The characters bisect and trisect one another, each touching only a part of the others in a chaos and maze of human relations. We begin to sense in the world of the novel the significance of Stevie's 'circles, circles, circles; innumerable circles, concentric, eccentric; a coruscating whirl of circles that by their tangled multitude of repeated curves, uniformity of form, and confusion of intersecting lines suggested a rendering of cosmic chaos, the symbolism of a mad art attempting the inconceivable' (p. 49). Not unlike Stevie, Conrad himself seems to be drawing endless circles in his novel: coins, spectacles, wheels, clock faces, haloed street lights, bowler hats, orange peel, billiard ball, the Professor's india-rubber ball, even the great dome of the observatory. And not just circles, but T-bars (the gas lights), triangles (not only Stott-Wartenheim's, also the triangular well of streets in front of Verloc's shop) – the novel fairly bristles with geometric images, as though Conrad were trying to squeeze some sort of order out of the chaos; as though he himself were trying to act out the embassy's injunction: 'What is required at present is not writing, but the bringing to light of a distinct, significant fact – I would almost say of an alarming fact' (p. 28).

The critical essay that tells us most about *The Secret Agent* is, of course, Conrad's own Preface, written in 1920 for a collected edition long after the novel's original publication early in 1907. Repeatedly, in the

Preface, Conrad uses Wurmt's image of 'bringing to light' as he speaks of 'illuminating facts', their 'illuminating quality', an 'illuminating impression'. He speaks of the idea precipitating like a geometry of bizarre and unexpected crystals in a colorless solution: 'Strange forms, sharp in outline, but imperfectly apprehended, appeared and claimed attention' (p. 11). As against the usual setting for Conrad's novels, the sea, 'reflector of the world's light', he now saw London as the 'background' for the story, 'a cruel devourer of the world's light'. 'Slowly the dawning conviction of Mrs Verloc's maternal passion grew up to a flame between me and that background.' 'At last the story of Winnie Verloc stood out complete . . . it had to be disengaged from its obscurity in that immense town,' brought 'out in front of the London background' (p. 11).

As one would expect from the Preface, light and dark are the key images in *The Secret Agent*, notably in that dark London with its 'sinister, noisy, hopeless, and rowdy night', 'sullen, brooding, and sinister', broken by 'solid blood-red light'. London becomes inner madness rendered as outer setting, and the city threatens throughout the novel to stifle, suffocate, submerge, overwhelm – Winnie is quite correct to fear in it hanging or drowning. London in the deepest sense is the engulfing sea or maze of irrationality – the very street numbers are as irrational as Stevie's circles. It is a 'slimy dampness', a 'slimy aquarium', 'an immensity of greasy slime' 'like a wet, muddy ditch'. Miss Claire Rosenfield has very astutely pointed out that balanced against these images of water are fish: the Assistant Commissioner is busy catching a 'sprat', Verloc, in order to get at the whale, dogfish, or witty fish, Vladimir.[4] At the moment he plunges into the murky depths of London, the Assistant Commissioner himself looks like a 'queer foreign fish', and, of course, Sir Ethelred is concerned throughout with his Fisheries Bill. At the end, Winnie is, as it were, thrown back into the sea.

Fishing provides the perfect symbol for the 'bringing to light of a distinct, significant fact', something all the men of the novel play at. Vladimir, Verloc, Heat, even Ossipon are all investigating – but lazily, fitfully. The novel concerns Greenwich Observatory, a place dedicated to bringing facts to light, but the novel uses the observatory only in a plot to destroy it. Ossipon invokes Lombroso as an Italian peasant would his saint. Heat's wisdom is not 'true wisdom', rather, 'His wisdom was of an official kind' (p. 79), and he is lazily willing to pin the crime on Michaelis. Two men stand out as exceptions to this general indolence.

The Assistant Commissioner really tries to find the truth – and, for that, he is twice described as Don Quixote. The other truth-seeker is, of course, the mad Professor. Confronted with 'this world of contradictions', 'the inexplicable mysteries of conscious existence', the rest of the men in the novel want simply to relax into such facile faiths as Heat's in his favorite racing form, the easy dogmas of the revolutionaries (which Conrad describes in religious images), or Verloc's belief that he could trust any woman who had given herself to him. 'Man', says Conrad, curiously echoing another melodramatic detective thriller, *Hamlet*, 'Man may smile and smile, but he is not an investigating animal. He loves the obvious' (p. 8).

Verloc's trust in his wife suggests the key to this cheerful oblivion: 'Mr Verloc loved his wife as a wife should be loved – that is, maritally, with the regard one has for one's chief possession.' 'She was mysterious, with the mysteriousness of living beings. The far-famed secret agent △ . . . was not the man to break into such mysteries' (p. 152). Possession substitutes for knowledge: thus Heat can rest secure on 'private friendship, private information, private use of it', and Verloc, with his air of having wallowed in bed all day, can glow in his belief that he has protected 'the town's opulence and luxury'. Ossipon can even speak of 'the even tenor of his revolutionary life'. He is fat, Verloc is fat, so also Heat and Michaelis. Winnie's mother has triple chins and her legs are so swollen she can scarcely move. For Yundt laziness is the *motif*: 'The famous terrorist had never in his life raised personally as much as his little finger against the social edifice' (p. 51). Appetite and eating image Verloc's grisly complacency at his murder, eating being another way in *The Secret Agent* of achieving the security of possession. For all the men in the story (save the Commissioner and the Professor), Silenus is the emblem. Lustful, lazy, fat, they rest and feed complacently on the obvious. *The Secret Agent* is, among other things, a study in sloth.

By contrast, the women are paragons of self-sacrifice. Winnie's mother commits herself through the failure of the male trustees to investigate her) to a death-like charitable home, all for the sake of the son, Stevie. And Winnie herself gave up her butcher-boy lover for the slothful eater Verloc so as to provide for Stevie. As for investigation – 'She felt profoundly that things do not stand much looking into' (pp. 150–1), a note that Conrad sounds again and again as her leitmotif. The women of the story (one could take Michaelis's patron as the prototype) do not probe the mysteries of the world;

instead, they offer to a world trusted and uninvestigated a bottomless compassion to the point where the only remedy for pain Stevie can even imagine is to be taken into his sister – mother's bed.

And yet, as the bed-wallowing Verloc finds out, it can be dangerous to relax into the sea of feminine compassion represented by Winnie. 'The protection she had extended over her brother had been in its origin of a fierce and indignant complexion' (p. 203), an 'ardour of protecting compassion exalted morbidly in her childhood' (p. 59). 'Mrs Verloc's temperament . . . when stripped of its philosophical reserve, was maternal and violent' – a curious pairing of adjectives (p. 199). Ossipon sees her 'twined round him like a snake, not to be shaken off. She was not deadly. She was death itself – the companion of life' (p. 237). Significantly, Winnie stabs Verloc as he is lolling on the sofa issuing his mating call.

In the moment of stabbing, Mrs Verloc literally becomes Stevie's avenging soul, that child who seems to bring to a focus the moral world of the novel. Stevie seems always to have alternated between being seduced and being beaten. His circles suggest the 'chaos and eternity' he found in human relations, a confusion of intersections and hidden sides. His response to deprivation is simple, primitive, and violent: 'Somebody, he felt, ought to be punished for it – punished with great severity' (p. 146), and this reaction pinpoints the pattern of anarchism (at least in Conrad's highly personal view of it): a morass of vague sentiments from which springs a mad retaliation. 'In the face of anything which affected directly or indirectly his morbid dread of pain, Stevie ended by turning vicious. . . . The tenderness of his universal charity had two phases as indissolubly joined and connected as the reverse and obverse sides of a medal. The anguish of immoderate compassion was succeeded by the pain of an innocent but pitiless rage' (p.144). He alternates between lazy, mindless compassion and sudden, violent action; Vladimir, Verloc, his sister-mother, and all the anarchists do the same.

Balanced against this moral and emotional anarchy are the police and the other forces of government, 'the House which is *the* House, *par excellence*,' but very distinctly not a compassionate home. Government tries to impose on this violence-in-violence some sort of control and order, a constant watch, 'rules of the game'. And it is the aim of Vladimir, Verloc, and the rest to provoke the very forces of control into anarchy. As the Professor puts it: 'To break up the superstition and worship of legality should be our aim. Nothing would please me more than to see Inspector Heat and his likes take to shooting us down in broad daylight with the approval of the public. Half our battle would be won then; the disintegration of the old morality would have set in its very temple' (p. 71). This theme of control brings us to Conrad himself. The idea that informs the novel is anarchy masked over by control or indolence. The 'secret agent' in human affairs, the 'unsuspected', is the potential for violence in each of us – and, presumably, in Conrad himself (who once sprang at Ford Madox Ford's throat when Ford interrupted his proofreading).

The Secret Agent seems to stand apart from the main line of Conrad's writing. It is set in the city, not the sea; government, not navigation, is his subject. Yet this novel is perhaps more deeply Conradian than any of the others. Albert Guerard has shown that Conrad's basic theme is the conflict between the mariner and the outlaw; between the man who seeks to establish control by finding his place among the hard, infallible objects of external reality and that other, darker figure who immerses himself in the destructive, chaotic jungle within and without. Although it is clearest, perhaps, in 'The Secret Sharer', between the anonymous captain and his outlaw double, we see the contrast all through Conrad's works: the twinned figures of Marlow and Kurtz, one returning from, one sinking into the 'Heart of Darkness'; MacWhirr battling the 'Typhoon' without and the passengers' riot within his ship; the skillful young captain threatened by the anarchic spirit of the dead one in 'The Shadow-Line'; Haldin and Razumov, the outlaw rejected and his betrayer in *Under Western Eyes*; the captain and crew of *The Nigger of the 'Narcissus'* striving to exorcise by seamanship the deadly thing within their ship; Lingard and Almayer in *Almayer's Folly*; Heyst and Jones in *Victory*; and we sometimes see the same dualism of control and anarchy, fidelity and betrayal, in single figures such as Lord Jim (notably) or Karain. Given such a preoccupation with the dualism of controller and controlled, how, in a sense, could Conrad have failed to write a novel about anarchy? And he wrote two, *The Secret Agent* and *Under Western Eyes*.

In *The Secret Agent*, the earlier of the two, we find Conrad's usual dualism doubled. There is controller and controlled, but then a doubleness to what is controlled: the police try to keep under surveillance and rule a violent, masculine rage which itself punctuates a

feminine, complacent compassion. Thus, the atmosphere of the novel
consists of indolence, obesity, dependence on women, bureaucracy,
compassion, Stevie's circles, and all this in the foggy, dark, damp, grimy
maze of London. In the night journey of Winnie's self-sacrificing
mother, Conrad brings all these elements together and at the same
moment sinks his novel to its deepest, most obscure point in the maze.
The action of the novel (as contrasted to its atmosphere) is best
described in the diplomat's phrase, 'the bringing to light of a distinct,
significant fact . . . an alarming fact': the explosion itself, the sacrifice of
the scapegoat Stevie, the emergence of his name-tape, the Professor's
detonator, the Commissioner's quest for Vladimir, or even Verloc's
bank account (the prosaic equivalent of the buried treasure in *Nostromo*
and other Conrad tales). But nothing is brought to light. Instead, at key
points in the novel, the lights are turned off. All this fishing in the slimy
dampness of London produces no catch: Winnie sinks into the ocean,
the buried treasure slips into Ossipon's pocket, and we are left with the
Professor, 'unsuspected and deadly'. 'An impenetrable mystery seems
destined to hang forever over this act of madness or despair' (p. 249).

Psychologically, it would be difficult and unnecessary to say what
that swamp or sea might have stood for in Conrad's mind – it
undoubtedly stood for many things. Death; passivity; sexuality; human
relations and communication; woman or the feminine side of Conrad's
own nature; betrayal or loss of fidelity, particularly the expatriate's
failure to carry on his forefathers' fight for Polish independence; the
writer landlocked at his farmhouse desk as against the onetime heroic
seaman; perhaps the irrational in the largest sense, particularly
irrational or self-destructive aggression (there is evidence that Conrad
himself once attempted suicide) – all these and many others may be
represented in that 'immensity of greasy slime' the novelist fought to
keep his head above. One thing, however, is clear: Conrad was deeply
tempted to let go his hold, lose control, and sink into it (as so many of his
heroes do). Not only *The Secret Agent*, but all his novels deal with the
control or punishment of such an impulse.

This problem of control creates not only the events and characters of
the Conradian novel, but also its form, for psychologically, form is to
content as defense is to impulse. It is surely no accident that a novelist so
preoccupied with action as a defense should choose a style which Henry
James saw was 'the way to do a thing that shall make it undergo most
doing'. As though Conrad felt the very writing of his stories as a

tempting but threatening anarchy, he interposed in most of them a dispassionate narrator, ironically commenting on and distancing us (and Conrad) from the fictive world. He thus defended against communicating not only with his material but also with his readers. A number of his stories (but most notably 'Amy Foster') deal with problems of communication; we hear from Ford Madox Ford about his Flaubertian search for *le mot juste* and his composing his richest sentences in French (for English was his third, not his second, language). Critics galore have noted (and some complained of) the fog of adjectives Conrad puts between his material and his reader.

In *The Secret Agent*, Conrad put aside the margin of safety the narrator represented (and his wife has written how depressed he became during the writing of this particular novel). He relied instead entirely on the adjectives. He created a comic, ironic style that swings between an involved periphrasis, almost neo-classic in manner, and sudden, grimy, realistic details. The result can be such delicious ironies as our last view of Ossipon: 'Already he bowed his broad shoulders, his head of ambrosial locks, as if ready to receive the leather yoke of the sandwich board' (p. 252). In sentence after sentence and scene after scene, a 'distinct, significant fact' comes to light against the prevailing murk: the fly on the window of Vladimir's office, for example, or the little cracked bell in the Verlocs' shop that marks each passing from the outer world to the inner. His artistic aim, Conrad said, was 'before all, to make you see'.

In structure no less than sentence style, we see him try either to flee the 'immensity of greasy slime' or to bring out from it some distinct fact that can then be seen and controlled. In *The Secret Agent*, Conrad (who was the first great writer to tackle the screenplay) constantly uses flashback, as though he were retreating from the immediate material into some safer matter elsewhere. *The Secret Agent* is a detective thriller – indeed, Alfred Hitchcock has made a film of it – but it does not grow as the usual thriller does from an initial problem to a mass of revelations at the end. Instead, Conrad gives us little secrets, as though he could not stand a sustained build-up of uncertainty and mystery; rather, there must be a constant 'bringing to light'.

Further, the novel, in its ending, pirouettes away from the complexities of politics and policing developed in its first three-quarters; at the end we are left with two characters so peripheral they become symbolic of the two poles of the novel: the morally complacent Ossipon and the madly violent Professor. Throughout the book, Conrad seems almost to be running away from his characters as his focus shifts successively from Verloc to Vladimir to the other anarchists to Heat to the Assistant Commissioner to Winnie Verloc's mother to Winnie to Ossipon and finally and ultimately to the Professor. We sense in the structure – or lack of it – another version of Stevie's circles, Conrad's flight from and return to his material: 'I had to fight to keep at arm's length the memories of my solitary and nocturnal walks all over London in my early days, lest they should rush in and overwhelm each page of the story' (p. 12).

By the structure of individual sentences and of the whole, Conrad enlists us in his defensive action of 'bringing to light a distinct, significant fact', but does he make us feel the need for the defense? In most of Conrad's works in which the characters sink into the moral swamp, he represents the morass as tempting or alluring, justified by compassion or sheer self-defense. *The Secret Agent* provides no such temptation for the fat, slimy, repellent world of the anarchists – except for one thing. Conrad plays on our curiosity; on just the first page, for example, we hear 'nominally', 'ostensible', 'discreetly but suspiciously', 'hinting at impropriety'. He tempts us to probe the secrets of the controllers and the controlled – but warns us they are both rather dreary. At only one point does he draw us into the novel unequivocally: the chapter of the murder where both the danger of being overwhelmed and the vengeful justification for overwhelming reach a peak. We come in on the side of Winnie and feel, as she does, the power of the terrible absurd urge to destroy and be destroyed into utter, total blackness. It is no wonder that all the many critics of this novel, though they differ as to its merits, find the murder its high point.

The critics, I think, are saying Conrad's special style (or character) succeeds in that chapter, much less so in the rest of the novel. But the novel as a whole is no less Conradian for that. In content, the novel lets us over the side, as it were, into the London sea of anarchy. Psychologically, such a content is a drive: Conrad describes as 'a fascinating temptation' the Assistant Commissioner's 'descent into the street . . . like the descent into a slimy aquarium' (p. 127). The defense becomes all Conrad's devices for extricating and distancing us from that tempting sea: the dry, ironic style, the shifting of focus from one character to another, flashback. Then, drive and defense, content and form come together as the style and theme of the whole, pervading and informing its individual sentences: 'the bringing to light of a distinct, significant fact . . . an alarming fact'. The style is indeed Conradian, for, as he defined his own aim in the Preface to *The Nigger of the 'Narcissus'*: 'The artist descends within himself, and in that lonely region of stress and strife,' if he succeeds, he can 'hold up unquestioningly, without choice and without fear the rescued fragment before all eyes . . .' 'And when it is accomplished – behold! – all the truth of life is there: a moment of vision, a sigh, a smile – and the return to an eternal rest.' The aim is a noble one, truly and stoically Conradian, and because we can understand his style psychologically, we can feel what he felt as something of the moral function of literature: to bring back to light, almost in the manner of a detective, a character and style of life buried in our own dark, anarchic past. . . .

SOURCE: extract from chapter 8 of *The Dynamics of Literary Response* (New York, 1969) pp. 225–37.

NOTES

1. Otto Fenichel, *The Psychoanalytic Theory of Neurosis* (New York: W. W. Norton, 1945) p. 467.
2. In my comments on the *The Secret Agent*, I am drawing in a general way upon a great many studies of Conrad, but most notably Albert Guerard's discussion of the ironic 'voice' in this novel in his superb *Conrad the Novelist* (Cambridge, Mass.: Harvard University Press, 1958).
3. My references are to page numbers in *The Secret Agent: A Simple Tale* (Garden City, N.Y.: Doubleday-Anchor Books, 1953).
4. Claire Rosenfield, *Paradise of Snakes: An Archetypal Analysis of Conrad's Political Novels* (Chicago and London: University of Chicago Press, 1967), ch.3.

Malcolm Bradbury

THE NOVELIST AS IMPRESARIO: JOHN FOWLES (1970)

> There is about the clothes, in the lavishly embroidered summer waistcoat, in the three rings on fingers, the panatella in its amber holder, the malachite-headed cane, a distinct touch of the flashy. He looks very much as if he had given up preaching and gone in for grand opera; and done much better at the latter than the former. There is, in short, more than a touch of the successful impresario about him.
>
> John Fowles, *The French Lieutenant's Woman*

I

Foppish, Frenchified, flashy and 'very minor', the lavish figure who inserts himself into the final chapter of *The French Lieutenant's Woman*, looking back at Mr. Rossetti's house in Chelsea 'as if it is some new theatre he has just bought and is pretty confident he can fill' and turning back time on his watch, is patently none other than a figure for the novelist John Fowles himself. He has, in fact, popped into the novel before, in several guises and voices, and we are used to his here faintly worried and there grandly confident, here contemporaneously nineteenth-century and there a-chronologically twentieth-century, presence. However, his final appearance in the guise of a stout impresario is not entirely creditable either to himself or to the ongoing novel, for it is as a confidence man he shows himself, a notably unresponsible intrusion that he makes and the small mechanical task he performs – setting the clock back a little in order utterly to transform the fortunes and futures of his two central characters, Charles Smithson and the French Lieutenant's Woman – he performs blandly, vainly, and trivially, out of an arrogant power and while en route for fresher pastures. He is the novelist in one of his less likeable guises.

Fortunately the writing continues in more reliable hands, for there is another John Fowles – a much more sober, sententious, and omniscient figure, capable of reporting and reflecting on events, and so of taking seriously the destiny of his characters and establishing with authority an ending which, however, may or may not have any authority whatsoever. The doubt arises because this narrator has already given us, in the previous chapter, one ending to his story. He has, for that matter, given us one two-thirds of the way through the novel, but that one he has rescinded in order to enforce deeper possibilities. But his two final endings have a different status. Both of them, we may say, are structured with all appropriate scruple out of the eventful plot; both of them are substantiations of the argumentative level of the book, or what used to be called its 'sentiments', closing in an aura of Arnoldian humanism, existentialist authenticity, and Marxist history, all of which textures of thought and feeling have been part of the work as a whole. Authorial authority is relativized not in order to lighten responsibility for the characters, thrusting it on the reader, but rather to take full responsibility for showing their freedom, their faculty of choice. The book closes and the reader can fall back only on recognitions themselves duplicitous; here is the writer's great power both to set his characters free to act and choose as they like, and his power to make them his victims, to set them free from his plot but by withdrawing his power himself exposing them more vigorously than if he had fulfilled it. The trickster and the voice of fact and authority; the manipulator and the humanist concerned in all good faith over the fate and the individual freedom of his characters; the plotter and the plot-escaper – these are co-existent presences in the novel and they produce an extraordinary resolution to it, a resolution in which the substantial action seems to end in one world and the substantiating *machinery*, the technical modes and means, in another.

Which is the real Fowles? Readers may disagree, and in disagreeing come up with extremely varied readings. We may take the book as a very Whig novel, a novel about emancipation through history, with Victorian hypocrisy and ignorance yielding up to modern truth and authenticity, to good faith and freedom, the whole enterprise aided by appropriately sympathetic techniques in which the characters are set free from the formal containments of traditional Victorian fiction. More obliquely and cunningly, we may take the book as a great pastiche novel, a novel of ironic counterpointings in which the present may make no such triumph over the past, in which emancipation is also a terrible exposure, a loss as well as a gain, and in which the substance of freedom is seen as something potentially other than that substance which the

modern theoreticians and rebellious theologians define it as, this whole
enterprise being aided by the way in which a modernist novel can be
balanced by contrast – so that the modes weigh equally in the scales.
There is a third possibility, which is that the modernist fiction is what is
questioned, being attenuated and modified by the substance and
realism of Victorian fiction. Certainly the novel crosses some of the
stranger boundaries of form and for that matter of criticism – above all
that between the nineteenth-century realist and the modern novel, a
perplexing barrier – which is precisely why it is baffling *to* criticism; it
invokes expectations, hypotheses, and probabilities we may best
describe in terms of one poetics while it engages us with the
sophisticated discourses of another. We may find our way through the
book as we might through a great realistic work, a work of liberal
realism attentive to character and social experience and the moral
expansions possible at their intersection; we may read it by modernist
canons and find it appropriately a work of self-conscious irony. In other
words, like some of the work of Nabokov or Barth or Borges, the book
seems to embody itself in the purist world of art while delighting in the
obligation to attend to reality; and like that kind of novel it tends to
expose our present critical debates and confusions and their greatest
point of uncertainty – the point where arises the question of whether
realistic or symbolistic norms of the novel can be reconciled, whether
criticism itself can find the same language for talking about a
nineteenth-century realist and a twentieth-century modernist novel.

   What, at any rate, is obvious is that John Fowles is – though we have
been slow to notice it – a sophisticated novelist; and it is worth asking
briefly how it is that this sort of sophistication can have emerged in
postwar English fiction. John Barth has taught us, whether truly or not,
that it is all-important for an artist to be technically up-to-date; on that
measure we have not had a wealth of contemporary English novelists to
turn to, though we have had some. We have, with Fowles, as with
writers like Nabokov and Barth and Borges, our difficulties in deciding
just how modern a novelist he is or wants to be, for there is, as with them,
a decided element of protective withdrawal from authoritative commitment to those elements of existential and revolutionary lore which his
work obviously copes with and comprehends – from, in fact, the
establishment 'modern' thought of our day. Nonetheless Fowles's work
is modern in the sense of Richard Poirier's definition, that it 'includes
the interpretation that will be made of it', and moves in the direction of

self-parody and solipsism.[1] But whatever his particular aesthetics, they have not been entirely commonplace in the English literary scene. It is universally acknowledged that criticism of contemporary writing is a difficult task and that its deceptions are many, that the literature of one's age needs sifting by the purging wisdom of time, that reviewing is one thing and criticism another; and in England one of the consequences of that truth has been that little accurate critical attention has been given to contemporary writing. But if criticism withdraws from creative discussion, or else treats contemporary writing as compelled into insignificance, there is likely to be a general diminution in critical discourse – which may help to explain the more or less low morale of the postwar English fictional scene, its lack of mythology and sociology about the nature of fiction and art. The enterprise of certain postwar English writers who, reacting against the Bloomsbury tradition of experimentalism, asserted an anti-experimental, socially documentary, very empirical purpose for the novel, did not receive much serious attention, even from critics whose responsiveness to earlier phases of realism was considerable; and when or where the emphasis was changed, and in different ways writers like Iris Murdoch, Muriel Spark, B. S. Johnson, and Christine Brooke-Rose attempted to distil a debate and an aesthetic speculativeness, they too got little close reading. The situation doubtless helped to encourage the disproportionately low impression of the quality of contemporary English fiction which has existed in international circles. The curious and surprising thing is that out of such an environment a novelist like John Fowles, whose emphases and concerns are very much of a piece with aesthetic speculation in the novel elsewhere, especially in the American novel, should emerge. The perfectly uncurious, unsurprising thing is that, when he did, he attracted almost no attention in England, and that most of his critical reputation, which has largely come with his last and most flamboyant book, has come in the United States, along with a considerable popular, indeed a best-selling, status as well. *The Collector* appeared in 1963; *The Magus* in 1966; *The French Lieutenant's Woman* in 1969, and it is only with the paperback edition of the last that his reputation in England has really become noticeable.

Yet there was always that in Fowles's work which might have attracted attention: a large intellectual and imaginative aspiration. The very scale of the enterprises he has undertaken as a novelist might well have stood out in any critical climate alive to such things. *The Magus,* for example, runs to 617 pages, and among other things it fairly clearly attempts a kind of history of the consciousness of the West in our present century, an act of recreation and invention carried out with remarkable range and deployment of intellect. *The French Lieutenant's Woman*, though somewhat shorter, is fairly clearly both a formal imitation of a Victorian novel and a very elegant endeavour at assessing the mental distance that must lie between a modern reader and a fiction of that sort – the result being a complex contrast between the psycho-social set of consciousness in the England of a hundred years ago, threaded through all the major areas of social, commercial, intellectual, and sexual life, and that of the present time in which the novelist consciously and articulately stands along with his reader. In one sense, the theme of Fowles's work is precisely cultural distillation, the task of rendering the way in which consciousness or structural coherence underlies all the parts of a society and produces a cultural unity between inner and outer worlds. That is why his novels are so broadly accumulative, so wide-ranging, so socially mobile or picaresque, so substantially populated and explored. Their task involves the interpenetration of many different levels of awareness or perception – requires, that is, social, emotional, and psychological exploration.

For a novelist who is sometimes described as 'existential', this is perhaps a curiously roundabout way of going at the writerly task; but then the reality with which Fowles is concerned is surely not exclusively a personal one, and when one looks to his aspiration, to the basis on which he has built his sophistication, it is not perhaps firstly or even primarily aesthetic. Or rather he presumes, and in this he resembles predecessors rather than contemporaries, that the aesthetic exists inside the problem rather than at the abstract level where the writer performs his arabesques of complication and coherence and resolution. Thus Fowles's last two books each have heroes for whom voyage, journey, evolving movement is a matter of social, emotional, and psychological exploration, carrying an obligation to discern a basis of personal authenticity. For each of them, the world is a theatre in which his role must be finally substantiated; the image or metaphor is precisely used, very much in the sense in which it has become a central metaphor for sociologists concerned with the hinterland where sociology and psychology meet. In that difficult world where modern man, seeking to validate some sense of authenticity, meets *homo psychologicus*, programmed via the unconscious, and *homo sociologicus*, programmed by

society, man as role-player, what Erving Goffman calls the 'drama-
turgical analogy', becomes a pervasive metaphor, touching not only on
the question of whether the theatre of society, in which we act our parts,
is substance or shadow, but whether the stage is one we can ever leave.[2]
The metaphor challenges authorship; it throws back at the playwright
or the novelist or the fiction-maker or the impresario a question about
the substantive reality of what he is creating: is it a copy of reality or a
competing fiction to set against a fiction? 'Perhaps what he was doing
sprang from some theory about the theatre – he had said it himself: *The
masque is only a metaphor*. A strange and incomprehensible new
philosophy? Metaphorism? Perhaps he saw himself as a philosopher in
an impossible faculty of ambiguity, a sort of Empson of the event.'
Nicholas Urfe's reflections on Conchis – the 'Magus' of the book of that
title – and his 'godgame' are therefore centralizing questions, which
touch on the relation of fictions to reality. And it seems clear enough
that part of the purpose of that novel is to create a world vigorously
dramatic, a world in which no part is ever inert, in which every street is
a theatre and every object a prop – or, as Robert Scholes has said, the
book seeks to give us back reality by passing beyond the inert banality
we have come to associate with that very term, reality, in the deadening
pages of the *nouveau roman*.[3]

It is in fact the achieved metaphorical energy of Fowles's novels that
gives them power over us; the novels live within themselves, are highly
inventive and linguistically vivid. Fowles puts right at the centre of his
work a superb generative energy, a history-making gift, a power of
what, until the word 'story' weakened in critical credit, was called story-
telling, of such an order that the philosophical and aesthetic articu-
lation of his works seems modified by its presence. The aesthetic
problem, the problem of fictions, is in fact created very deep inside *The
Magus*, made less an aspect of its construction and management than of
its theme. It remains, of course, a book about art; it is the sort of book a
novelist might write in order to assert, for himself and others, a sense of
the possibilities open to fiction in a time when our ideas and notions of
freedom, of selfhood, and of significant order are in ferment, and
complex problems of modern history, modern psychic life or consciousness, modern notions of selfhood and of reality, and modern aesthetics of
form have to be synthesized. These, we may propose, though the
reviewers did not, are the inner themes of *The Magus*; and the
hypothesis has a fair confirmation in *The French Lieutenant's Woman*,

where a number of these themes rise explicitly to the presentational surface, implicating the novelist himself and becoming part of his technical self-questioning and self-development. In both books the hero is led towards a state of exposure or self-discovery, led out of one state of consciousness into another, in a world in which the historical determinants of consciousness are extremely significant and in which the capacity to learn through fictions is central.

If it is the case that we live in a time when it is difficult for a writer to establish the literal reality of plot and character as coherent meanings, and to express a fiction as a coherent linear development of knowledge; if language and structure have become quizzical properties for many of our writers, then Fowles is clearly an author who has come to know and explore such suspicions. The novelist who intrudes so carefully yet so flashily into the last pages of *The French Lieutenant's Woman* in the guise of impresario has earlier made it clear that he has, like any good student in a new university, duly read and digested his Roland Barthes and his Alain Robbe-Grillet, and knows what a novel 'in the modern sense of the word' is, which is not an omniscient narrative. Fowles understands and expresses an awareness of the status fictions and myths have with us; and he not only embodies the resulting technicalities but explores the version of history by which such a thing might be asserted. As his fictional world moves from superego to id, from stability to exposure, so does his sense of the commanding novelist move through a similar trajectory:

The novelist is still a god, since he creates (and not even the most aleatory *avantgarde* modern novel has managed to extirpate its author completely); what has changed is that we are no longer the gods of the Victorian image, omniscient and decreeing; but in the new theological image, with freedom our first principle, not authority.

It is perhaps worth noting, though, that Fowles does not dissolve the tradition of realism completely, and that in many respects his aim, like Iris Murdoch's, seems to be to preserve as much humanism for the novel as can be got. If the traditional novel may, by the linearity and rigour of its plot and by authorial omniscience, seem to control and limit, the modernist one may, by the placing of character in long formal perspectives, tend to dehumanize, to ironize. Fowles has reason to claim his contemporaneity, but also some to question it; and both these things

I think he does. He knows his modernity, systematically, as a deep structure in consciousness; and his essential theme, the encounter of his heroes with the dreadful freedom pushed upon us out of history, supports his more flamboyant aesthetic pretensions. But his work has something of the air of forcing itself towards a formal self-consciousness of surface, rather than inherently needing it. So in *The French Lieutenant's Woman* one feels left, as I have said, with a sense of mystification. The realistic Victorian mode of the novel, in which Fowles seems capable of working at high intensity, is also represented as authoritarian and containing; the modern mode, which comports with Sarah's modernizing consciousness and also opens the door of formal opportunity, allows for unpredictability and contingency. Yet Fowles's real intensity of achievement lies above all in what he does in the former mode, and what he does there is only to be explained in terms of a realistic aesthetic that responds to the intensities created by living with the object or person the writer invents and develops. The larger framing apparatus has the air of being functional and enabling, and in some ways doesn't so much free the material as reify and distance it. The book actually succeeds, I suspect, on the level of its sheer impurity. Fowles is, in the end, an ethical novelist with a predilection for disguise; and he requires, clearly, many 'liberal' constituents in his novel which are not present in the formal wholeness of a novel by, say, Robbe-Grillet. His typical novel is perhaps a bridging enterprise, an aesthetic marriage of phrases of style. This may explain something of the oddity of *The Magus*, a rather more mysterious and I think commanding novel than *The French Lieutenant's Woman*, and therefore an excellent place to look at Fowles's tactics – and his distinction – in more detail.

II

The novelist today may feel himself under a growing need to present his fictions as fictive – because the problems of presenting the structure of a novel as authoritative or somehow co-equal with life are intensified and obscured where there are no communal myths or ethics; because in an age of prolix contingencies the novelist is hard put to it to give them in any necessary order. This self-consciousness he may represent by manifesting the unreality or the oddity of his own role as narrator; or he may delegate the function by creating the figure of a substitute artist who raises the problem. A number of modern fictions have therefore turned to the strategy of ambiguous revelation; there is within them a substitute author-figure who is both powerful and deceptive, the bearer of some supra-rational wisdom which he holds in quizzical status. The psychopomp figures of Iris Murdoch's early novels – Hugo Belfounder, Mischa Fox, Honor Klein – with their ambiguous philosophical or anthropological charisma, are much of this kind: voices of forces beyond and outside the familiar orders of society and its states of mind, possessors of ambiguous myths that yet contain both truth and falsehood. And this, it seems to me, is a primary premise of *The Magus*, a book in which a myth, a myth about consciousness and history, is offered to us, shown in its psychic power, yet questioned in its status – and the question touches the status of all fictions, including that of the novel we are reading. Fictions are not existence; hence an element of the charlatan exists in the novelist's own role. To some extent, then, *The Magus* is concerned with the familiar obsessions of modernism – with the hope that beyond the ordinary, contingent, and disillusioned world of real life there lies a meaning of fullness, balance, and regard for mystery, and the suspicion that this transcendent hope is one beyond life and time and therefore can only be a translucent, literary image. But it is also very much aware of the unsatisfactoriness of asserting simply a formal salvation, hope of redemption through an aesthetic unity. And Fowles does indeed manage to create the sense that his structures and obsessions are not borrowed properties but fulfil a logical need to consider how the imagination now may design, shape, and give meaning to the world.

The Magus begins in a world of familiar day-to-day reality; it shifts into a universe of theatrical mysteries; and it finally returns us to the day-to-day world conscious that the mysteries are not simply a theatrical extravaganza but a species of vision about our own needs and desires. Fowles does this by creating around his central character and first-person narrator, Nicholas Urfe, a vast and complicated psycho-drama enacted, at great and improbable expense, for his benefit. Urfe is a young man recently down from Oxford; a rationalist, an agnostic, and a hedonist, he also possesses poetic ambitions and a strong feeling of 'inauthenticity'. In London, unsure what to do with his future, he meets and begins living with an Australian girl named Alison. Nicholas, through the British Council, gets a post as schoolmaster on a Greek island, Phraxos, and sees this in a familiar philhellenic way as a possible route to a fuller life. It becomes clear that Alison has fallen in love with him, but Nicholas really doesn't want the entanglement and is indeed incapable of adjusting to it; he goes off to Greece with vague feelings of having won an emotional victory over her. But once he gets there and begins his job, sensations of isolated despair, deeper convictions of inauthenticity, and an increased knowledge of the deathly element within him bring him to the brink of suicide. But he stops short, insufficiently 'authentic' even for self-murder, and resigns himself to a condition of *mauvaise foi*.

Up to this point, the story, though well-presented, is a 'conventional' modern tale. But the mood of the book now changes, and another kind of action starts to develop. Nicholas comes across a villa in another part of the island and meets his Prospero figure – Maurice Conchis, its owner, reputed to have been a collaborator with the Germans and to have some strange influence over the school. At his villa, Conchis is surrounded by magnificent, if sometimes obscene, *objets d'art*; he has the air of possessing a pleasured and privileged view of the world; and his life seems vaguely to contain meanings somehow related to Nicholas's fortunes. On invitation, Urfe starts to spend most of his weekends at the villa. Gradually the mysteries he encounters there take on a sequential form; they become a vast and continuing drama. First Conchis introduces Urfe to pamphlets on science and witchcraft; he also begins telling stories about his own life which move through some of the basic historical events of the century – its changes in style and thought, its two world wars. At the same time these events suddenly start to be mysteriously recreated, first at a distance from Nicholas, then, more and more, around him, involving him and threatening him. A girl called Lily, a figure from Conchis's past life supposedly dead during the First World War, appears on the scene. Nicholas, trying to penetrate rationalistically to the truth about these fantasies, starts to provide himself with an explanation – 'Lily' is actually, as she reveals, an actress named Julie. But now that the masques begin to interlock with real life, what to begin with was a spectacle becomes a web around him.

Nicholas tries to break away from his involvement by going off to Athens, where he meets Alison again. But this is no solution; he rejects Alison for Lily – Julie, and does so basically because of the latter's role as an Edwardian girl, for she lies somewhere beyond the sexual directness of the 'androgynous twentieth-century mind'. (The same sort of trans-historical encounter appears, in reverse, as the main theme of *The French Lieutenant's Woman*, in the person of the 'modernized' Sarah Woodruff.)

When Nicholas gets back to the island again, he is much more involved in the power of the mysteries and begins to see a line through them; they are a kind of fable of the action of the godless twentieth-century mind, and also provide a field of symbols and insights that might indeed give it meaning. Shortly after this, Conchis reaches the culmination of his own story – his experiences with the Germans on the island during the Second World War. The Germans order him to kill three resistance fighters; if he does not, he and eighty hostages from the island will be killed. Conchis refuses, in a vision of freedom – a modern freedom which is 'beyond morality' but which 'sprang out of the very essence of things – that comprehended all, the freedom to do all, and stood against only one thing – the prohibition not to do all.' This idea of freedom is ambiguously left, as a force of transcendence and a power of destruction; it is placed in the modern world and the history of Europe; it is the theme of the fables that have gone before.

This seems to mark the end of the mysteries. The masques cease; the party appears to conclude. And Urfe claims Julie, whom he believes loves him. But the final movement of the story is concerned with the complete penetration of all that has gone before into Nicholas's own life and his 'real' world. Urfe is carried off as a prisoner to the Greek mainland and undergoes a mock-trial. The masque-makers have now emerged with disguises from myth and classical legend and cease to be figures from Conchis's personal history. Then in the course of the trial they take on new roles – they reveal themselves as social psychologists, conducting a vast experiment on Urfe, whose life they know in full detail and document in the language of neo-science. In a magnificent set-piece scene, Urfe is taunted with all his psychic weaknesses and portrayed by his tormentors as a characteristic and typically distorted personality type of the modern world – autoerotic, autopsychotic, repetitiously hostile, dependent on aggressive sexual relationships. A parodied withdrawal-therapy follows. Urfe is made to watch as Julie is shown to him in a pornographic film; then she makes love to a Negro in his presence. After all this, he is told by Conchis that he is now 'elect' – he is an initiate into the cruelty of freedom.

But Urfe, though released, is hardly set free of the web that has been built up around him. After being dismissed from his job, he goes to Athens and there sees Alison, who is also mysteriously assimilated into the Conchis world. So are most of his friends and acquaintances, most of his life; no individual is reliably out in the world of unmanipulated reality, and no past event in his life is free from intrusion. In the final scene of the book, Urfe is led back to Alison, who has been escaping him. The question remains, is she still within the world of the plot, or is she free of it? And has it been a plot against him, or a plot *for* him – a plot to lead him to wisdom? The final pages are ambiguous; we do not know whether Urfe has been saved or damned by his experiences, whether the mysterious powers have withdrawn or remain in his life, whether he accepts Alison or ends the novel in renewed isolation. Above all we are left doubtful about whether the masques and mysteries, which have been given such fictional density as an experience, are a diabolic trap or a species of recovery and revelation.

III

The Magus is generically a mythic novel or perhaps rather a romance, and this kind of fiction of the mysterious web has a long and honourable ancestry. Indeed, Fowles himself draws on a number of significant literary allusions. Conchis is Prospero, magician, psychopomp – the mysterious creator of mysteries, the symbolist of the world of the unseen, the agent of the supernatural, the psychic force that can lead us through to a new version of reality. He is a splendid impresario, rather like the figure of the author who appears, in his lavishly embroidered summer waistcoat, to spy on the agents of *The French Lieutenant's Woman*. But Fowles deals with him in an ambiguous way, though in a way not unfamiliar in much modern fiction. An obvious comparison can be made to Iris Murdoch, some of whose novels – *A Severed Head*, *The Unicorn*, and others – involve a mythic universe in which mystery suggests the problems of a lost order or structure not available in liberal-conventional notions of reality. Like Iris Murdoch, Fowles is clearly concerned not simply with mystery for its own sake, or the vague evocation of powers undreamt of in our philosophy, but with forces and structures that underlie our rational being, socio-psychic forces that are not readily registered in the fiction of documentary modes. In Iris Murdoch it is, I think, fairly evident that we are invited 'out' of society in order to see the powers which underpin it, powers which presume new relationships and new risks with selfhood that must by necessity be explored. The problem of the mode is that it characteristically involves a high degree of fictional faking, and there is a strong temptation for the novelist to create a sense of mystery and special insight which is no more than a numinously dramatic satisfaction, a building up of myth for its own splendid sake. Fowles obviously piles on the suspense by making Urfe at times less aware of what has to be going on than he should be, and the elaborate forgeries and ruses employed by Conchis require a kind of good luck to sustain the illusion which Fowles as novelist always grants.

Fowles's way of working the story is to make his reader identify with Urfe and so, to a considerable extent, to sustain his desire for a rational explanation, an unmasking of what Conchis calls his 'godgame'. Urfe belongs to the world of the real and ordinary, and he is a natural violator of myths; because he is cautious of being drawn into illusion the reader moves in with him when he does yield. In Urfe, then, Fowles catches many instincts, tones, obsessions and above all ambiguities in our culture – its distrust of myth, its sense of the validity of the real and familiar world, its suspicion of revelation and authority, yet also its desire for metaphor, its wish to transcend the environment which gives only a literal meaning, its search for density of being. All these things in Urfe – together with his appreciation of the more spacious relationships of the past, his sense of the possibility of being a limited psychic type – make him available as a neophyte for the world for which Conchis stands. But that world itself is caught equally well and with a like density and ambiguity. Conchis is on the one hand the higher rationalist, who comprehends all that Urfe knows and is one jump ahead – he unmasks the desire to unmask, he historically or psychologically locates the sentiments and fears amid which Urfe lives and finally does so in a language he understands. His 'godgame' is not only an exercise in timeless and traditional hermetic symbolism; it is also a masque and myth about contemporary history. He thus provides a structure for the comprehension of Urfe's world, though it is uncertain whether Urfe does or can accept it. His dark but ultimate wisdom – the wisdom of serene endurance, the wisdom of the archaic smile that holds experience complete and stands above it, and which is vouchsafed to Alison in the final scene – is enacted within the terms of modern experience. It has the prophetic pull of Honor Klein's dark wisdom in *A Severed Head*, and the same sense that it is a knowledge beyond the novel's capacity to register; only an image will do. The primary action is conducted in relation to a hero less far along life's path; and, as with *A Severed Head*, the rationalistic underpinning of day-to-day life, with its casual sexual relationships and its vague codes of personal relations, is left behind, yet without our knowing clearly what is put in its place.

But Conchis is of course not only the wise magician but also the faker, the sleight-of-hand artist enabled by his wealth, his gift of persuasion, and his mysterious authority to dominate and transform his environment. As Fowles's epigraph to the book suggests, the Magus is both the mountebank and, in the world of Tarot symbolism, the magician who operates the cards. The duplicity of role is structural to the book, though of course it also leaves it in an insoluble ambiguity; can a trick which reveals so much and costs so much in goods and spirit really be only a trick? And what, apart from fictive purposes, would be its point? Fowles leaves the interpretation open. If Conchis could be destroyed by Urfe's rational search, he would be nothing; in fact, he always dominates Urfe's world of 'reality' as well as the fantasy world which at first is all Urfe credits him with creating. But if he were the total mystic, his wisdom would have to be rare indeed; he would have to provide a total version of the modern world. What in fact he serves to do is to draw us towards transcendental images which lead us outside the world, yet create a sense that there is a density missing from the rational view of experience. It is evident, at the end – when it seems the watching eyes are withdrawn, the theatre in which Urfe has so long conducted his actions has disappeared, when he feels at once escape and loss of 'their' interest – that Urfe is the man in the Platonic myth of the cave in a modern variant: the man who has seen the real and then returned to life. The powers that he has seen are not, however, only those of art in its sense of an observed theatrical drama; they are those of art seen as psychic revelation. The dilemma it concludes with – that of how the orders and symbols which transcend life but also reveal and order it can really be mingled with it – is the dilemma of the artist himself, and it is in this sense that the book is a self-conscious inquiry into its own structure.

IV

So of course the real Magus in the novel is the novelist himself. The creation of myth in our modern employment of language is itself a precarious exercise. We use language to explore contingent reality and not to create systematic and numinous orders. But the rationalistic use of language (here roughly associated with Urfe) implies no logic, no structural unity. For realism and rationalism, our basic ways of making discourse, are a-mythic species of description; it is in this sense that we live in an age of No-Style. Fowles's purpose in the novel is therefore to create a context of illusion and a language of illusion which has the capacity to go beyond theatrical play and display and actually create structural myths. This, by confronting and connecting the world of rationalism and the world of illusion, feeding the former into the latter and then withdrawing it in its incompleteness, he does. Urfe's dilemma is at the beginning of the book that of loss of structure, and this he knows; that part of him which is the poet, the lover, and the man seeking a meaningful history of his age, in order that he might have an identity and an authenticity, seeks and values the Magus. And the Magus, whatever his deceptions, provides precisely that – a structure for feeling art, and history, which makes possible not only a fantastic world beyond 'reality' but art itself. In order to create this awareness, Fowles has in the book effectively to create another language or at least another order of notation. To do that, a large part of the action of the book has to develop in a world of feigning, convention, stylization, which we historically associate with high art, art as play and display. At one point in the action, Conchis makes a comment about novels: they are, he says, artefacts that make inferior orders. Fowles feeds the literal events of his novel into the hands of the myth-makers he has created within it, and so is able to create a sense of a higher artefact. But this of course leads him into a consciousness of the fictiveness of the enterprise; and if on the one hand he is able to make the shift from illusory theatricals to a suggestion of a more binding structure for modern experience, he must also sustain the fictiveness of that structure. It is in accomplishing this delicate balance, I think, that the success of the book lies – whatever its local failures. In an age of No-Style, this sort of painstaking yet finally questioned mythography is about as far as the novel can go; and this, I think, is the artistic encounter that must finally interest us in the book. It involves, that is, a real encounter between modern man and art, and does justice to the dilemmas of both. Fowles, then, not only registers the fictiveness of fiction, the spuriousness of structure, but also its inevitable claim and its psychic urgency, and he does this against modern history. In doing that, he shifts the resources of the current English novel in a significant way, and so manages to suggest the power fiction may still retain, to create fresh and inquisitive new alignments of experience.

SOURCE: Chapter 16 of *Possibilities* (London, 1973) pp. 256–71.

The essay originally appeared as a contribution to *Sense and Sensibility in Twentieth-Century Writing*, ed. Brom Weber (Carbondale, Ill., 1970).

NOTES

1. Richard Poirier, *The Performing Self: Compositions and Decompositions in the Languages of Contemporary Life* (London, 1971) pp. 27–44.

2. Erving Goffman, *The Presentation of Self in Everyday Life* (New York, 1959; London, 1969).

3. Robert Scholes, 'The Orgiastic Fiction of John Fowles', *The Hollins Critic*, VI 5 (Dec 1969) 1–12.

Raymond Williams

WESSEX AND THE BORDER (1973)

Thomas Hardy was born a few miles from Tolpuddle, a few years after the deportation of the farm labourers who had come together to form a trade union. This fact alone should remind us that Hardy was born into a changing and struggling rural society, rather than the timeless backwater to which he is so often deported. It reminds us also that he wrote in a period in which, while there were still local communities, there was also a visible and powerful network of the society as a whole: the law and the economy; the railways, newspapers and the penny post; a new kind of education and a new kind of politics.

The Hardy country is of course Wessex: that is to say mainly Dorset and its neighbouring counties. But the real Hardy country, we soon come to see, is that border country so many of us have been living in: between custom and education, between work and ideas, between love of place and an experience of change. There can be no doubt at all of Hardy's commitment to his own country, and in a natural way to its past, as we can see in his naming of Wessex. But his novels, increasingly, are concerned with change. They are set within the period from just before his own birth to the actual time when he was writing: the last and deepest novels, *Tess* and *Jude the Obscure*, are significantly the most contemporary. There is always a great deal in them of an old rural world: old in custom and in memory, but old also in a sense that belongs to the new times of conscious education, the oldness of history and indeed of prehistory: the educated consciousness of the facts of change. Within the major novels, in several different ways, the experiences of change and of the difficulty of choice are central and even decisive.

It is this centrality of change, and of the complications of change, that we miss when we see him as a regional novelist: the incomparable chronicler of his Wessex, the last voice of an old rural civilization. That acknowledgement, even that warm tribute, goes with a sense that the substance of his work is getting further and further away from us: that he is not a man of our world or the nineteenth-century world, but simply the last representative of old rural England or of the peasantry.

The very complicated feelings and ideas in Hardy's novels, including the complicated feelings and ideas about country life and people, belong very much in a continuing world. He writes more consistently and more deeply than any of our novelists about something that is still very close to us wherever we may be living: something that can be put, in abstraction, as the problem of the relation between customary and educated life; between customary and educated feeling and thought. This is the problem we saw in George Eliot and that we shall see again in Lawrence. It is the ground of their significant connection. . . .

In this characteristic world, rooted and mobile, familiar yet newly conscious and self-conscious, the figure of Hardy stands like a landmark. It is not from an old rural world or from a remote region that Hardy now speaks to us; but from the heart of a still active experience, of the familiar and the changing, which we can know as an idea but which is important finally in what come through as personal pressures – the making and failing of relationships, the crises of physical and mental personality – which Hardy as a novelist at once describes and enacts.

But of course we miss all this, or finding it we do not know how to speak of it and value it, if we have picked up, here and there, the tone of belittling Hardy. It is now very common.

When the ladies retired to the drawing-room I found myself sitting next to Thomas Hardy. I remember a little man with an earthy face. In his evening clothes, with his boiled shirt and high collar, he had still a strange look of the soil.[1]

This is Somerset Maugham, with one of his characteristic tales after dinner. It is a world, one may think, Hardy should never have got near; never have let himself be exposed to. But the tone and the response are significant, all the way from that dinner-table and that drawing-room to the 'look of the soil', in the rural distance. All the way, for some of us, to the land, the work, that comes up in silver as vegetables, or to the labour that enters that company – the customary civilized company – with what is seen as an earthy face. It is there again when Henry James speaks of 'the good little Thomas Hardy' or when F. R. Leavis says that *Jude the Obscure* is impressive 'in its clumsy way'.

A tone of social patronage, supported by crude and direct suppositions about origin, connects interestingly with a tone of literary patronage and in ways meant to be damaging with a strong and directing supposition about the substance of Hardy's fiction. If he was a countryman, a peasant, a man with the look of the soil, then this is the point of view, the essential literary standpoint, of the novels. That is to say the fiction is not only about Wessex peasants, it is by one of them who of course had managed to get a little (though hardly enough) education. Some discriminations of tone and fact have then to be made.

First, we had better drop 'peasants' altogether. Where Hardy lived and worked, as in most other parts of England, there were, as we have seen, virtually no peasants, although 'peasantry' as a generic word for country people was still used by writers. The actual country people were landowners, tenant farmers, dealers, craftsmen and labourers, and that social structure – the actual material, in a social sense, of the novels – is radically different, in its variety, its shading, and many of its basic human attitudes from the structure of a peasantry. Secondly, Hardy is none of these people. Outside his writing he was one of the many professional men who worked within this structure, often with uncertainty about where they really belonged in it. A slow gradation of classes is characteristic of capitalism anywhere, and of rural capitalism very clearly. Hardy's father was a builder who employed six or seven workmen.Hardy did not like to hear their house referred to as a cottage, because he was aware of this employing situation. The house is indeed quite small but there is a little window at the back through which the men were paid, and the cottages down the lane are certainly smaller. At the same time, on his way to school, he would see the mansion of Kingston Maurward (now fortunately an agricultural college) on which his father did some of the estate work, and this showed a sudden difference of degree which made the other distinction comparatively small though still not unimportant. In becoming an architect and a friend of the family of a vicar (the kind of family, also, from which his wife came) Hardy moved to a different point in the social structure, with connections to the educated but not the owning class and yet also with connections through his family to that shifting body of small employers, dealers, craftsmen and cottagers who were themselves never wholly distinct, in family, from the labourers.

Within his writing his position is similar. He is neither owner nor tenant, dealer nor labourer, but an observer and chronicler, often again with uncertainty about his actual relation. Moreover he was not writing for them, but about them, to a mainly metropolitan and unconnected literary public. The effect of these two points is to return attention to where it properly belongs, which is Hardy's attempt to describe and value a way of life with which he was closely yet uncertainly connected, and the literary methods which follow from the nature of this attempt. As so often when the current social stereotypes are removed the critical problem becomes clear in a new way.

It is the critical problem of so much of English fiction, since the actual yet incomplete and ambiguous social mobility of the nineteenth century. And it is a question of substance as much as of method. It is common to reduce Hardy's fiction to the impact of an urban alien on the 'timeless pattern' of English rural life. Yet though this is sometimes there the more common pattern is the relation between the changing nature of country living, determined as much by its own pressures as by pressures from 'outside', and one or more characters who have become in some degree separated from it yet who remain by some tie of family inescapably involved. It is here that the social values are dramatized in a very complex way and it is here that most of the problems of Hardy's actual writing seem to arise.

One small and one larger point may illustrate this argument, in a preliminary way. Nearly everyone seems to treat Tess as simply the passionate peasant girl seduced from outside, and it is then surprising to read quite early in the novel one of the clearest statements of what has become a classical experience of mobility:

Mrs Durbeyfield habitually spoke the dialect; her daughter, who had passed the Sixth Standard in the National School under a London-trained mistress, spoke two languages: the dialect at home, more or less; ordinary English abroad and to persons of quality.[2]

Grace in *The Woodlanders*, Clym in *The Return of the Native*, represent this experience more completely, but it is in any case a continuing theme, at a level much more important than the trivialities of accent. And when we see this we need not be tempted, as so often and so significantly in recent criticism, to detach *Jude the Obscure* as a quite separate kind of novel.

A more remarkable example of what this kind of separation means and involves is a description of Clym in *The Return of the Native* which belongs in a quite central way to the argument I traced in *Culture and Society*:

Yeobright loved his kind. He had a conviction that the want of most men was knowledge of a sort which brings wisdom rather than affluence. He wished to raise the class at the expense of individuals rather than individuals at the expense of the class. What was more, he was ready at once to be the first unit sacrificed.[3]

The idea of sacrifice relates in the whole action to the familiar theme of a vocation thwarted or damaged by a mistaken marriage, and we shall have to look again at this characteristic Hardy deadlock. But it relates also the general action of change which is a persistent social theme. As in all major realist fiction the quality and destiny of persons and the quality and destiny of a whole way of life are seen in the same dimension and not as separable issues. It is Hardy the observer who sets this context for personal failure:

In passing from the bucolic to the intellectual life the intermediate stages are usually two at least, frequently many more; and one of these stages is sure to be worldly advance. We can hardly imagine bucolic placidity quickening to intellectual aims without imagining social aims as the transitional phase. Yeobright's local peculiarity was that in striving at high thinking he still cleaved to plain living – nay, wild and meagre living in many respects, and brotherliness with clowns. He was a John the Baptist who took ennoblement rather than repentance for his text. Mentally he was in a provincial future, that is, he was in many points abreast with the central town thinkers of his date. . . . In consequence of this relatively advanced position, Yeobright might have been called unfortunate. The rural world was not ripe for him. A man should be only partially before his time; to be completely to the vanward in aspirations is fatal to fame. . . . A man who advocates aesthetic effort and deprecates social effort is only likely to be understood by a class to which social effort has become a stale matter. To argue upon the possibility of culture before luxury to the bucolic world may be to argue truly, but it is an attempt to disturb a sequence to which humanity has been long accustomed.[4]

The subtlety and intelligence of this argument from the late 1870s come from a mind accustomed to relative and historical thinking, not merely in the abstract, as he learned from Mill or from Darwin, but in the process of observing a personal experience of mobility. This is not country against town, or even in any simple way custom against conscious intelligence. It is the more complicated and more urgent historical process in which education is tied to social advancement within a class society, so that it is difficult, except by a bizarre personal demonstration, to hold both to education and to social solidarity ('he wished to raise the class'). It is the process also in which culture and affluence come to be recognized as alternative aims, at whatever cost to both, and the wry recognition that the latter will always be the first choice, in any real history.

The relation between the migrant and his former group is then exceptionally complicated. His loyalty drives him to actions which the group can see no sense in, its overt values supporting the association of education with personal advancement which his new group has already made but which for that very reason he cannot accept.

'I am astonished, Clym. How can you want to do better than you've been doing?'

'But I hate that business of mine . . . I want to do some worthy things before I die.'

'After all the trouble that has been taken to give you a start, and when there is nothing to do but keep straight on towards affluence, you say you . . . it disturbs me, Clym, to find you have come home with such thoughts . . . I hadn't the least idea you meant to go backward in the world by you own free choice . . .

'I cannot help it,' said Clym, in a troubled tone.

'Why can't you do . . . as well as others?

'I don't know, except that there are many things other people care for which I don't . . .'

'And yet you might have been a wealthy man if you had only persevered . . . I suppose you will be like your father. Like him, you are getting weary of doing well.'

'Mother, what is doing well?'[5]

The question is familiar but still after all these years no question is more relevant or more radical. Within these complex pressures the return of the native has a certain inevitable nullity, and his only possible overt actions can come to seem merely perverse. Thus the need for social identification with the labourers produces Clym's characteristic negative identification with them; becoming a labourer himself and making his original enterprise that much more difficult: 'the monotony of his occupation soothed him, and was in itself a pleasure'. . . .

Hardy's writing, or what in abstraction can be called his style, is obviously affected by the crisis – the return of the native – which I have been describing. We know that he was worried about his prose and was reduced by the ordinary educated assumptions of his period to studying Defoe, Fielding, Addison, Scott and *The Times*, as if they could have helped him. His complex position as an author, writing about

country living to people who almost inevitably saw the country as
empty nature or as the working-place of their inferiors, was in any case
critical in this matter of language. What have been seen as his
strengths – the ballad form of narrative, the prolonged literary imitation of traditional forms of speech – seem to me mainly weaknesses.
This sort of thing is what his readers were ready for: a 'tradition' rather
than human beings. The devices could not in any case serve his major
fiction where it was precisely disturbance rather than continuity which
had to be communicated. It would be easy to relate Hardy's problem of
style, to the two languages of Tess: the consciously educated and the
unconsciously customary. But this comparison, though suggestive, is
inadequate, for the truth is that to communicate Hardy's experience
neither language would serve, since neither in the end was sufficiently
articulate: the educated dumb in intensity and limited in humanity; the
customary thwarted by ignorance and complacent in habit. The marks
of a surrender to each mode are certainly present in Hardy but the main
body of his mature writing is a more difficult and complicated
experiment. For example:

The season developed and matured. Another year's instalment of flowers,
leaves, nightingales, finches, and such ephemeral creatures, took up their
positions where only a year ago others had stood in their place when these were
nothing more than germs and inorganic particles. Rays from the sunrise drew
forth the buds and stretched them into long stalks, lifted up sap in noiseless
streams, opened petals, and sucked out scents in invisible jets and breathings.
    Dairyman Crick's household of maids and men lived on comfortably,
placidly, even merrily. Their position was perhaps the happiest of all positions
in the social scale, being above the line at which neediness ends, and below the
line at which the *convenances* began to cramp natural feeling, and the stress of
threadbare modishness makes too little of enough.
    Thus passed the leafy time when arborescence seems to be the one thing
aimed at out of doors. Tess and Clare unconsciously studied each other, ever
balanced on the edge of a passion, yet apparently keeping out of it. All the while
they were converging, under an irresistible law, as surely as two streams in one
vale.[6]

This passage is neither the best nor the worst of Hardy. Rather it shows
the many complicated pressures working within what had to seem a
single intention. 'The leafy time when arborescence' is an example of
inflation to an 'educated' style, but the use of '*convenances*', which might
appear merely fashionable, carries a precise feeling. 'Instalment' and

'ephemeral' are also uses of a precise kind, within a sentence which shows mainly the strength of what must be called an educated point of view. The consciousness of the natural process, in 'germs and inorganic particles' (he had of course learned it from Darwin who with Mill was his main intellectual influence) is a necessary accompaniment, for Hardy's purpose, of the more direct and more enjoyed sights and scents of spring. It is loss not gain when Hardy reverts to the simpler and cruder abstraction of 'Dairyman Crick's household of maids and men', which might be superficially supposed to be the countryman speaking but is actually the voice of the detached observer at a low level of interest. The more fully Hardy uses the resources of the whole language, as a precise observer, the more adequate the writing is. There is more strength in 'unconsciously studied each other', which is at once educated and engaged, than in the 'two streams in one vale', which shared with the gesture of 'irresistible law' a synthetic quality, here as of a man playing the countryman novelist.

Hardy's mature style is threatened in one direction by a willed 'Latinism' of diction or construction, of which very many particular instances can be collected (and we have all done it, having taken our education hard), but in the other direction by this much less noticed element of artifice which is too easily accepted, within the patronage we have discussed, as the countryman speaking (sometimes indeed it is literally the countryman speaking, in a contrived picturesqueness which is now the novelist's patronage of his rural characters). The mature style itself is unambiguously an educated style, in which the extension of vocabulary and the complication of construction are necessary to the intensity and precision of the observation which is Hardy's essential position and attribute.

The grey tones of daybreak are not the grey half-tones of the day's close, though the degree of their shade may be the same. In the twilight of the morning, light seems active, darkness passive; in the twilight of evening, it is the darkness which is active and crescent, and the light which is the drowsy reverse.[7]

This is the educated observer, still deeply involved with the world he is watching, and the local quality of this writing is the decisive tone of the major fiction.

The complication is that this is a very difficult and exposed position for Hardy to maintain. Without the insights of consciously learned history and of the educated understanding of nature and behaviour he cannot really observe at all, at a level of extended human respect. Even the sense of what is now called the 'timeless' – in fact the sense of history, of the barrows, the Roman remains, the rise and fall of families, the tablets and monuments in the churches – is, as I have said, a function of education. That real perception of tradition is available only to the man who has read about it, though what he then sees through it is his native country, to which he is already deeply bound by memory and experience of another kind: a family and a childhood; an intense association of people and places, which has been his own history. To see tradition in both ways is indeed Hardy's special gift: the native place and experience but also the education, the conscious inquiry. Yet then to see living people, within this complicated sense of past and present, is another problem again. He sees as a participant who is also an observer; this is the source of the strain. For the process which allows him to observe is very clearly in Hardy's time one which includes, in its attachment to class feelings and class separations, a decisive alienation.

If these two noticed Angel's growing social ineptness, he noticed their growing mental limitations. Felix seemed to him all Church; Cuthbert all College. His Diocesan Synod and Visitations were the mainsprings of the world to the one; Cambridge to the other. Each brother candidly recognized that there were a few unimportant scores of millions of outsiders in civilized society, persons who were neither University men nor Churchmen; but they were to be tolerated rather than reckoned with and respected.[8]

This is what is sometimes called Hardy's bitterness, but in fact it is only sober and just observation. What Hardy sees and feels about the educated world of his day, locked in its deep social prejudices and in its consequent human alienation, is so clearly true that the only surprise is that critics now should still feel sufficiently identified with that world – the world which coarsely and coldly dismissed Jude and millions of other men – to be willing to perform the literary equivalent of that stalest of political tactics: the transfer of bitterness, of a merely class way of thinking, from those who exclude to those who protest. But the isolation which can follow, while the observer holds to educated procedures but is unable to feel with the existing educated class, is severe. It is not the countryman awkward in his town clothes but the more significant tension – of course with its awkwardness and its spurts of bitterness and nostalgia – of the man caught by his personal history in the general crisis of the relations between education and class, relations which in practice are between intelligence and fellow-feeling. As he observes the Clare brothers: 'Perhaps, as with many men, their opportunities of observation were not so good as their opportunities of expression.'[9] That after all is the nullity, in a time in which education is used to train members of a class and to divide them from other men as surely as from their own passions (for the two processes are deeply connected). Hardy can see it as a process in others, in a class, but the real history of his writing is that he knew, in himself, the experience of separation: a paradoxical separation, for a more common experience was still close and real.

It is with this complex pressure in mind that we must look at the country which Hardy was describing. He could respond so closely because his own mobility was in a mobile and changing society. It is how he saw others, in his fine essay on the *Dorsetshire Labourer* (which can be compared with Jefferies' on the *Wiltshire Labourer*): 'They are losing their individuality, but they are widening the range of their ideas, and gaining in freedom. It is too much to expect them to remain stagnant and old-fashioned for the pleasure of romantic spectators.'[10] This double movement, of loss and liberation, of exposure and of advantage, is the characteristic he shares with his actual rural world. 'A modern Wessex of railways, the penny post, mowing and reaping machines, union workhouses, lucifer matches, labourers who could read and write, and National school children.'[11]

The point is not only Hardy's recognition of this modernity, but the fact that virtually every feature of it that he lists preceded his own life (the railway came to Dorchester when he was a child of seven). The effects of the changes of course continued, and the complex effects of the movement of the general economy with its contrasting effects on different areas and sections of a rural society from which there was still a general movement to the towns, worked their slow way through. The country was not timeless but it was not static either; indeed, it is because the change was long (and Hardy knew it was long) that the crisis took its particular forms. It was with a fine detail, seeing the general effects from the society as a whole but also the internal processes and their complicated effects on the rural social structure, that Hardy recorded and explained this process, as here in *Tess*:

All the mutations so increasingly discernible in village life did not originate entirely in the agricultural unrest. A depopulation was also going on. The village had formerly contained, side by side with the agricultural labourers, an interesting and better-informed class, ranking distinctly above the former – the class to which Tess's father and mother had belonged – and including the carpenter, the smith, the shoemaker, the huckster, together with nondescript workers other than farm-labourers; a set of people who owed a certain stability of aim and conduct to the fact of their being life-holders like Tess's father, or copy-holders, or, occasionally, small freeholders. But as the long holdings fell in they were seldom again let to similar tenants, and were mostly pulled down, if not absolutely required by the farmer for his hands. Cottagers who were not directly employed on the land were looked upon with disfavour, and the banishment of some starved the trade of others, who were thus obliged to follow. These families, who had formed the backbone of the village life in the past, who were the depositaries of the village traditions, had to seek refuge in the larger centres; the process, humorously designated by statisticians as 'the tendency of the rural population towards the large towns' being really the tendency of water to flow uphill when forced by machinery.[12]

Here there is something much more than the crude and sentimental version of the rape of the country by the town. The originating pressures within rural society itself are accurately seen, and are given a human and social rather than a mechanical dimension.

Indeed we miss almost all of what Hardy has to show us if we impose on the actual relationships he describes, a neo-pastoral convention of the countryman as an age-old figure, or a vision of a prospering countryside being disintegrated by Corn Law repeal or the railways or agricultural machinery. It is not only, for example, that Corn Law repeal and the cheap imports of grain made less difference to Dorset: a county mainly of grazing and mixed farming in which the coming of the railway gave a direct commercial advantage in the supply of milk to London: the economic process described with Hardy's characteristic accuracy in *Tess*:

They reached the feeble light, which came from the smoky lamp of a little railway station; a poor enough terrestrial star, yet in one sense of more importance to Talbothays Dairy and mankind than the celestial ones to which it stood in such humiliating contrast. The cans of new milk were unladen in the rain, Tess getting a little shelter from a neighbouring holly tree. . . .
. . . ' Londoners will drink it at their breakfasts tomorrow, won't they?' she asked. 'Strange people that we have never seen? . . . who don't know anything of us, and where it comes from, or think how we two drove miles across the moor tonight in the rain that it might reach 'em in time?'[13]

The new real connection, and yet within it the discontinuities of knowledge and of condition, are the specific forms of this modern rural world. What happened now in the economy as a whole, in an increasingly organized urban and industrial market, had its partly blind effects – a new demand here, collapse and falling prices elsewhere – on an essentially subordinated and now only partial domestic rural economy. But the market forces which moved and worked at a distance were also deeply based in the rural economy itself: in the system of rent and trade; in the hazards of ownership and tenancy; in the differing conditions of labour on good and bad land, or in socially different villages (as in the contrast between Talbothays and Flintcomb Ash); and in what happened to people and to families in the interaction between general forces and personal histories – that complex area of ruin or survival, exposure or continuity. This was Hardy's actual society, and we cannot suppress it in favour of a seamless abstracted 'country way of life'. . . .

One of the most immediate effects of mobility, within a structure itself changing, is the difficult nature of the marriage choice. This situation keeps recurring in terms which are at once personal and social: Bathsheba choosing between Boldwood and Oak; Grace between Giles and Fitzpiers; Jude between Arabella and Sue. The specific class element, and the effects upon this of an insecure economy, are parts of the personal choice which is after all a choice primarily of a way to live, of an identity in the identification with this or that other person. And here significantly the false marriage (with which Hardy is so regularly and deeply concerned) can take place either way: to the educated coldness of Fitzpiers or to the coarseness of Arabella. Here most dramatically the condition of the internal migrant is profoundly known. The social alienation enters the personality and destroys its capacity for any loving fulfilment. The marriage of Oak and Bathsheba is a case of eventual stability, after so much disturbance, but even that has an air of inevitable resignation and lateness. It is true that Hardy, under pressure, sometimes came to generalize and project these very specific failures into a fatalism for which in the decadent thought of his time the phrases were all too ready. In the same way, seeing the closeness of man and the land being broken by the problems of working the land, he sometimes projected his insistence on closeness and continuity into the finally negative images of an empty nature and the tribal past of Stonehenge and the barrows, where the single observer, at least, could feel a direct flow of knowledge. Even these, however, in their deliberate hardness – the uncultivable heath, the bare stone relics – confirm the human negatives, in what looks like a deliberate reversal of pastoral. In them the general alienation has its characteristic monuments, though very distant in time and space from the controlling immediate disturbance.

But the most significant thing about Hardy, in and through these difficulties, is that more than any other major novelist since this difficult mobility began he succeeded, against every pressure, in centring his major novels in the ordinary processes of life and work. It is this that is missed when in the service of an alienating total view – an abstraction of rural against urban forces – what he deliberately connected is deliberately taken apart. The best-known case is the famous description, in *Tess*, of the threshing-machine, which has often been abstracted to argue that the essential movement of the fiction is alien industrialism against rural humanity:

Close under the eaves of the stack, and as yet barely visible, was the red tyrant that the women had come to serve – a timber-framed construction, with straps and wheels appertaining – the threshing machine which, whilst it was going, kept up a despotic demand upon the endurance of their muscles and nerves.
A little way off there was another indiscreet figure; this one black, with a sustained hiss that spoke of strength very much in reserve. The long chimney running up beside an ash-tree, and the warmth which radiated from the spot, explained without the necessity of much daylight that here was the engine which was to act as the primum mobile of this little world. By the engine stood a dark motionless being, a sooty and grimy embodiment of tallness, in a sort of trance, with a heap of coals by his side: it was the engineman. The isolation of his manner and colour lent him the appearance of a creature from Tophet, who had strayed into the pellucid smokelessness of this region of yellow grain and pale soil, with which he had nothing in common, to amaze and to discompose its aborigines.[14]

But this powerful vision of an alien machine must not blind us to the fact that this is also an action in a story – the action of a real threshing-machine. It stands in that field and works those hours because it has been hired, not by industrialism but by a farmer. And there are whole human beings trying to keep up with it and with him:

Thus the afternoon dragged on. The wheat-rick shrank lower, and the straw-rick grew higher, and the corn-sacks were carted away.

At six o'clock the wheat-rick was about shoulder-high from the ground. But the unthreshed sheaves remaining untouched seemed countless still, notwith-standing the enormous numbers which had been gulped down by the insatiable swallower, fed by the man and Tess, through whose two young hands the greater part of them had passed. . . .

. . . A panting ache ran through the rick. The man who fed was weary, and Tess could see that the red nape of his neck was encrusted with dirt and husks. She still stood at her post, her flushed and perspiring face coated with the corn-dust, and her white bonnet embrowned by it. She was the only woman whose place was upon the machine so as to be shaken bodily by its spinning, and the decrease of the stack now separated her from Marian and Izz, and prevented their changing duties with her as they had done. The incessant quivering, in which every fibre of her frame participated, had thrown her into a stupefied reverie in which her arms worked on independently of her consciousness.[15]

We can see here the relation to Crabbe, in the attention to the faces and the bodies of labourers, but also the development from him: the decisive development to an individuation which yet does not exclude the common condition. For this is Tess the girl and the worker: the break between her consciousness and her actions is as much a part of her emotional as of her working life. It is while she is working, here and elsewhere, that her critical emotional decisions are taken; it is through the ache and dust of the threshing-machine that she again sees Alec. Hardy thus achieves a fullness which is quite new, at this depth, in all country writing: the love and the work, the aches of labour and of choice, are in a single dimension.

Nor is this only an emphasis of pressure or of pain. Hardy often sees labour, with a fine insight, as a central kind of learning and relationship:

They had planted together, and together they had felled; together they had, with the run of the years, mentally collected those remoter signs and symbols which seen in few are of runic obscurity, but all together made an alphabet. From the light lashing of the twigs upon their faces when brushing through them in the dark, they could pronounce upon the species of tree whence they stretched; from the quality of the wind's murmur through a bough, they could in like manner name its sort afar off.[16]

This, from *The Woodlanders*, is the language of the immediate apprehen-sion of 'nature', but it is also more specifically the language of shared work, in 'the run of the years'. Feeling very acutely the long crisis of separation, and in the end coming to more tragically isolated catas-trophes than any others within this tradition, he yet created continually the strength and the warmth of people living together: in work and in love; in the physical reality of a place.

To stand working slowly in a field, and feel the creep of rainwater, first in legs and shoulders, then on hips and head, then at back, front, and sides, and yet to work on till the leaden light diminishes and marks that the sun is down, demands a distinct modicum of stoicism, even of valour. Yet they did not feel the wetness so much as might be supposed. They were both young, and they were talking of the time when they lived and loved together at Talbothays Dairy, that happy green tract of land where summer had been liberal in her gifts: in substance to all, emotionally to these.[17]

The general structure of feeling in Hardy would be much less convincing if there were only the alienation, the frustration, the separation and isolation, the final catastrophes. What is defeated but not destroyed at the end of *The Woodlanders* or the end of *Tess* or the end of *Jude* is a warmth, a seriousness, an endurance in love and work that are the necessary definition of what Hardy knows and mourns as loss. Vitally – and it is his difference from Lawrence, as we shall see; a difference of generation and of history but also of character – Hardy does not celebrate isolation and separation. He mourns them, and yet always with the courage to look them steadily in the face. The losses are real and heartbreaking because the desires were real, the shared work was real, the unsatisfied impulses were real. Work and desire are very deeply connected in his whole imagination. The passion of Marty or of Tess or of Jude is a positive force coming out of a working and relating world; seeking in different ways its living fulfilment. That all are frustrated is the essential action: frustrated by very complicated processes of division, separation and rejection. People choose wrongly but under terrible pressures: under the confusions of class, under its misunderstandings, under the calculated rejections of a divided separating world.

   It is important enough that Hardy keeps to an ordinary world, as the basis of his major fiction. The pressures to move away from it, to enter a more negotiable because less struggling and less divided life, were of course very strong. And it is even more important, as an act of pure affirmation, that he stays, centrally, with his central figures; indeed moves closer to them in his actual development, so that the affirmation of Tess and of Jude – an affirmation in and through the defeats he traces and mourns – is the strongest in all his work.

'Slighted and enduring': not the story of man as he was, distant, limited, picturesque; but slighted in a struggle to grow – to love, to work with meaning, to learn and to teach; enduring in the community of this impulse, which pushes through and beyond particular separations and defeats. It is the continuity not only of a country but of a history and a people.

SOURCE: extracts from chapter 18 of *The Country and the City* (London, 1973) pp. 239–40, 241–6, 247–53, 255–8.

NOTES

1. In Preface to *Cakes and Ale* (1970).
2. *Tess of the D'Urbervilles*, ch. 3.
3. *The Return of the Native*, Book Third, ch. 2.
4. Ibid.
5. Ibid.
6. *Tess of the D'Urbervilles*, ch. 20.
7. Ibid.
8. Ibid., ch. 25.
9. Ibid.
10. Repr. in *Hardy's Personal Writings*, ed. H. Orel (London, 1967) p. 181
11. From the Preface to *Far from the Madding Crowd*.
12. *Tess of the D'Urbervilles*, ch. 51.
13. Ibid., ch. 30.
14. Ibid., ch. 47.
15. Ibid., ch. 48.
16. *The Woodlanders*, ch. 44.
17. *Tess of the D'Urbervilles*, ch. 43.

David Craig

FICTION AND THE 'RISING INDUSTRIAL CLASSES' (1973)

One of the more massive tasks to which the nineteenth-century novelists rose with such energy and plenitude of imagination was making sense of the more far-flung and powerful social forces that reach into the lives of all of us. The contemporary changes in living were so fast, they embroiled such quantities of peoples and materials and forced elements so new and disquieting onto the attention, that the writers, for all their energy and plenitude, tended to fall back on methods suited to the much smaller units that hitherto had been their natural scene – the village, the family, the big house. The smaller the unit and the more domestic the life, the more easily it could be managed by the masterful or goodhearted individual (or undermined by a single fiend or villain). Hence the unreal manipulations so often brought in to resolve the ramifications of a novel by Scott or Dickens or Tolstoy or George Eliot. As John B. Mitchell puts it:

This formal plot element . . . becomes more and more dominant as the book nears its end, while the social critique, though still remaining strong, becomes more and more a by-product of the formal plot. So, artistically, the latter sections of Dickens's novels (for that matter it seems to me the last sections of the vast majority of eighteenth or nineteenth-century English novels) tend to fall considerably short of the rest of the book.[1]

If the critic fails to recognise this – both the phenomenon and its cause – he is left with no way of either defining or explaining the weaknesses that follow, in novels that have set themselves large subjects, from pivoting too wide a significance on personal relations between individuals. For example here are the conclusions (in a run-together form) of a recent study of *Bleak House*, 'acquisitiveness', and the 'rising industrial classes':

Rosa (standing for reinvigorated tradition) is united with honourable industrialism. It is a human solution to a rivalry of powers. The sins of the 'fathers' are resolved in and through love. Dickens's emblematic marriage, although perfectly at home at the level of character, suggests a solution to the urgent problems of the time. Provided the personal relationship is right, it will spread out and cleanse society. It will oil Chancery procedure, invigorate Parliament, reform slum landlords, and make telescopic philanthropists re-align their sights. Dickens does not show us a system actually reformed but we are meant to recognise that the varieties of System will get cured of their constrictive or self-regarding ailments as soon as a personal love directs itself outward socially. Dickens knows, on the realistic level, that in fact one tyranny is competing with another; but he has offered his social diagnosis elsewhere in *Bleak House*. The union of Rosa and Watt signifies his social prescription.[2]

This seems to waver between recognising the fallacies of overpersonalising a large social situation and falling into them. Mr Blount's first use of 'resolved' is all right since it refers only to the rounding off of the work of art, but when it turns into a 'solution', and to the urgent problems of the time no less, the fallacy has come in, since this can only mean that someone (whether Dickens or Mr Blount) does believe that, somehow, more individual efforts at friendliness, between strategically right parties, could reform a heartless social order and that, if one believed so, one could work in a practical way towards that end. This is such arrant wishful thinking that it is then half withdrawn – Dickens 'does not show us a system actually reformed', he knows that 'in fact one tyranny is competing with another'. But a final effort to clinch the question of whether personal relations could possibly be managed so as to better society – or, if not, what else could – is then fudged, or shelved, by the phrase 'on the realistic level'. If Dickens did know on the realistic level that in his society one tyranny (the hereditary landlords, the Dedlocks) was competing with another (the new industrial capitalists, the Rouncewells), it was presumably on the unrealistic level that he suggested his social prescription of a spreading, cleansing personal love. In that case, what is left of his suggestion, as anything like a serious effort to understand modern society, that love could melt or wish away exploitation and acquisitiveness?

Some such fallacy has so hovered round the discussion of literary and social matters alike that the question can best be taken further through a novel that leads directly from matters of literary treatment to the main history of the industrial epoch – George Eliot's *Felix Holt* (1866), subtitled 'The Radical', another important book from the decades which followed the Hungry Forties and the start of the 'second Industrial Revolution'. Chapter 30 of *Felix Holt*, like the chapter of Lawrence's *Women in Love* called 'The Industrial Magnate', opens out endless perspectives into those lines of social development that have brought us to where we are now. It presents, in the speeches of the nameless trade-unionist and of Felix at an election meeting, two kinds of radicalism: the first a rendering of what must have been said on many a platform from about 1815 onwards, and the second George Eliot's own kind of ardent humanism. The workman's speech is the most plausible and telling political utterance I know of in our literature,[3] and from the first images of the man we sense that we are getting the real thing: 'a grimy man in a flannel shirt, hatless and with turbid red hair, who was insisting on political points with much more ease than had seemed to belong to the gentlemen speakers on the hustings', his 'bare arms . . . powerfully muscular, though he had the pallid complexion of a man who lives chiefly amidst the heat of furnaces'. The man's speaking style is equally well done, over a stretch of several pages: it has the momentum, the insistences and repetitions, the immediate striking-power which are indispensable if such utterance is to carry across. This quality of writing shows George Eliot to have been quite unusually open to the view point, idiom, and whole culture of the underdog and militant mass-representative. But her final sympathy is not with this man.

His speech is written to show him as a fully enlightened spokesman for his class: he doesn't care only for immediate party ends:

'It isn't a man's share just to mind your pin-making, or your glass-blowing, and higgle about your wages, and bring up your family to be ignorant sons of ignorant fathers, and no better prospect; that's a slave's share; we want a freeman's share, and that is to think and speak and act about what concerns us all, and see whether these fine gentlemen who undertake to govern us are doing the best they can for us. They've got the knowledge, say they. Very well, we've got the wants. . . .'

Just before this Felix has given a loud 'Hear hear!' and the crowd have looked round at him with his 'well-washed face and educated expression'. The speaker then puts his main arguments for democratic control over the legislature – in which he echoes Gerrard Winstanley the Digger's classic appeal for justice *in this life* – and ends with a point that roots the speech perfectly in real politics. He has attacked the ruling-class, but in that post-1832 pre-1867 England he must make do with a member of it as his representative: hence the business-like bluntness with which he ends up, 'And if any of you have acquaintance among county voters, give 'em a hint that you wish 'em to vote for Transome', and he steps down from the stone and quickly walks off.

The whole thing is so right and complete that one can't think of anything (except perhaps more responses from the crowd) that is either necessary or plausible for the dramatic rendering of such a piece of life from such a time. The author's clinching comment, however, in introducing the immediately following speech, is that Felix's expression 'was something very different from the mere acuteness and rather hard-lipped antagonism of the trades-union man'. These phrases are in themselves perfectly apt; what is not acceptable is the implication that there was some finer alternative attitude which could replace or seriously compete with that kind of militancy. The state of social struggle at that time was such that *only* antagonism, allied to acuteness, could conceivably have made any headway in quickening people to a sense of all they lacked. This was the age in which the miners were moulding bullets in their cottages and the government was building barracks all over England because it could no longer trust the soldiers not to be subverted if they were lodged in billets.[4] It was the age in which a wave of slump was liable to throw one-third of the workers in a textile town into pauperdom.[5] When the people gathered to protest against these conditions, they were attacked and sabred by men of Harold Transome's class – the gentleman-volunteers at Peterloo. When things have reached such a pass, hard-lipped antagonism is so irresistibly wished upon people of spirit that to try and base one's ideal 'above it all' is to place veils between oneself and reality.

Unreality is indeed what mainly tinges the image of Felix in what follows. He wears a working man's brown velveteens but the author is careful to make him an odd man out, 'with a dress more careless than that of most well-to-do workmen on a holiday', and this oddity she of course presents as a virtue. This virtue is not one which she is able to ground in convincingly-rendered mien, behaviour, or speech:

Even lions and dogs know a distinction between men's glances; and doubtless those Duffield men, in the expectation with which they looked up at Felix, were unconsciously influenced by the grandeur of his full yet firm mouth, and the calm clearness of his grey eyes, which were yet somehow unlike what they were accustomed to see along with an old brown velveteen coat, and an absence of chin-propping. When he began to speak, the contrast of voice was still stronger than that of appearance. The man in the flannel shirt had not been heard – had probably not cared to be heard – beyond the immediate group of listeners. But Felix at once drew the attention of persons comparatively at a distance.

We are not told by what mesmerism or miracle of elocution Felix draws people from afar. The association of 'clear' eyes with moral loftiness is of course sentimental pot-boiler's stock-in-trade, and that blurred 'some-how' is quite unlike George Eliot's typical good prose. It is vague in order to be evasive, and what she is evading is saying, with the open snobbery of an ordinary 'lady novelist', that Felix has the supposed virtues of a 'gentleman' in spite of his 'low origins'. The alleged 'grandeur' of his presence is not done in words that bring to the mind's senses an image anything like solid enough to bear the moral weight laid on it. In the speech itself, as in all Felix's dialogue, proletarian directness is meant to be done by the occasional homely phrase, 'he pours milk into a can without a bottom' and the like. But the run of the speech, especially the prearranged syntax and smoothly sequential linking of the sentences, doesn't suggest any kind of utterable English, unlike the trade-unionist's speech in which one phrase triggers off another. What Felix comes out with is really Victorian printed homily. It might be argued that a self-educated Victorian artisan would in fact have expressed himself rather stiffly. But this is not pointed up in any way, it is not distinctly marked off from the author's own moralising prose, and the effect in dramatic terms, especially coming after the lifelike trade-unionist, is to shrink Felix's speech to the status of a message coming at us direct from the author.

This message is that the vote (and the other democratic demands then being put by the Chartists) matters little unless 'men's passions, feelings, desires' can be refined:

'That's very fine,' said a man in dirty fustian, with a scornful laugh. 'But how are we to get the power without votes?'
'I'll tell you what's the greatest power under heaven,' said Felix, 'and that is public opinion – the ruling belief in society about what is right and what is wrong, what is honourable and what is shameful. . . . How can political freedom make us better, any more than a religion that we don't believe in, if people laugh and wink when they see men abuse and defile it? And while public opinion is what it is – while corruption is not felt to be a damning disgrace – while men are not ashamed in Parliament and out of it to make public questions which concern the welfare of millions a mere screen for their

own petty private ends, – I say, no fresh scheme of voting will much help men in our condition. . . .'

and he goes off on a denunciation of 'treating' voters till they are too drunk to know what they're doing and vote for the men who brought them the beer. It is a sorry anti-climax after the building up of Felix as a saviour and sole mouthpiece of the redeeming truth. Studies of mid-nineteenth-century voting suggest that fear of eviction was often a more potent influence than the treating. But the paramount factor here, which George Eliot manages to evade, is that corruption was petty compared with the fundamental class bias in the political system. Insofar as Felix is arguing that the trade unions 'expected voting to do more' towards an equal society than it possibly could, we can agree, for the mass of people had largely helped towards a middle-class hegemony in society by allowing their own power to be channelled into the struggle to enfranchise the £10 householders. As the most penetrating contemporary journalist put it, 'They had united all *property* against all *poverty*.'[6] But Felix is shaped to embody quite a different sort of protest. He stands for a moral betterment that is above mere politics, and thus he has behind him the wishful liberalism of George Eliot's tradition. In this respect it is only the distinction of her style that sets her off from the claptrap typified by Charles Kingsley in *Alton Locke* (1850), a novel expressly aimed at removing politics to the realm of pious philanthropy:

'Yes,' she continued, 'Freedom, Equality, and Brotherhood are here. Realise them in thine own self, and so alone thou helpest to make them realities for all. Not from without, from Charters and Republics, but from within, from the Spirit working in each; not by wrath and haste, but by patience made perfect through suffering, canst thou proclaim their good news to the groaning masses, and deliver them, as thy Master did before thee, by the cross, and not the sword.[7]

The unreality of the position shows through in Felix's promise that 'if you go the right way to work you may get power sooner without votes'. All this could mean in practice would be something like syndicalism, and of course George Eliot does not mean that! – any more than Felix actually produces his 'right way' in the course of the novel. All George Eliot can offer, through Felix, is high-mindedness, unrooted in any particular activity or movement.

This was not only preachifying in mid-air. In its place and time it ignored the crucial truth, more and more evident as each political phase wore on, that the struggle for the vote and other democratic rights was itself a deep-reaching force for moral growth. This was seen early on, by Francis Place the tailor, who knew the campaign for the 1832 Reform from the inside. In that year he wrote that militancy 'has impressed the morals and manners, and elevated the character of the working-man. . . . In every place as reform has advanced, drunkenness has retreated.'[8] Place of course did not make speeches on the moral insignificance of the franchise but worked for it with every ounce of his devotion and shrewdness. By the end of George Eliot's life (1880) or shortly after it, with the growing union organisation of the unskilled, those closest to the struggle could see time and again how the militancy despised and feared as barbarous by the middle and upper classes was in fact a civilising force. Once the East End worker 'develops his own type and makes it count by means of organisation', as Engels put it in a letter of 1889, 'scenes like those which occurred during Hyndman's pro-cession through Pall Mall and Piccadilly will then become impossible and the rowdy who will want to provoke a riot will simply be knocked dead.' A foremost leader of labour in those years, Tom Mann of the Amalgamated Society of Engineers, saw how this was working in the north of England. In a letter of about 1888 he wrote that as Marxism spread in Lancashire and the Social Democratic Federation developed more branches, 'The Blackburn men will testify that as a result they became respected where they had formerly had to be constantly ready for fisticuff work, & Darwen developed even better.'[9] This was not at all confined to an exceptional few advanced socialists. In a passage that seems to me classic – it deserves to be known as a milestone in the growth of our civilisation – Ben Tillett, the dockers' leader, sums up the after-effects of the 1889 agreement on a higher minimum wage, a rate for overtime, regular gangs, notice or money when men were dismissed, and regular signing-on times (to stop the bestial fight for work-tickets at the docks):

We had established a new spirit; the bully and the thief, for a time at least, were squelched; no more would the old man be driven and cursed to death by the younger man, threatened and egged on to murder by an overmastering bully. The whole tone and conduct of work, or management of the men, was altered, and for the best.

The goad of the sack was not so fearful; the filthiness and foulness of language was altered for an attempt at courtesy, which, if not refined, was at least a recognition of the manhood of our brothers.

From a condition of the foulest blackguardism in directing the work, the men found a greater respect shown them; they, too, grew in self-respect, and the men we saw after the strike were comparable to the most self-respecting of the other grades of labour.

The 'calls' worked out satisfactorily; organisation took the place of the haphazard; the bosses who lazed and loafed on their subordinates were perforce obliged to earn instead of thieving their money; the work was better done; the men's lives were more regular as their work was – the docker had, in fact, become a man!

The man became greater in the happiness of a better supplied larder and home; and the women folk with the children, shared the sense of security and peace the victory at the docks had wrought.[10]

There is how modern man has won his way forwards, developing himself in the course of meeting those needs with which his way of life has faced him. Yet – deflected and domineered-over, it seems, by the old notions of salvation for the individual soul – thinking about such matters is still weak in the sense of what we are collectively. The novel, which is bound to work through the characterising of individuals – whatever may be made of this in sum – has suffered accordingly. The first critic to realise the quality of *Felix Holt* and, in doing so, to distinguish between the implausible Felix and the fine Transome part was F. R. Leavis; yet in discussing *why* it was that George Eliot couldn't help idealising Felix he can only suggest that she was 'relying on her "moral consciousness" unqualified by first-hand knowledge'.[11] At least as important, I would have thought – for she did know the country workman yet still idealised Adam Bede – is the tendency in our culture to value the purely moral above the merely social, to set a space between practical and ideal activities. For this comes in again and again to deform the presentation of society in the best of our classic novels since the Industrial Revolution. In *Women in Love* Lawrence takes the critique of 'hard-lipped antagonism' to an extreme and can see *nothing* but smash and grab and a debased levelling-down in the concerted struggles of the working people at the start of this century. At least this is only a minor element in that novel and, as I argue below, one that Lawrence fails to incorporate into the valid drama of the book. In the case of *Howards End*, which is E. M. Forster's attempt at the sort of comprehensive coverage of modern civilisation that Leavis claims for *Women in Love*, the novelist tries to embody a *rapprochement* between intelligentsia and businessmen through the central relationship of the book, the

Wilcox - Schlegel marriage. The tantalising thing about it is that Forster with part of himself quite realises that individual love or friendship cannot bring together a whole people deeply divided by interest, upbringing, and way of life: he emphasises, for example, the futility of Margaret and Helen's hoping to change Leonard Bast (to make him the free and developed person he craves to be) by taking him home for tea-parties with intelligent conversation. Yet by having Margaret marry Mr Wilcox, with her eyes open, and with no final loss of her loving attachment to him even in the teeth of his repeated flouting of what she holds most valuable, Forster is staging what he has already shown to be unrealistic; indeed, time after time he almost openly challenges us to demur.[12]

Forster's social radicalism has been keen but intermittent,[13] and it is significant that the experiences which, for a time, floated him off the shoals of barrenness as a writer were those he had in India, where the facts of inequality, inhumanity, and exploitation were so clamant that wishful ideals could hardly have survived. In *A Passage to India*, which has recently been praised by a distinguished psychologist for showing how colonialism vitiates relations between people,[14] the only vestige of the over-personalising fallacy is the occasional aphorism – 'One touch of regret . . . would have made . . . the British Empire a different institution', 'Indians know whether they are liked or not . . . and that is why the British Empire rests on sand', and so on.[15] But nothing in the body of the drama supports this kind of view of the empire: the frictions between races – which in many ways have replaced those between classes, with the evolution of capitalism into imperialism – are followed out unflinchingly, from the touches of unease that mar Fielding's friendship with Aziz, down to the last, perfectly-imagined moment of acknowledged conflict between Indian and Englishman as they ride along the rocky trail.

It is easier to face matters squarely when they are sited abroad, and this must be one of the reasons why during the past sixty years more good novels by English writers have been set abroad than in their own country.[16] When the situation is close to us, we are prone to retreat into ideals rather than face the lifetime of wearing practical effort that a genuinely social solution necessarily demands: for example, we pretend to ourselves that far-flung communal matters could be solved by a 'charge of heart' or by pursuing some 'higher purpose' or abstract end not grounded in the situation in which we find ourselves. In a world moulded by industrial revolutions it would be more sensible to realise that man makes himself by meeting specific needs, most often of a social – practical kind, in the course of which his human nature is changed and new ideas arise. This is not to subordinate feelings and relationships to some brute process but rather to see more exactly why the course of our lives – including feelings, relationships, and thoughts – is as it is.

SOURCE: chapter 6 of *The Real Foundations* (London, 1973)
pp. 131–42

NOTES

1. John B. Mitchell, 'Problems of the Development of the Proletarian Revolutionary Novel in 19th-century Britain', *Zeitschrift für Anglistik und Amerikanistik*, II (1963) pp. 253–8.
2. Trevor Blount, 'The Ironmaster and the New Acquisitiveness: Dickens's Views on the Rising Industrial Classes as Exemplified in *Bleak House*', *Essays in Criticism*, xv 3 (Oct 1965).
3. Not that the competition is strong; the only immediately comparable thing is the conversation among the miners which Disraeli dramatises convincingly in Book 3, ch. 1, of *Sybil*.
4. Hammond and Hammond, *The Town Labourer*, vol. 1, pp. 91–5.
5. Arnold Toynbee, 'Are Radicals Socialists?', in his *The Industrial Revolution* (1884) pp. 221–2.
6. Bronterre O'Brien, quoted by Asa Briggs in *Chartists Studies*, p. 295.
7. *Alton Locke* (1889 edition) ch. 41, p. 304.
8. Graham Wallas, *Life of Francis Place*, p. 145.
9. *On Britain*, p. 521; Torr, *Tom Mann and His Times*, p. 255.
10. Ben Tillett, *A Brief History of the Dockers' Union* (1910), quoted from Tom Mann, *Memoirs*, pp. 89–90.
11. F. R. Leavis, *The Great Tradition*, p. 52.
12. Especially the end of ch. 22 when Margaret is looking into Wilcox's eyes: 'What was behind their competent stare? She knew, but was not disquieted.'
13. The only place where Forster aligns himself with the have-nots, as distinct from ironically exposing the failings of his own class, appears to be the essay 'Me, Them and You' in *Abinger Harvest*.
14. G. M. Carstairs, Foreword to Frantz Fanon, *A Dying Colonialism* (1970 ed.) p. 8.
15. *A Passage to India*, chs 5, 29 (Penguin ed.) pp. 50, 253.
16. E.g. by Conrad, Forster, Lawrence, L. H. Myers, Joyce Cary, Graham Greene.

PART FOUR

Some Contemporary Authors Speaking

Iris Murdoch

AGAINST DRYNESS: A POLEMICAL SKETCH (1961)

The complaints which I wish to make are concerned primarily with prose, not with poetry, and primarily with novels, not with drama; and they are brief, simplified, abstract, and possibly insular. They are not to be construed as implying any precise picture of 'the function of the writer'. It is the function of the writer to write the best book he knows how to write. These remarks have to do with the background to present-day literature, in Liberal democracies in general and Welfare States in particular, in a sense in which this must be the concern of any serious critic.

We live in a scientific and anti-metaphysical age in which the dogmas, images, and precepts of religion have lost much of their power. We have not recovered from two wars and the experience of Hitler. We are also the heirs of the Enlightenment, Romanticism, and the Liberal tradition. These are the elements of our dilemma: whose chief feature, in my view, is that we have been left with far too shallow and flimsy an idea of human personality. I shall explain this.

Philosophy, like the newspapers, is both the guide and the mirror of its age. Let us look quickly at Anglo-Saxon philosophy and at French philosophy and see what picture of human personality we can gain from these two depositories of wisdom. Upon Anglo-Saxon philosophy the two most profound influences have been Hume and Kant: and it is not difficult to see in the current philosophical conception of the person the work of these two great thinkers. This conception consists in the joining of a materialistic behaviourism with a dramatic view of the individual as a solitary will. These subtly give support to each other. From Hume through Bertrand Russell, with friendly help from mathematical logic and science, we derive the idea that reality is finally a quantity of material atoms and that significant discourse must relate itself directly

or indirectly to reality so conceived. This position was most pictures-
quely summed up in Wittgenstein's *Tractatus*. Recent philosophy,
especially the later work of Wittgenstein and the work of Gilbert Ryle
derivative therefrom, alters this a little. The atomic Humian picture is
abandoned in favour of a type of conceptual analysis (in many ways
admirable) which emphasises the structural dependence of concepts
upon the public language in which they are framed. This analysis has
important results in the philosophy of mind, where it issues in modified
behaviourism. Roughly: my inner life, for me just as for others, is
identifiable as existing only through the application to it of public
concepts, concepts which can only be constructed on the basis of overt
behaviour.

This is one side of the picture, the Humian and post-Humian side. On
the other side, we derive from Kant, and also Hobbes and Bentham
through John Stuart Mill, a picture of the individual as a free rational
will. With the removal of Kant's metaphysical background this
individual is seen as alone. (He is in a certain sense alone on Kant's view
also, that is: not confronted with real dissimilar others.) With the
addition of some utilitarian optimism he is seen as eminently educable.
With the addition of some modern psychology he is seen as capable of
self-knowledge by methods agreeable to science and common sense. So
we have the modern man, as he appears in many recent works on ethics
and I believe also to a large extent in the popular consciousness.

We meet, for instance, a refined picture of this man in Stuart
Hampshire's book *Thought and Action*. He is rational and totally free
except in so far as, in the most ordinary lawcourt and commonsensical
sense, his degree of self-awareness may vary. He is morally speaking
monarch of all he surveys and totally responsible for his actions.
Nothing transcends him. His moral language is a practical pointer, the
instrument of his choices, the indication of his preferences. His inner life
is resolved into his acts and choices, and his beliefs, which are also acts,
since a belief can only be identified through its expression. His moral
arguments are references to empirical facts backed up by decisions. The
only moral word which he requires is 'good' (or 'right'), the word which
expresses decision. His rationality expresses itself in awareness of the
facts, whether about the world or about himself. The virtue which is
fundamental to him is sincerity.

If we turn to French philosophy we may see, at least in that section of it which has most caught the popular imagination, I mean in the work of Jean Paul Sartre, essentially the same picture. It is interesting how extremely Kantian this picture is, for all Sartre's indebtedness to Hegelian sources. Again, the individual is pictured as solitary and totally free. There is no transcendent reality, there are no degrees of freedom. On the one hand there is the mass of psychological desires and social habits and prejudices, on the other hand there is the will. Certain dramas, more Hegelian in character, are of course enacted within the soul; but the isolation of the will remains. Hence *angoisse*. Hence, too, the special anti-bourgeois flavour of Sartre's philosophy which makes it appeal to many intellectuals: the ordinary traditional picture of personality and the virtues lies under suspicion of *mauvaise foi*. Again the only real virtue is sincerity. It is, I think, no accident that, however much philosophical and other criticism Sartre may receive, this powerful picture has caught our imagination. The Marxist critics may plausibly claim that it represents the essence of the Liberal theory of personality.

It will be pointed out that other phenomenological theories (leaving aside Marxism) have attempted to do what Sartre has failed to do, and that there are notable philosophers who have offered a different picture of the soul. Yes; yet from my own knowledge of the scene I would doubt whether any (non-Marxist) account of human personality has yet emerged from phenomenology which is fundamentally unlike the one which I have described and can vie with it in imaginative power. It may be said that philosophy cannot in fact produce such an account. I am not sure about this, nor is this large question my concern here. I express merely by belief that, for the Liberal world, philosophy is not in fact at present able to offer us any other complete and powerful picture of the soul. I return now to England and the Anglo-Saxon tradition.

The Welfare State has come about as a result, largely, of socialist thinking and socialist endeavour. It has seemed to bring a certain struggle to an end; and with that ending has come a lassitude about fundamentals. If we compare the language of the original Labour Party constitution with that of its recent successor we see an impoverishment of thinking and language which is typical. The Welfare State is the reward of 'empiricism in politics'. It has represented to us a set of thoroughly desirable but limited ends, which could be conceived *in non-theoretical terms*; and in pursuing it, in allowing the idea of it to dominate the more naturally theoretical wing of our political scene, we have to a large extent lost our theories. Our central conception is still a debilitated form of Mill's equation: happiness equals freedom equals personality. There should have been a revolt against utilitarianism; but for many reasons it has not taken place. In 1905 John Maynard Keynes and his friends welcomed the philosophy of G. E. Moore because Moore reinstated the concept of experience, Moore directed attention away from the mechanics of action and towards the inner life. But Moore's 'experience' was too shallow a concept; and a scientific age with simple attainable empirical aims has preferred a more behaviouristic philosophy.

What have we lost here? And what have we perhaps never had? We have suffered a general loss of concepts, the loss of a moral and political vocabulary. We no longer use a spread-out substantial picture of the manifold virtues of man and society. We no longer see man against a background of values, of realities, which transcend him. We picture man as a brave naked will surrounded by an easily comprehended empirical world. For the hard idea of truth we have substituted a facile idea of sincerity. What we have never had, of course, is a satisfactory Liberal theory of personality, a theory of man as free and separate and related to a rich and complicated world from which, as a moral being, he has much to learn. We have bought the Liberal theory as it stands, because we have wished to encourage people to think of themselves as free, at the cost of surrendering the background.

We have never solved the problems about human personality posed by the Enlightenment. Between the various concepts available to us the real question has escaped: and now, in a curious way, our present situation is analogous to an eighteenth-century one. We retain a rationalistic optimism about the beneficent results of education, or rather technology. We combine this with a romantic conception of 'the human condition', a picture of the individual as stripped and solitary: a conception which has, since Hitler, gained a peculiar intensity.

The eighteenth-century was an era of rationalistic allegories and moral tales. The nineteenth-century (roughly) was the great era of the novel; and the novel throve upon a dynamic merging of the idea of person with the idea of class. Because nineteenth-century society was dynamic and interesting and because (to use a Marxist notion) the type and the individual could there be seen as merged, the solution of the eighteenth-century problem could be put off. It has been put off till now. Now that the structure of society is less interesting and less alive than it was in the nineteenth-century, and now that Welfare economics have removed certain incentives to thinking, and now that the values of science are so much taken for granted, we confront in a particularly dark and confusing form a dilemma which has been with us implicitly since the Enlightenment, or since the beginning, wherever exactly one wishes to place it, of the modern Liberal world.

If we consider twentieth-century literature as compared with nineteenth-century literature, we notice certain significant contrasts. I said that, in a way, we were back in the eighteenth-century, the era of rationalistic allegories and moral tales, the era when the idea of human nature was unitary and single. The nineteenth-century novel (I use these terms boldly and roughly: of course there were exceptions) was not concerned with 'the human condition', it was concerned with real various individuals struggling in society. The twentieth-century novel is usually either crystalline or journalistic; that is, it is either a small quasi-allegorical object portraying the human condition and not containing 'characters' in the nineteenth-century sense, or else it is a large shapeless quasi-documentary object, the degenerate descendant of the nineteenth-century novel, telling, with pale conventional characters, some straightforward story enlivened with empirical facts. Neither of these kinds of literature engages with the problem that I mentioned above.

It may readily be noted that if our prose fiction is either crystalline or journalistic, the crystalline works are usually the better ones. They are what the more serious writers want to create. We may recall the ideal of 'dryness' which we associate with the symbolist movement, with writers such as T. E. Hulme and T. S. Eliot, with Paul Valéry, with Wittgenstein. This 'dryness' (smallness, clearness, self-containedness) is a nemesis of Romanticism. Indeed it *is* Romanticism in a later phase. The pure, clean, self-contained 'symbol', the exemplar incidentally of what Kant, ancestor of both Liberalism and Romanticism, required art to be, is the analogue of the lonely self-contained individual. It is what is left of the other-worldliness of Romanticism when the 'messy' humanitarian and revolutionary elements have spent their force. The temptation of art, a temptation to which every work of art yields except the greatest ones, is to console. The modern writer, frightened of technology and (in England) abandoned by philosophy and (in France) presented with simplified dramatic theories, attempts to console us by myths or by stories.

On the whole: his truth is sincerity and his imagination is fantasy. Fantasy operates either with shapeless day-dreams (the journalistic story) or with small myths, toys, crystals. Each in his own way produces a sort of 'dream necessity'. Neither grapples with reality: hence 'fantasy', not 'imagination'.

The proper home of the symbol, in the 'symbolist' sense, is poetry. Even there it may play an equivocal role since there is something in symbolism which is inimical to words, out of which, we have been reminded, poems are constructed. Certainly the invasion of other areas by what I may call, for short, 'symbolist ideals', has helped to bring about a decline of prose. Eloquence is out of fashion; even 'style', except in a very austere sense of this term, is out of fashion.

T. S. Eliot and Jean-Paul Sartre, dissimilar enough as thinkers, both tend to undervalue prose and to deny it any *imaginative* function. Poetry is the creation of linguistic quasi-things; prose is for explanation and exposition, it is essentially didactic, documentary, informative. Prose is ideally transparent; it is only *faute de mieux* written in words. The influential modern stylist is Hemingway. It would be almost inconceivable now to write like Landor. Most modern English novels indeed are not *written*. One feels they could slip into some other medium without much loss. It takes a foreigner like Nabokov or an Irishman like Beckett to animate prose language into an imaginative stuff in its own right.

Tolstoy who said that art was an expression of the religious perception of the age was nearer the truth than Kant who saw it as the imagination in a frolic with the understanding. The connection between art and the moral life has languished because we are losing our sense of form and structure in the moral world itself. Linguistic and existentialist behaviourism, our Romantic philosophy, has reduced our vocabulary and simplified and impoverished our view of the inner life. It is natural that a Liberal democratic society will not be concerned with techniques of improvement, will deny that virtue is knowledge, will emphasise choice at the expense of vision; and a Welfare State will weaken the incentives to investigate the bases of a Liberal democratic society. For political purposes we have been encouraged to think of ourselves as totally free and responsible, knowing everything we need to know for the important purposes of life. But this is one of the things of which Hume said that it may be true in politics but false in fact; and is it really true in politics? We need a post-Kantian unromantic Liberalism with a different image of freedom.

The technique of becoming free is more difficult than John Stuart Mill imagined. We need more concepts than our philosophies have furnished us with. We need to be enabled to think in terms of degrees of freedom, and to picture, in a non-metaphysical, non-totalitarian, and non-religious sense, the transcendence of reality. A simple-minded faith in science, together with the assumption that we are all rational and totally free, engenders a dangerous lack of curiosity about the real world, a failure to appreciate the difficulties of knowing it. We need to return from the self-centred concept of sincerity to the other-centred concept of truth. We are not isolated free choosers, monarchs of all we survey, but benighted creatures sunk in a reality whose nature we are constantly and overwhelmingly tempted to deform by fantasy. Our current picture of freedom encourages a dream-like facility; whereas what we require is a renewed sense of the difficulty and complexity of the moral life and the opacity of persons. We need more concepts in terms of which to picture the substance of our being; it is through an enriching and deepening of concepts that moral progress takes place. Simone Weil said that morality was a matter of attention not of will. We need a new vocabulary of attention.

It is here that literature is so important, especially since it has taken over some of the tasks formerly performed by philosophy. Through literature we can re-discover a sense of the density of our lives. Literature can arm us against consolation and fantasy and can help us to recover from the ailments of Romanticism. If it can be said to have a task, now, that surely is its task. But if it is to perform it, prose must recover its former glory, eloquence and discourse must return. I would connect eloquence with the attempt to speak the truth. I think here of the work of Albert Camus. All his novels were *written*; but the last one, though less striking and successful than the first two, seems to me to have been a more serious attempt upon the truth: and illustrates what I mean by eloquence.

It is curious that modern literature, which is so much concerned with violence, contains so few convincing pictures of evil.

Our inability to imagine evil is a consequence of the facile, dramatic and, in spite of Hitler, optimistic picture of ourselves with which we work. Our difficulty about form, about images – our tendency to produce works which are either crystalline of journalistic – is a symptom of our situation. Form itself can be a temptation, making the work of art into a small myth which is a self-contained and indeed self-satisfied individual. We need to turn our attention away from the consoling dream necessity of Romanticism, away from the dry symbol, the bogus individual, the false whole, towards the real impenetrable human person. That this person is substantial, impenetrable, in-dividual, indefinable, and valuable is after all the fundamental tenet of Liberalism.

It is here, however much one may criticise the emptiness of the Liberal idea of freedom, however much one may talk in terms of restoring a lost unity, that one is forever at odds with Marxism. Reality is not a given whole. An understanding of this, a respect for the contingent, is essential to imagination as opposed to fantasy. Our sense of form, which is an aspect of our desire for consolation, can be a danger to our sense of reality as a rich receding background. Against the consolations of form, the clean crystalline work, the simplified fantasy-myth, we must pit the destructive power of the now so unfashionable naturalistic idea of character.

Real people are destructive of myth, contingency is destructive of fantasy and opens the way for imagination. Think of the Russians, those great masters of the contingent. Too much contingency of course may turn art into journalism. But since reality is incomplete, art must not be too much afraid of incompleteness. Literature must always represent a battle between real people and images; and what it requires now is a much stronger and more complex conception of the former.

In morals and politics we have stripped ourselves of concepts. Literature, in curing its own ills, can give us a new vocabulary of experience, and a truer picture of freedom. With this, renewing our sense of distance, we may remind ourselves that art too lives in a region where all human endeavour is failure. Perhaps only Shakespeare manages to create at the highest level both images and people; and even *Hamlet* looks second-rate compared with *Lear*. Only the very greatest art invigorates without consoling, and defeats our attempts, in W. H. Auden's words, to use it as magic.

SOURCE: *Encounter*, January 1961, 16–20.

Angus Wilson

'TRUST THE TALE' (1963)

. . . An analysis of the making of that first short story ['Raspberry Jam',
written in November 1946 – Ed.] may suggest some of the ways in which
a novelist unconsciously comes to make one moral statement while
supposing he is making another. The story, the first fictional work of my
life, was written in feverish excitement in one day. . . . It tells of a boy of
thirteen, the lonely son of conventional, self-centred upper middle class
parents in an English village. He has only two friends in the village: two
old sisters of gentle birth, now impoverished, drunken and the subject of
village scandal. While an adult group at his mother's house gossip about
the two old women, ostensibly asking whether they are suitable friends
for the boy, Johnnie returns in his mind to the episode that, unknown to
his family, has brought his friendship with them to an end, a terrible and
traumatic episode for him. The two old women had invited him to tea.
When he arrived they were clearly half-tipsy and they plied him with
drink. They then brought in a bullfinch – 'the prisoner' – and tortured
it to death in front of him. The act, of course, though to the boy it is just
an incredible horror, is in fact a culmination of rising paranoia
produced in the simple, imaginative, generous old women by the
narrow-minded malice, jealousy and frightened detestation that their
originality has aroused in the village. The irony is that in their drunken
craziness they destroy their friendship with Johnnie which alone gave
any natural play to their generosity and childlike imaginative needs,
perhaps destroy for ever the innocence of the boy himself.

When I wrote this story I saw the two old women as the embodiment
of that saintliness which the mediocrity of the world seeks to destroy; by
this reading, their craziness and their destruction of their young friend's
peace of mind is not their 'fault' but that of the world which has failed to
cherish them. Yet, as I have subsequently thought of the story, I have
felt this to be a disturbingly illogical pattern, at variance with the shape
of the story as it unfolds. I see now that what the story *says*, as opposed to

what I thought I was saying, is that those, who like my old women, seek to retain a childlike (childish) innocence, and in particular a childlike (childish) ignorance, however 'good' their conscious motives, will inevitably destroy themselves and in all probability those they love. It is not insignificant, perhaps, that Johnnie, who at the age of thirteen might reasonably live in a world of childlike (childish) fantasy, is shown, without my realizing it as I wrote, using this fantasy to protect himself from the reality of his parents' demands upon him to grow up – although their conception of growing up, of course, is an inadequate one.

The character was drawn directly from myself as I had been at that age, but I felt only sympathy with my childhood self as I wrote, and did not notice the sting in the tale. Further, the old women, intended to strengthen the concept of childlike (childish) goodness, but really undermining it, were taken from two old women I knew much later in my life, at the age of twenty or so. And with these women, far from successfully creating an imaginative bond, I rather seriously failed to make any *rapport* at all, whereas a brother of mine was beloved by them. This was the brother next to me who at the age of thirteen had endured his nose being put out of joint by my unexpected birth. He was a saintly and exceedingly selfless man, and I only fear that the old ladies' preference for him showed a greater insight than I granted them; for in real life I regarded them not as receptacles of sanctity, but, like the village in the story, thought of them solely as a crazy nuisance, the more crazy since they did not respond to my charms. I seem in fiction to have righted any disappointment I may have felt by making them the intimates of my own starved affections at a much earlier age.

Such falsification in fact, unconscious at the time of writing (I had no conscious memory of the old women and was only vaguely aware that Johnnie came out of myself) suggests the way in which fiction can be constructed out of protective falsehood. The moral truth of the story was still deep in my unconscious; the conscious mind was soothed with fact unconsciously rearranged to propose a more flattering, untrue moral thesis. But the shape of the narrative defies this falsification. . . .

SOURCE: extract from *The Wild Garden* (London, 1963) pp. 23,
24–6.

John Fowles

'AN AUTHOR'S SELF-CONSCIOUSNESS' (1969)

For the drift of the Maker is dark, an Isis hid by the veil. . . .
                                        Tennyson, *Maud* (1855)

I do not know. This story I am telling is all imagination. These characters I create never existed outside my own mind. If I have pretended until now to know my characters' minds and innermost thoughts, it is because I am writing in (just as I have assumed some of the vocabulary and 'voice' of) a convention universally accepted at the time of my story: that the novelist stands next to God. He may not know all, yet he tries to pretend that he does. But I live in the age of Alain Robbe-Grillet and Roland Barthes; if this is a novel, it cannot be a novel in the modern sense of the word.

So perhaps I am writing a transposed autobiography; perhaps I now live in one of the houses I have brought into the fiction; perhaps Charles is myself disguised. Perhaps it is only a game. Modern women like Sarah exist, and I have never understood them. Or perhaps I am trying to pass off a concealed book of essays on you. Instead of chapter headings, perhaps I should have written 'On the Horizontality of Existence', 'The Illusions of Progress', 'The History of the Novel Form', 'The Aetiology of Freedom', 'Some Forgotten Aspects of the Victorian Age' . . . what you will.

Perhaps you suppose that a novelist has only to pull the right strings and his puppets will behave in a lifelike manner; and produce on request a thorough analysis of their motives and intentions. Certainly I intended at this stage (*Chap. Thirteen – unfolding of Sarah's true state of mind*) to tell all – or all that matters. But I find myself suddenly like a man in the sharp spring night, watching from the lawn beneath that dim upper window in Marlborough House; I know in the context of my book's reality that Sarah would never have brushed away her tears and leant down and delivered a chapter of revelation. She would instantly have turned, had she seen me there just as the old moon rose, and disappeared into the interior shadows.

But I am a novelist, not a man in a garden – I can follow her where I like? But possibility is not permissibility. Husbands could often murder their wives – and the reverse – and get away with it. But they don't.

You may think novelists always have fixed plans to which they work, so that the future predicted by Chapter One is always inexorably the actuality of Chapter Thirteen. But novelists write for countless different reasons: for money, for fame, for reviewers, for parents, for friends, for loved ones; for vanity, for pride, for curiosity, for amusement: as skilled furniture-makers enjoy making furniture, as drunkards like drinking, as judges like judging, as Sicilians like emptying a shotgun into an enemy's back. I could fill a book with reasons, and they would all be true, though not true of all. Only one same reason is shared by all of us: *we wish to create worlds as real as, but other than the world that is*. Or was. This is why we cannot plan. We know a world is an organism, not a machine. We also know that a genuinely created world must be independent of its creator; a planned world (a world that fully reveals its planning) is a dead world. It is only when our characters and events begin to disobey us that they begin to live. When Charles left Sarah on her cliff-edge, I ordered him to walk straight back to Lyme Regis. But he did not; he gratuitously turned and went down to the Dairy.

Oh, but you say, come on – what I really mean is that the idea crossed my mind as I wrote that it might be more clever to have him stop and drink milk . . . and meet Sarah again. That is certainly one explanation of what happened; but I can only report – and I am the most reliable witness – that the idea seemed to me to come clearly from Charles, not myself. It is not only that he has begun to gain an autonomy; I must respect it, and disrespect all my quasi-divine plans for him, if I wish him to be real.

In other words, to be free myself, I must give him, and Tina, and Sarah, even the abominable Mrs Poulteney, their freedoms as well. There is only one good definition of God: the freedom that allows other freedoms to exist. And I must conform to that definition.

The novelist is still a god, since he creates (and not even the most aleatory avant-garde modern novel has managed to extirpate its author completely); what has changed is that we are no longer the gods of the Victorian image, omniscient and decreeing; but in the new theological image, with freedom our first principle, not authority.

I have disgracefully broken the illusion? No. My characters still exist, and in a reality no less, or no more, real than the one I have just broken. Fiction is woven into all, as a Greek observed some two and a half thousand years ago. I find this new reality (or unreality) more valid; and I would have you share my own sense that I do not fully control these creatures of my mind, any more than you control – however hard you try, however much of a latter-day Mrs Poulteney you may be – your children, colleagues, friends, or even yourself.

But this is preposterous? A character is either 'real' or 'imaginary'? If you think that, *hypocrite lecteur*, I can only smile. You do not even think of your own past as quite real; you dress it up, you gild it or blacken it, censor it, tinker with it . . . fictionalize it, in a word, and put it away on a shelf – your book, your romanced autobiography. We are all in flight from the real reality. That is a basic definition of *Homo sapiens*.

So if you think all this unlucky (but it *is* Chapter Thirteen) digression has nothing to do with your Time, Progress, Society, Evolution and all those other capitalized ghosts in the night that are rattling their chains behind the scenes of this book . . . I will not argue. But I shall suspect you.

I report, then, only the outward facts: that Sarah cried in the darkness, but did not kill herself; that she continued, in spite of the express prohibition, to haunt Ware Commons. . . .

———

. . . For a while his travelling companion took no notice of the Sleeping Charles. But as the chin sank deeper and deeper – Charles had taken the precaution of removing his hat – the prophet-bearded man began to stare at him, safe in the knowledge that *his* curiosity would *not* be surprised.

His look was peculiar: sizing, ruminative, more than a shade disapproving, as if he knew very well what sort of man this was (as Charles had believed to see very well what sort of man *he* was) and did not much like the knowledge or the species. It was true that, unobserved, he looked a little less frigid and authoritarian a person; but there remained about his features an unpleasant aura of self-confidence – or if not quite confidence in self, at least a confidence in his judgment of others, of how much he could get out of them, expect from them, tax them.

A stare of a minute or so's duration, of this kind, might have been explicable. Train journeys are boring; it is amusing to spy on strangers; and so on. But this stare, which became positively cannibalistic in its intensity, lasted far longer than a minute. It lasted beyond Taunton, though it was briefly interrupted there when the noise on the platform made Charles wake for a few moments. But when he sank back into his slumbers, the eyes fastened on him again in the same leechlike manner.

You may one day come under a similar gaze. And you may – in the less reserved context of our own century – be aware of it. The intent watcher will not wait till you are asleep. It will no doubt suggest something unpleasant, some kind of devious sexual approach . . . a desire to know you in a way you do not want to be known by a stranger. In my experience there is only one profession that gives that particular look, with its bizarre blend of the inquisitive and the magistral; of the ironic and the soliciting.

Now could I use you?

Now what could I do with you?

It is precisely, it has always seemed to me, the look an omnipotent god – if there were such an absurd thing – should be shown to have. Not at all what we think of as a divine look; but one of a distinctly mean and dubious (as the theoreticians of the *nouveau roman* have pointed out) moral quality. I see this with particular clarity on the face, only too familiar to me, of the bearded man who stares at Charles. And I will keep up the pretence no longer.

Now the question I am asking, as I stare at Charles, is not quite the same as the two above. But rather, what the devil am I going to do with you? I have already thought of ending Charles's career here and now; of leaving him for eternity on his way to London. But the conventions of Victorian fiction allow, allowed no place for the open, the inconclusive ending; and I preached earlier of the freedom characters must be given. My problem is simple – what Charles wants is clear? It is indeed. But what the protagonist wants is not so clear; and I am not at all sure where she is at the moment. Of course if these two were two fragments of real life, instead of two figments of my imagination, the issue to the dilemma is obvious: the one want combats the other want, and fails or succeeds, as the actuality may be. Fiction usually pretends to conform to the reality: the writer puts the conflicting wants in the ring and then describes the fight – but in fact fixes the fight, letting that want he himself favours win. And we judge writers of fiction both by the skill they show in fixing the fights (in other words, in persuading us that they were not fixed) and by the kind of fighter they fix in favour of: the good one, the tragic one, the evil one, the funny one, and so on.

But the chief argument for fight-fixing is to show one's readers what one thinks of the world around one – whether one is a pessimist, an optimist, what you will. I have pretended to slip back into 1867; but of course that year is in reality a century past. It is futile to show optimism or pessimism, or anything else about it, because we know what has happened since.

So I continue to stare at Charles and see no reason this time for fixing the fight upon which he is about to engage. That leaves me with two alternatives. I let the fight proceed and take no more than a recording part in it; or I take both sides in it. I stare at that vaguely effete but not completely futile face. And as we near London, I think I see a solution; that is, I see the dilemma is false. The only way I can take no part in the fight is to show two versions of it. That leaves me with only one problem: I cannot give both versions at once, yet whichever is the second will seem, so strong is the tyranny of the last chapter, the final, the 'real' version.

I take my purse from the pocket of my frock-coat, I extract a florin, I rest in on my right thumbnail, I flick it, spinning, two feet into the air and catch it in my left hand.

So be it. And I am suddenly aware that Charles has opened his eyes and is looking at me. There is something more than disapproval in his eyes now; he perceives I am either a gambler or mentally deranged. I return his disapproval, and my florin to my purse. He picks up his hat, brushes some invisible speck of dirt (a surrogate for myself) from its nap and places it on his head.

We draw under one of the great cast-iron beams that support the roof of Paddington station. We arrive, he steps down to the platform, beckoning to a porter. In a few moments, having given his instructions, he turns. The bearded man has disappeared in the throng.

SOURCE: extracts from chapters 13 and 55 of *The French Lieutenant's Woman* (London, 1969) pp. 97–9, 388–90.

SELECT BIBLIOGRAPHY

This list of further reading is a small selection from a large body of interesting and significant writing. The student is also referred to the works listed in 'Notes on Contributors' by the authors anthologised in this Casebook.

COLLECTIONS

Miriam Allott, *Novelists on the Novel* (London, 1959).
Malcolm Cowley (ed.), *Writers at Work* (London, 1958).
John Halperin (ed.), *The Theory of the Novel: New Essays* (London, 1974).
David Lodge (ed.), *Twentieth Century Criticism: A Reader* (London, 1972).
William van O'Connor, *Forms of Modern Fiction* (Minneapolis, 1948).
Philip Stevick (ed.), *The Theory of the Novel* (New York, 1967).
Stratford-upon-Avon Studies 12: Contemporary Criticism (London, 1970).

INDIVIDUAL BOOKS AND ARTICLES

Joseph Conrad, Preface to *The Nigger of the 'Narcissus'* (London, 1897).
Virginia Woolf, 'Modern Fiction' (1919) and 'Mr Bennett and Mrs Brown' (1924) in *Collected Essays* (London, 1966).
Percy Lubbock, *The Craft of Fiction* (London, 1921).
E. M. Forster, *Aspects of the Novel* (London, 1927).
Q. D. Leavis, *Fiction and the Reading Public* (London, 1932).
Mark Schorer, 'Technique as Discovery', *Hudson Review* I (Spring 1948) 67–87.
A. A. Mendilow, *Time and the Novel* (London, 1952).
Dorothy van Ghent, *The English Novel: Form and Function* (New York, 1953).
Ian Watt, *The Rise of the Novel* (Berkeley, 1957).
Simon O. Lesser, *Fiction and the Unconscious* (Boston, 1957).
Richard Stang, *The Theory of the Novel in England, 1850–1870* (New York, 1959).
C. B. Cox, *The Free Spirit* (London, 1963).
A. Friedman, *The Turn of the Novel* (London, 1966).
Bernard Bergonzi, *The Situation of the Novel* (London, 1970).
Gabriel Josipovici, *The World and the Book* (London, 1971).

PERIODICALS

Specifically devoted to fiction are *Modern Fiction Studies* and *Novel: a Forum on Fiction*. (The latter ran a series of articles in 1967–9 under the running title 'Towards a Poetics of Fiction'.)

NOTES ON CONTRIBUTORS

WAYNE C. BOOTH (b. 1921). George M. Pullman Professor of English, University of Chicago. Publications include *The Rhetoric of Fiction* (1961) and *The Rhetoric of Irony* (1974).

MALCOLM BRADBURY (b. 1932). Professor of American Studies, University of East Anglia. His critical writings include *Evelyn Waugh* (1964), *The Social Context of Modern English Literature* (1971) and *Possibilities* (1973). He is also a novelist: *Eating People is Wrong* (1959), *Stepping Westward* (1965), *The History Man* (1975).

DAVID CRAIG (b.1932). Senior Lecturer in English, University of Lancaster. Publications include *Scottish Literature and the Scottish People* (1961), *The Real Foundations* (1973) and editions of *Hard Times* and of Hugh MacDiarmid.

JOHN FOWLES (b. 1926). Novelist: *The Collector* (1958), *The Magus* (1966), *The French Lieutenant's Woman* (1969), *The Ebony Tower: Collected Novellas* (1974).

BARBARA HARDY. Professor of English Literature, Birkbeck College, University of London. Novel criticism includes *The Appropriate Form* (1964), *The Moral Art of Dickens* (1970) and *Tellers and Listeners* (1975).

NORMAN N. HOLLAND (b. 1927). Professor of English and Director of the Center for the Psychological Study of the Arts, State University of New York, Buffalo. Publications include *Psychoanalysis and Shakespeare* (1966) and *Poems in Persons* (1973).

HENRY JAMES (1843–1916). Writer. Notable amongst his own collections of his criticism are *Partial Portraits* (1888) and *Notes on Novelists* (1914); there is a useful selection in Morris Shapira (ed.), *Henry James: Selected Literary Criticism* (1963). His specially-written Prefaces for the New York edition of his novels are gathered by R. P. Blackmur as *The Art of the Novel* (1934).

FRANK KERMODE (b. 1919). Fellow of King's College, Cambridge and formerly (1974–82) King Edward VII Professor of English Literature, University of Cambridge. Publications include *The Romantic Image* (1957), *The Sense of an Ending* (1967), *Continuities* (1968) and *Modern Essays* (1971).

DAVID HERBERT LAWRENCE (1885–1930). Writer. His *Studies in Classic American Literature* (1924) and *Reflections on the Death of a Porcupine* (1925) contain writing about the novel. E. D. McDonald (ed.), *Phoenix* (1936) and Warren Roberts and Harry T. Moore (eds), *Phoenix II* (1968) contain other fiction criticism, most of it previously uncollected, and including 'Study of Thomas Hardy'. See also A. Beal (ed.), *D. H. Lawrence: Selected Literary Criticism* (1964) and A. A. H. Inglis (ed.), *A Selection from Phoenix* (1971).

F. R. LEAVIS (1895–1978). Literary, social, and educational critic. Editor, at Cambridge, of *Scrutiny* (1932–53). Publications include *The Great Tradition* (1948), *Anna Karenina and Other Essays (1967)*, *Dickens: The Novelist* (1970) with Q. D. Leavis, *Nor Shall my Sword* (1972), and *Thought, Words, and Creativity* (1976).

DAVID LODGE (b.1935). Professor of English Literature, University of Birmingham. Publications include *The Language of Fiction* (1969), *The Novelist at the Crossroads* (1971). His novels include *Changing Places: A Tale of Two Campuses* (1975).

IRIS MURDOCH (b. 1919). Novelist; Fellow in Philosophy, St Anne's College, Oxford, 1948–63. Non-fictional publications include *Sartre: Romantic Rationalist* (1953) and *The Sovereignty of Good* (1971).

ROBERT SCHOLES (b. 1929). Professor of English, Brown University, Providence, Rhode Island. Publications include *Approaches to the Novel* (1961), *The Nature of Narrative* (1966) with Robert L. Kellogg, and *Structuralism in Literature* (1974).

LIONEL TRILLING (1905–75). Late Professor of English at Columbia University. His works in criticism and the history of ideas include *The Liberal Imagination* (1950), *The Opposing Self* (1955), *Beyond Culture* (1965) and *Sincerity and Authenticity* (1973). There has been a recent revival of interest in his novel *The Middle of the Journey* (1947).

RAYMOND WILLIAMS (b. 1921). Professor of Drama, University of Cambridge. Writings on literature and cultural history include *Culture and Society, 1780–1950* (1958), *The Long Revolution* (1961) and the *English Novel from Dickens to Lawrence* (1970). The most widely read of his three novels is the first, *Border Country* (1960).

ANGUS WILSON, C.B.E, F.R.S.L. (b. 1913). Novelist. Professor of English Literature, University of East Anglia. His writings about the novel include *Emile Zola* (1952), *The Wild Garden* (1963) and *The World of Charles Dickens* (1970).

INDEX

Figures in italic denote essays or extracts reprinted in this volume.